mothes Petaford
487. 3679

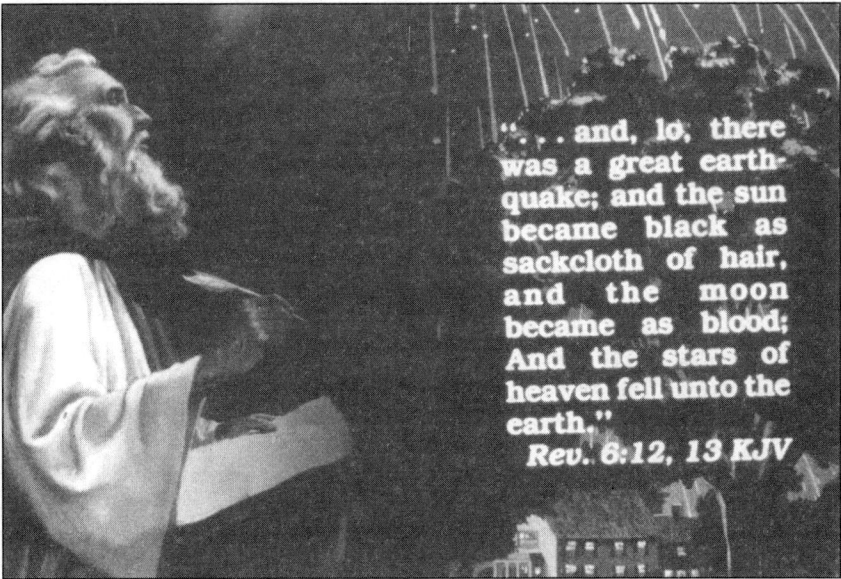

". . . and, lo, there was a great earthquake; and the sun became black as sackcloth of hair, and the moon became as blood; And the stars of heaven fell unto the earth."
Rev. 6:12, 13 KJV

Restoration

of the

Apostolic Church

VOLUME 2
in the series
GENUINE CHRISTIANITY

By
Ronald Thompson

TEACH Services, Inc.
Brushton, New York

The author assumes full responsibility for the accuracy
of all facts and quotations as cited in this book.

FRONT COVER
COURTESY RISCHGITZ

ISBN 1–57258–147–6
Library of Congress Catalog Card No. 98–88854

Published by

TEACH Services, Inc.
254 Donovan Road
Brushton, New York 12916

DEDICATED
TO
LAYMEN, SEMINARIANS
AND THEOLOGIANS
OF
PROTESTANTISM
To Commemorate St. Columba's contribution
to Christianity on the occasion
of the
1400th ANNIVERSARY
of St. Columba's death
(597–1997)

Table of Contents

PICTURES

ILLUSTRATIONS

ACKNOWLEDGMENTS

First and foremost I acknowledge God's hand in this writing enterprise. I am humbly grateful for His direction. Some aspects I consider Providential—such as the unexpected arrival of *The Celtic Church in Britain*, sent by the Publisher Teach Services, Inc., given to me as a sample or exhibit of their kind of printing. Since I was going to write about the Celtic Church I needed a book of this nature, a condensation of a doctoral dissertation on the *beliefs* of the Celtic Church, a unique subject that is rarely, if ever discussed. As a researcher, I don't believe I would have ferreted out this recently published book. This book arrived unexpectedly like a "bolt from the blue"—a heavenly surprise, and right on time, just when I needed such a book.

Another new book containing thirty three original historical documents also came to me as a "godsend," fulfilling a similar scenario. This time it was from my son, Glynn Thompson, M.D., F.A.C.O.G., who was interested in my treatise, and thought I could make use of it. I sure did, for without it my book would have been incomplete and less compelling—such is the value of primary sources.

Thanks Glynn for the use of your computer and technical advice to sort out snags, while preparing a disk for the publisher. I extend a special thanks to my wife, Dawn, for typing the text of this book on this computer.

Extensive travel for this work has not been necessary, since the Kimbel Library of Coastal Carolina University, South Carolina, is close at hand to facilitate the borrowing of rare books through Interlibrary Loan. This courtesy was extended to me gratis, as a visiting professor, and all books were obtained efficiently, and on time as needed—Bravo!

Last, but not least, a word of thanks is due to Carlota Brown, an unofficial research assistant to me, for locating obscure material and sending "scads" of photostatic copies to me. I am reminded of the expression: "search was made in the archives, where the treasures were stored" (Ezra 6:1, NKJV), when I think of the treasures of source documents Carlota has access to, in the archives of Andrews University, Michigan. It is known as the Advent Source Collection, the largest of its kind in the world.

FOREWORD

The multiplicity of denominations, congregations and movements taking the name "Christian" today staggers the mind. Where does one begin to try to sort out the various truth claims and traditions?

Dr. Ronald Thompson suggests that we go back to the start of it all—to the church of the apostles. He aims to identify the marks of Christianity as it emerged among the first followers of Jesus Christ, and then trace these marks as they were perpetuated or lost during the succeeding centuries.

The scope of this undertaking is large: Dr. Thompson paints on a broad canvas that stretches to our times. Twenty centuries of Christian history is a huge bite to swallow. But the author isn't attempting to write another history of the church per se—he wants to trace the history of what he calls "apostolic" Christianity.

Thompson writes from a firmly Protestant stance, as one for whom *sola scriptura* is the watchword. Every reader who takes the Bible seriously will find this work challenging—and probably provocative as well. For the author ultimately is concerned with far more than the trail of apostolic Christianity down through the centuries: he wants to discover if its ancient marks find expression even today.

That is a quest that anyone who seeks to know and follow truth must welcome.

William G. Johnsson, Ph.D.

PREFACE

The purpose of this book is to recognize that the Christian Church eventually "fell away" from its former faith as prophesied by Paul (2 Thessalonians 2:3, 4), and also left its "first love," as prophesied by John (Revelation 2:4). Waldenses and Anabaptists located the "fall" in the synthesis—a sell-out to worldly power and compromise with the world, in which Christianity became the religion of an empire, rather than the religion of personally committed believers.

To elaborate further, it is acknowledged that the Christian Church made a wrong turn somewhere in its history, which resulted in the loss of something which earlier generations had. And if that is the case, it calls for a RESTITUTION, or RESTORATION of that earlier *primitive Christianity*, epitomized in the Apostolic Church of the first century, delineated in the Gospels, the Acts, and the Epistles.

Aside from the movement of reform under Martin Luther, based on the concept of the Scriptures alone—*sola Scriptura*, restitutionist, or models for religious reform, assume implicitly or explicitly that the earliest Christians, who lived closest to Christ and the apostles, are the model for the church to follow throughout history. Ten qualities of the model Apostolic Church of the First Century, including the "apostles' doctrine" (Acts 2:42) will be described in Chapter 1.

Now, as far as the Celtic Church is concerned, it developed independently, and therefore *maintained* the fundamentals of the Apostolic Church. The extension of Celtic Christianity in the British Isles and Europe will make exciting reading in Chapter 2.

On the other hand, Chapter 2 also demonstrates how the Waldenses and Anabaptists *restored* the fundamentals of the Apostolic Church against great odds.

Chapter 3 takes the reader into the nineteenth century to discover a very different Christian atmosphere, one of religious freedom and brotherly love, an awareness of living in the "time of the end," and fostered by an awakening in the British Isles and Europe, that the Second Advent of Christ was near at hand. This generated an unprecedented searching of the Prophetic Scriptures.

In this setting it is thought that the Christian Church had lost something—that is the Spiritual Gifts first evident in the early Apostolic Church. Hence there emerges the Catholic Apostolic Church, that ostensibly restores all the Spiritual Gifts with special emphasis on apostles, prophecy, healing and tongues. Such phenomena will be examined, scrutinized, and tested for authenticity in Chapter 4.

Chapter 5 through 8 considers the Second Advent Awakening and Movement in America, with the Emergence and Restoration of the Apostolic Church of the Last Days.

SPECIAL ANNOUNCEMENT: HOLD YOUR BREATH!

This book will reveal some home truths from the nineteenth century that are baffling many Christians today. It will reveal:

(1) The Origin of the Futurist Interpretation of Prophecy and the attack on the Historicist Interpretation of Prophecy;

(2) The Origin of Dispensationalism;

(3) The Origin of the Charismatic Movement;

(4) Why Christ failed to Return in 1844;

(5) Where and when the teaching of the Secret Rapture and Two-Stage Second Coming Originated;

(6) What constitutes the Restoration of the Apostolic Church of the Last Days.

From another perspective this treatise presents the nineteenth century as a great battleground, almost on a par with the sixteenth century, in which the forces of good and evil have locked horns in a titanic struggle. The conflict is over truth and error. Unknown monumental truths sally forth, "driving a straight furrow" in the proclamation of truth (2 Timothy 2:15, NEB), to be recognized, accepted, and believed, *only* to be negated, confused, and beaten back by opposing forces. These opposing forces introduce strange, fanciful, erroneous doctrines "to tickle their ears," and "stop their ears to the truth and turn to mythology" (2 Timothy 4:3, 4, NEB).

This conflict over the separation of truth from error in the nineteenth century, will engage the imagination, and grip the attention of every earnest reader, and seeker for truth and enlightenment—"no punches are pulled."

Shalom!

"Doctor "

RONALD C. THOMPSON

Fellowship = spells > associate partners,
                                        1

Chapter 1

APOSTOLIC CHURCH OF THE
FIRST CENTURY

In order to gain perspective of the Apostolic Church of the First Century one needs to read the passage of Scripture pertaining to it, found in Acts of the Apostles, Chapter Two as follows:

v.36. Therefore let all the house of Israel know assuredly, that God hath made that same Jesus, whom ye have crucified, both Lord and Christ.

v.37. Now when they heard this, they were pricked in their heart, and said unto Peter and to the rest of the apostles, Men and brethren, what shall we do?

v.38. Then Peter said unto them, Repent and be baptized every one of you in the name of Jesus Christ for the remission of sins, and ye shall receive the gift of the Holy Ghost.

v.39. For the promise is unto you, and to your children, and to all that are afar off, even as many as the Lord our God shall call.

v.40. And with many other words did he testify and exhort, saying, Save yourselves from this untoward generation.

v.41. Then they that gladly received his word were baptized: and the same day there were added unto them about three thousand souls.

v.42. And they continued stedfastly in the apostles' doctrine and fellowship, and in breaking of bread, and in prayers. The word the apostles preached & teach,

v.43. And fear came upon every soul: and many wonders and signs were done by the apostles.

v.44. And all that believed were together, and had all things in common;

v.45. And sold their possessions and goods, and parted them to all men, as every man had need.

v.46. And they, continuing daily with one accord in the temple, and breaking bread from house to house, did eat their meat with gladness and singleness of heart. ⊃ Fellowship

v.47. Praising God, and having favour with all the people. And the Lord added to the church daily such as should be saved.

Authorized King James Version

No period of the Christian Church's sojourn on this earth is more full of interest than the period of its inception in the first century of the Christian era. The period covered by the book of Acts is unique, in that it marked the immediate transition, when God set aside Judaism, with its entrenched and privileged status, and suddenly introduced the Christian Church. One moment there was no church; the next, there it was—the Apostolic Church born in power on the Day of Pentecost, exhibiting ten distinctive qualities as outlined in Acts of the Apostles, Chapter Two.¹ These qualities that marked the Apostolic Church will now be considered under ten headings.

I. SAVED BY FAITH (Acts 2:36–38)

The Apostolic Church was Saved by Faith. Peter's presentation of the crucified Jesus as both Lord and Christ brought conviction by faith in Christ—they were pricked in their heart, their consciences were aroused, and they called out, "What shall we do?" That's a good state of mind to be in. Peter immediately replied, "Repent!" Repentance not only means sorrow for sin, but a turning away from sin with abhorrence. And unless there is an entire turning away from sin and a confession of it, there is no real change of heart or life; and "except a man be born again he cannot see the kingdom of God" (John 3:3)—which brings us to the next distinctive quality.

II. SEPARATED BY BAPTISM (Acts 2:38)

The Apostolic Church was Separated by Baptism. After Peter told his convicted audience to Repent, he added, "Be baptized every one of you in the name of Jesus Christ for the remission of sins" (Acts 2:38). The spiritual rebirth, or regeneration, is climaxed in the public testimony of baptism by immersion in water, for, "except a man be born of water and of the Spirit, he cannot enter the kingdom of God" (John 3:5). In response to Peter's call for baptism, the resultant baptism of 3,000 souls was phenomenal, as they "gladly received his word" (Acts 2:41).

III. SPIRIT ENDOWED (Acts 2:38)

There is no question about it, that the Apostolic Church was Spirit Endowed, born in the power of the Spirit—"ye shall receive the gift of the Holy Ghost" (Acts 2:38). The gift of the Holy Spirit was an enabling power: (1) to be witnesses to the "uttermost part of the earth" (Acts 1:8); (2) to speak the "word of God with boldness" (Acts 4:31); (3) to give "gifts unto men" (Ephesians 4:8). "And he gave some, apostles; and some prophets; and some evangelists; and some pastors and teachers; For the perfecting of the saints" (Ephesians 4:11,12). One must not forget that the initial power of the Holy Spirit was in the gift of *tongues, so "that every man heard them speak in his own language" (Acts 2:4,6); even if Paul placed tongues at the end of his list of gifts at 1 Corinthians 12, verse 28.*

IV. STEADFAST IN THE APOSTLES' DOCTRINE (Acts 2:42)

Although the book of Acts is a record of the events of the Apostolic Church, it does demonstrate the doctrine of salvation climaxed in baptism, and relates some of the apostles' doctrine. But the Apostolic

Church that unfolds historically in Acts, unfolds theologically and doctrinally in the Epistles of Paul, Peter, and John. Following are seven areas of the apostles' doctrine found in the Acts and the Epistles.

Christ's High Priestly Ministry

We may rejoice in God through our Lord Jesus Christ, by whom we have now received the atonement, or reconciliation (Romans 5:11). But the application of the atonement of Christ to the believer, is accomplished by the High Priestly Ministry of Christ, that commenced at His Ascension. The book of Hebrews drives home the ministry of Christ in the heavenly sanctuary: "For Christ is not entered into the holy places made with hands, which are the figures of the true; but into heaven itself, now to appear in the presence of God for us" (Hebrews 9:24). Again we read about Christ's effecting salvation for us: "Wherefore he is able also to *save* them to the uttermost that come unto God by him, seeing he ever liveth to make *intercession* for them" (Hebrews 7:25; Italics supplied). It is clearly stated that "we have such an high priest, who is set on the right hand of the throne of the Majesty in the heavens; a minister of the sanctuary, and of the true tabernacle, which the Lord pitched and not man" (Hebrews 8:1,2). Finally, other references may be cited for Christ as Mediator (Hebrews 8:6; 1 Timothy 2:5) and Advocate (1 John 2:1). John saw Jesus in the heavenly sanctuary among the seven candlesticks of the first apartment, clothed in high priestly garb with a golden girdle (Revelation 1:12,13).

Christ's Seat of Judgment

Apart from Christ's mediatorial ministry in the heavenly sanctuary as High Priest, He included another phase—that of Judge. "For we must all appear before the judgment seat of Christ; that every one may receive the things done in his body, according to that he hath done, whether it be good or bad" (2 Corinthians 5:10). The thought is repeated at Romans 14, verses 10 and 11, to "give account of himself before God." Jesus himself said, "every idle word that men shall speak, they shall give account thereof in the day of judgment (Matthew 12:36). That's serious business—no one is excluded, it involves the righteous and the unrighteous. Peter relates the order of the judgment, "that judgment must *begin at the house of God:* and if it first begin at us, what shall be the end of them that *obey not the gospel of God*" (1 Peter 4:17; Italics supplied). There is to be a judgment for believers followed by a judgment for unbelievers. The Apostolic Church of the first century did not know when the judgment would occur. Paul in addressing Felix reasoned of "judgment to come," and he trembled at the thought (Acts 24:25). Nevertheless, Paul announced God had appointed a day, in which He will judge the world (Acts 17:31). John prophesied that the first angel's message declared "the hour of His judgment is come" (Revelation 14:6,7). But the impact of John's prophecy was lost on the Apostolic Church of the first century. It was to make an impact on the restored Apostolic Church of the last days (See Chapter 7).

Christ's Second Coming

The Apostolic Church of the first century looked forward to the single climactic event, when Christ shall "appear the second time without sin unto salvation" (Hebrews 9:28). They believed in a literal, personal, audible and visible Second Coming as related by Paul: "For the Lord *himself* shall descend from heaven, with a *shout*, with the *voice* of the archangel, and with the *trump* of God: and the *dead in Christ* shall rise *first*: Then we *which are alive and remain* shall be caught up together with them in the clouds, to meet the Lord in the air: and so shall we ever be with the Lord" (1 Thessalonians 4:16,17; Italics supplied). There was no doubt in their minds that the Second Coming would be visible to all mankind—nothing secret about the event. The Apostolic Church believed that at the Second Coming the righteous dead would be raised, leaving the wicked in the state of death, or oblivion. They believed the righteous living would be translated to join the righteous multitude raised from the dead. But the wicked who "obey not the gospel," who were living on the earth at the time of the Second Coming, would be totally destroyed (2 Thessalonians 1:7–9).

One of the clearest descriptions of the *manner* of Christ's Second Coming is given in Acts of the Apostles, Chapter 1, following:

v.9. And when he had spoken these things, while they beheld, he was taken up; and a *cloud* received him out of their sight.

v.10. And while they looked stedfastly toward heaven as he went up, behold, two men stood by them in white apparel;

v.11. Which also said, Ye men of Galilee, why stand ye gazing up into heaven? this *same Jesus*, which is taken up from you into heaven, shall *so come in like manner as you have seen him go into heaven.*
Authorized King James Version (Italics supplied)

These verses from the Acts make a striking parallel between the Ascension of Christ and His Second Advent. Jesus literally ascended in person, not as a phantom, while a cloud received Him out of their vision. The *same* person of Jesus will literally descend from heaven in His Second Advent, surrounded by clouds and visible to all mankind. John bears out a similar description: "Behold he cometh with *clouds*; and *every eye shall see him*, and they also which pierced him: and *all kindreds of the earth shall wail because of him*" (Revelation 1:7; Italics supplied).

Christ's Teaching on the Sleep of Death

Referring to the succinct description of the Second Coming in 1 Thessalonians 4:16, 17 it is interesting to note that the three verses before this description, namely verses 13 to 15, refer to those who "sleep in Jesus" being equated with the "dead in Christ" (verse 16). Jesus also likened the death of Lazarus to sleep—that is the sleep of death (John 11:11, 14). The Apostolic Church of the first century also believed in the sleep of death, when they observed the stoning of Stephen, who while expiring, cried out "receive my spirit" (Greek: *pneuma* equated with breath) and then "he fell asleep" (Acts 7:59, 60). But they knew that the deathly sleep of Stephen was not merely unconsciousness—it was total oblivion and extinction.

Such an understanding and belief is based upon what David said on the subject of death: "His breath goeth forth, he returneth to his earth; in that very day his thoughts perish"—that is extinction (Psalms 146:4). Death, therefore, is the reverse of creation—when "the Lord God formed man of the *dust of the ground*, and breathed into his nostrils the *breath of life*, and man became a living soul" (Genesis 2:7; Italics supplied). Clearly when a person dies the body is buried and returns to the dust of the earth, and the essence of life, couched in symbolic language as the breath, or spirit, "shall return unto God who gave it" (Ecclesiastes 12:7).

The spirit, or breath of life, is not an entity in itself. It has no existence, personality, or form and shape apart from the body. There is no conscious entity that enters the body at birth, or leaves it after death, that can think, act, or do anything apart from the body. There is only life upon the *union* of the body and the essence of life breathed by God. Simply put, when a person dies, God turns off the current of life. "In the resurrection at the last day" (John 11:24) when Jesus comes, God will recreate the body, and breathe into it the breath of life, and "this *mortal shall have put on immortality*, and death is swallowed up in victory" (1 Corinthians 15:54; Italics supplied).

The doctrine of the immortality of the soul is an ancient pagan doctrine. The first profane historian Herodotus (born 484 B.C.) stated, "The Egyptians also were the first who asserted the doctrine that the soul of man is immortal" (*Herodotus*, Euter. 2, par. 123). But the Scriptures assert that it is God, "Who only hath immortality" (1 Timothy 6:16; 1:17). Man is mortal by nature. Nevertheless, immortality and eternal life will be conferred upon the saved, "who by patient continuance in well doing seek" for it (Romans 2:7). The late Archbishop of Canterbury, Primate of Great Britain, Dr. William Temple, said:

> Man is not immortal by nature nor of right;
> but he is capable of immortality, and there
> is *offered* to him resurrection from the
> dead and *life eternal*, if he will
> receive it from God and on God's terms.[2]
>
> (Italics supplied)

With regard to the destiny of the wicked the Scriptures run counter to the doctrine of the immortality of the soul. Jesus settled the matter when he said: "fear him which is able to destroy both soul (Greek: *psuche*, also translated *life*) and body in hell" (Matthew 10:28;

See Appendix A). Thus, the wicked are DESTROYED, they do not live and exist in hell. Further, the wicked are *not disembodied spirits in hell*. Hell fire destroys *both the soul, which is life, and the body*.

Jude says Sodom and Gomorrah "are set forth for an example, suffering the vengeance of eternal fire" (Jude 7). Because the word "eternal" is used it does not mean these cities are still burning eternally. Evidence shows the fire of destruction has burned out, but the *results* of total destruction are eternal. Peter clarifies the matter stating, "And turning the cities of Sodom and Gomorrah into *ashes*, condemned them to *destruction*, making them an example to those who afterward would live *ungodly* " (2 Peter 2:6, NKJV; Italics supplied). The complete destruction of these cities, reducing them to *ashes*, is an *example* of the annihilation of the *ungodly* at the end of time. Peter goes on and describes the final dissolution of the elements in a conflagration of the atmospheric heavens and the earth, in which everything will be "burned up." This is the final "day of judgment and perdition of ungodly men" (excerpted from 1 Peter 3:7–11).

The sleep of death, and the non-immortality of the soul, including the annihilation of the wicked, comprised the apostles' doctrine, steadfastly held by the Apostolic Church of the first century.

The Ten Commandments

The Apostolic Church observed the ten commandments not in order to be saved, but because they were saved by grace through faith (Ephesians 2:8). Since repentance includes a sorrow for sin and a turning away from it, it is absolutely essential to know what sin is. John defines sin saying, "sin is the transgression of the law" (1 John 3:4). Paul says, "by the law is the knowledge of sin" (Romans 3:20). Paul goes on, "I had not known sin, but by the law: for I had not known lust, except the law had said, *Thou shalt not covet* " (Romans 7:7; Italics supplied). Hence the ten commandments come into sharp focus to the repentant soul, they flash conviction of sin upon the soul. He stands guilty before God, for breaking any or all of the commandments of God.

The ten commandments have defined sin, and condemned the sinner. But now the law of ten commandments takes on another function. It acts the part of a severe schoolmaster: "wherefore the law was our schoolmaster, to *bring us unto Christ*, that we might be *justified by faith* " (Galatians 3:24; Italics supplied). The law is a whip to the soul, having driven the believer to Christ, where he may confess his sins, where he may wash his robes and make them white in the blood of the Lamb (Revelation 7:14). He is no longer under the condemnation of the law—he is under the grace of God (Romans 6:14). He is forgiven for his sin, and is cleansed from it. Like the publican in the parable, who pled for mercy because of his sin, the believer is justified (Luke 18:13, 14). He goes on his way rejoicing, establishing the law of God (Romans 3:31) and upholding it as "holy, and just, and good" (Romans 7:12).

The Sabbath

Since the Apostolic Church observed the ten commandments, the fourth commandment (Exodus 20:8–11), demonstrating love to God (Matthew 22:37, 38), would naturally fall into place. Such motivation was demonstrated by the women attending to Christ's burial, who "prepared spices and ointments; and rested the Sabbath day *according to the commandment*" (Luke 23:56; Italics supplied).

The observance of the Sabbath involved more than the cessation of labor (Exodus 20:9–11)—it was to be kept "holy" (Exodus 20:8). How else could it be kept holy, than to direct attention to the worship of God. And Jesus demonstrated that, when "he came to Nazareth, where he had been brought up: and as his custom was, he went into the *synagogue on the Sabbath day*, and stood up for to read" (Luke 4:16; Italics supplied). Likewise, the apostles, while maintaining the "apostles' doctrine," followed the example of Jesus, and according to the account "they came to Antioch in Pisidia, and went into the *synagogue on the Sabbath day*, and sat down. And after the reading of the law and the prophets the rulers of the synagogue sent unto them, saying, ye men and brethren, if ye have any word of exhortation for the people, say on. Then Paul stood up," and preached (Acts 13:14–16; Italics supplied).

Paul's Christ-centered preaching in Antioch was a triumph, because after preaching to the Jews, "the Gentiles besought that these words might be preached to them the next Sabbath. And the next Sabbath day came almost the whole city together to hear the word of God" (Acts 13:42, 44).

The book of Acts is replete with acts of worship and preaching on the Sabbath day. In Philippi, Paul "went out of the city by a river side" and prayed and worshiped with a group of women (Acts 16:12, 13). In Thessalonika Paul entered the synagogue and "three Sabbath days reasoned with them out of the scriptures" (Acts 17:1, 2). In Corinth Paul spent eighteen months teaching the word of God, "and he reasoned in the synagogue every Sabbath, and persuaded the Jews and the Greeks" (Acts 18:1, 11, 4). If we were to add up all the Sabbath meetings recorded in Acts we would come up with a total of eighty four Sabbath services.

While the preponderance of evidence favors the worship of God on the Sabbath day, there are those who think that a change to worship on Sunday, the first day of the week, is detectable. Two references are cited in view of this apparent change—Acts 20, verse 7, and 1 Corinthians 16, verses 1 and 2. However, close scrutiny of the references does not support the contention.

The first-day reference for a meeting, actually turns out to be a meeting held Saturday night, quoting the New English Bible: "On the Saturday night, in our assembly for the breaking of bread, Paul, who was to leave next day, addressed them, and went on speaking until midnight" (Acts 20:7). Obviously, Paul, who had spent the Sabbath (Saturday) with the believers in Troas, was loathe to leave them until midnight, way after the close of the Sabbath at sunset. It so happened that Paul stayed on "till break of day," being Sunday, at which time he "departed," walking a good twenty miles to Assos, where he boarded ship to sail on (Acts 20:11–14). It is clear that Paul attached no significance to Sunday sacredness by undertaking this strenuous journey.

The second reference to Sunday, the first day of the week, has nothing to do with Sunday sanctity—there is no gathering for worship, or any preaching. Paul was calling for the use of Sunday, not for worship, but for some book-keeping to be done; to check out one's private profits, and lay aside some money, ready to be picked up promptly, to relieve the poor at Jerusalem. The New English Bible says: "And now about the collection in aid of God's people: you should follow my directions to our congregations in Galatia. Every Sunday each of you is to put aside and keep by him a sum in proportion to his gains, so that there may be no collecting when I come" (1 Corinthians 16:1, 2).

Bishop Sylvester 1 of Rome, a contemporary of Constantine the Great, reputedly decreed that Sunday should not be called the "venerable day of the sun," according to Constantine's Sunday Law, 321 A.D., but it should be called the *Lord's Day*. Since the term Lord's Day has stuck ever since, it is no wonder that the term Lord's Day would be applied to Sunday, when one reads about John saying, "I was in the Spirit on the Lord's Day" (Revelation 1:9). But the Scriptures do not support this application. The fourth commandment describes the Sabbath as "the Sabbath of the Lord" (Exodus 20:10)—therefore the Sabbath *is* the Lord's Day. Christ Himself acknowledged that He, "The Son of Man is Lord even of the Sabbath day" (Matthew 12:8; See Mark 2:27, 28). If Christ is the Lord of the Sabbath, then it follows that the *Sabbath is the Lord's Day*, and not Sunday. Since the Apostolic Church of the first century accepted Jesus as "both Lord and Christ" (Acts 2:36) they had no problem in observing the true Lord's Day—the seventh-day Sabbath.

The Body Temple

When God demonstrated by the vision of the sheet full of unclean creatures, that Peter "should not call any man common or unclean" (Acts 10:28) such as the Gentiles, we notice another important point in the experience. When the voice told Peter to eat the creatures on the sheet, Peter was adamant and replied, "I have never eaten any thing that is common or unclean" (Acts 10:14), like the pig. He is to be commended for his stanch stand. He had lived up to the Levitical dietary prohibition, that outlined unclean creatures not to be eaten on land, in the waters, and in the air (Leviticus 11). In fact he was also obedient to the entire Levitical Health Code, as were many others.

Remember, in Old Testament times, Daniel "would not *defile* himself with the portion of the king's meat, nor with the wine which he drank," and requested rather a vegetarian diet (Daniel 1:8, 12; Italics supplied). We owe it to Paul who carried over these dietary and health principles to the era of the Apostolic Church, by molding them into the "apostles' doctrine" of the Body Temple, declaring at 1 Corinthians, Chapter 3:

v.16. Do you not know that you are the temple of God and that the Spirit of God dwells in you?

v.17. If any man *defiles the temple of God*, God will destroy him. For the temple of God is holy which temple you are.

(Italics supplied)
The New King James Version

Whatever defiles the Body Temple, be it unclean meat, like pork, or intoxicating alcoholic liquor, or any other defiling substance taken into the body, it is considered a great offense by God. In this context, even he who commits fornication, sins against his own body (1 Corinthians 6:18, 19).

Apart from the motivation to maintain a pure healthy Mind and Body, free from any injury, or defilement that is physical or mental, there is another much stronger motivation. And that is as Christians we are "bought with a price"—the precious blood of Jesus was shed to pay the price of our salvation (Acts 20:28). Therefore, since our bodies are bought, and we are saved thereby, we should be only too glad, consequent to our salvation, to glorify God in our body, and in our spirit, which belongs to God (1 Corinthians 6:20).

V. STRONG IN FELLOWSHIP (Acts 2:42)

The Apostolic Church was not only steadfast in the apostles' doctrine regarding seven major areas as outlined above, but was strong in the apostles' fellowship "not forsaking the assembling of ourselves together" (Hebrews 10:25). "No more strangers and foreigners, but fellow citizens with the saints, and of the household of God" (Ephesians 2:19).

VI. SIMPLE IN WORSHIP (Acts 2:42)

The simplicity of worship among the believers of the Apostolic Church is stated in one meaningful sentence. "They, continuing daily with one accord in the temple, and breaking bread from house to house" (Acts 2:46). Into this setting one must bring in the important ingredient of worship—prayer, since God's house is a house of prayer for all nations (Mark 11:17).

VII. SANCTIFIED IN LIFE (Acts 2:43)

The simple account of the believers of the Apostolic Church is that "fear came upon every soul" (Acts 2:43). The Godly fear and love of God was supreme. They were serious about their salvation and wanted to "grow in grace" (2 Peter 3:18), "for therein is the righteousness of God revealed from faith to faith" (Romans 1:17). They were justified by faith and had peace with God (Romans 5:1). And the very God of peace sanctified them wholly, and they were preserved blameless (1 Thessalonians 5:23).

VIII. SOLD ON THE GOSPEL ECONOMY (Acts 2:44, 45)

The Apostolic Church practised a Gospel economy, by helping one another materially, based on the law of sympathy, self-denial, and equality, rather than on the law of self-interest and competition. Upon the degree of need, they distributed the proceeds of the sale of possessions and goods without extravagance. The account says: "all that believed were together, and had all things common; and sold their possessions and goods, and parted them to all men, as every man had need" (Acts 2:44, 45).

IX. SINGING FROM THE HEART (Acts 2:46, 47)

True joy and happiness comes in knowing the Lord. The joy and gladness of these Christians of the Apostolic Church had the connotation of being exultant. With such emotions stirring within, they would naturally overflow in torrents of praise to God, and these Christians would enjoy the favor of all people (Acts 2:46, 47).

X. SUCCESSFUL IN WITNESS (Acts 2:47)

In fulfillment of the promise, that when the Holy Spirit was poured out at Pentecost they would be witnesses (Acts 1:8), 3000 souls were baptized, and the "Lord added to the church daily such as should be saved" (Acts 2:41, 47). But the promise extended to the "uttermost part of the earth." And before the first century concluded, the Apostolic Church advanced with the Gospel, in the face of terrible persecution, of entrenched dislike, and growing hatred and scorn. Nevertheless, it was Successful in Witness, and Paul could claim that the Gospel had been "preached to every creature which is under heaven" (Colossians 1:23).

These ten qualities including the "apostles' doctrine" were distinctive characteristics of the Apostolic Church of the first century. It was the model church—the paradigm. Chapter 2 will show how the Celtic Church *maintained* the fundamentals of the Apostolic Church. And since the Roman Church fell away from these fundamentals, we trace the *restoration* of the Apostolic Church by the Waldenses and Anabaptists—a thrilling episode in Redemptive history.

Chapter 2

RESTORATION OF THE APOSTOLIC CHURCH AMONG CELTS, WALDENSES, AND ANABAPTISTS

The Apostolic Church was " built upon the foundation of the apostles and prophets, Jesus Christ himself being the chief corner stone" (Ephesians 2:20). But, no sooner had it established itself on the foundation of the "apostles' doctrine" (Acts 2:42) than the seeds of apostasy were beginning to germinate. Although the Apostolic Church of the first century exhibited a pure, primitive godliness, Paul warned that after his death "shall grievous wolves enter in among you, not sparing the flock. Also of your own selves shall men arise, speaking perverse things, to draw away disciples after them" (Acts 20:29, 30).

The Apostasy of the Church, by attacking the Commandments

Writing to the Thessalonian church, who expected an imminent Second Coming, Paul warned, "Let no man deceive you by any means: for that day shall not come, except there come a FALLING AWAY FIRST" (Greek: a definite apostasy) a falling away of the church (2 Thessalonians 2:3; Capitalization supplied). Paul added, this "mystery of lawlessness is already at work" (2 Thessalonians 2:7, NKJV).

Since the devil could not destroy the early church with outright persecution, he resorted to compromise with Roman paganism. Soon after Constantine's Edict of Milan, 313 A.D., that resulted in the toleration and legalization of Christianity, an apostasy, or falling away is detectable, in making overtures to pagan philosophies and superstitions. After Constantine's Sunday law went into effect in 321, the church followed up with a subtle compromise at the Council of Laodicea, in 364, that enjoined:

> Christians shall not Judaize and be idle on Saturday [Sabbath], but shall work on that day; but the Lord's day they shall especially honour, and, as being Christians, shall, if possible, do no work on that day. If, however, they are found Judaizing, they shall be shut out from Christ.[1]

Such was the blatant attack on the fourth commandment, regarding the Sabbath, carried out by the Roman Church, fulfilling the apostasy, or "falling away," predicted by Paul. The "mystery of lawlessness" was also at work, subtly attacking the second commandment—forbidding the making of images and the worship of them (Exodus 20:3–6). By the time of the reign of Constantine the worship of relics was well established in the Roman Church. It was believed that the veneration of the so-called remains of martyrs and 'saints', or the objects that may have been associated with them, brought special merit to the worshiper and gave access to God in prayer. Pagan temples taken over by the church were to be consecrated with relics. The worship of relics led to the veneration of images and saint worship. The traffic in the trade of relics was enormous. From the discovery of the purported true cross by Constantine's mother, Helena, there were so many splinters and pieces of the cross paraded, that one could almost build a ship with them.

Maintaining the Fundamentals of the Apostolic Church

At this juncture we introduce the Celtic Church that endeavored to maintain the pristine purity of the early gospel, that primitive Christianity found in the Apostolic Church. While such an attack was made on the commandments of God by the Roman Church the early Celtic Church, of the sixth and seventh centuries in the British Isles, had a profound respect for the Ten Commandments—not an antinomian thought was ever indulged in, whether spoken or written. The ten commandments were recited in early Celtic services. The commandments were written first and foremost in the Celtic manual described as the "books of the Law" (*Liber ex Lege Moisi*), containing thirty five Biblical texts from the Pentateuch, excluding Genesis.[2]

From a theological point of view the Celtic Church understood the role of the commandments based upon the "apostles' doctrine" (Acts 2:42) of the Apostolic Church. The Celtic Christian recognized that the transgression of any one, or more of the commandments constituted sin. He believed they led him to Christ where he obtained forgiveness and power to observe them. Since Jesus came to save man from sin (Matthew 1:21), it was vital to the Celtic Christian's salvation, that his sin may be revealed by the law, in order for him to turn away from it, and be saved.

Apart from the Celtic manual, the *Liber*, containing all the ten commandments, the fifth Biblical text cited, specified the keeping of the Sabbath.[3] As mighty guardians of the Sabbath truth of the Apostolic Church, Celtic missionaries from the Emerald Isle, Ireland, traveled across to Scotland, planted their banner of the Sabbath truth there, and went on to capture England and Wales for that truth, and then turned to Europe and planted their banner in France, Germany, Switzerland, and Italy. These brave missionaries left home base without any assistance, negotiating the sea in frail coracles of wicker and hide to bring Christ, the Lord of the Sabbath, to the pagans of North Britain. Although hundreds of missionaries traveled to distant lands unknown, their accomplishments far exceeded their expectations, wielding an influence greatly disproportionate to their numbers. These self-sacrificing Celtic missionaries emanating from Ireland, Christianized Scotland, and the Anglo-Saxons of England, including the foreigners of Europe. Bear in mind that the greatest accomplishments of the missionary phase of the Celtic Church began with Columba in the year 563, and ended with the Council of Whitby in 664, when the tide of Roman Catholic opposition turned against the Celtic

Church. Nevertheless, the achievements of the missionary phase of the Celtic Church in that brief one hundred years, enters the annals of history as one of the most outstanding eras for the extensive proclamation of a pure Gospel, that made an impact on early Medieval civilization. The rest of the story after 664, is one in which any advance steps attempted by the Celtic Church were thwarted at every turn. But scattered remnants persisted in maintaining their faith in Britain, until their last bastion of faith—the Sabbath fell in the eleventh century, and they were eventually absorbed by the Roman Church.

Moreover for the Celtic Church to maintain the Sabbath truth for five centuries—from the sixth to the eleventh century—is a marvelous achievement, worthy of five-star recognition in the annals of ecclesiastical history.

It fell to the lot of Catholic Queen Margaret of Scotland, in 1060, to bring about the collapse of the Sabbath that was defended and observed by the Celtic Church. Since the Scottish Church was a church of the people, the Queen, displaying much zeal for her own church, was determined to unite church and state, and make it the church of the monarch. She summoned the remnants of Celtic Christian leaders to attend three days of grueling sessions in a congress, in which the commanding figure of the Queen attacked Celtic beliefs, especially the Sabbath. The well known Catholic historian Dr. Bellesheim described the scene:

> The Queen further protested against the prevailing abuse of Sunday desecration. 'Let us', she said, 'venerate the Lord's day, inasmuch as upon it our Saviour rose from the dead: let us do no servile work on that day'....The Scots in this matter had no doubt kept up the traditional practise of the ancient monastic Church of Ireland, which observed Saturday rather than Sunday as a day of rest.[4]

Is it not strange, that after all that Queen Margaret had done to wipe out the Celtic Church of Scotland, she had contributed to honor their founder, Columba, as a Roman Catholic Saint. Needless to say, his forerunner Patrick, was also enrolled as a Roman saint—all done in good faith of course to bolster the Roman Church policy of absorption.

What happened to the Scottish branch of the Celtic Church befell the Welsh branch also. "There is much evidence that the Sabbath prevailed in Wales universally until A.D. 1115, when the first Roman bishop was seated at St. David's."[5]

Having discussed the Celtic Church's adherence to the ten commandments, especially the Sabbath commandment, we go back to study its beginning, its strategy of operations, including the leadership and direction taken by the church, plus its beliefs, and the impact it made on early Medieval civilization.

There is no doubt, but that the Celtic Church was Spirit Endowed to be "witnesses unto the uttermost part of the earth" (Acts 1:8). They were Successful in Witness, like the Apostolic Church, because they believed in the reception of the Spiritual Gifts of: Apostles, evangelists, and pastor-teachers (Ephesians 4:11).

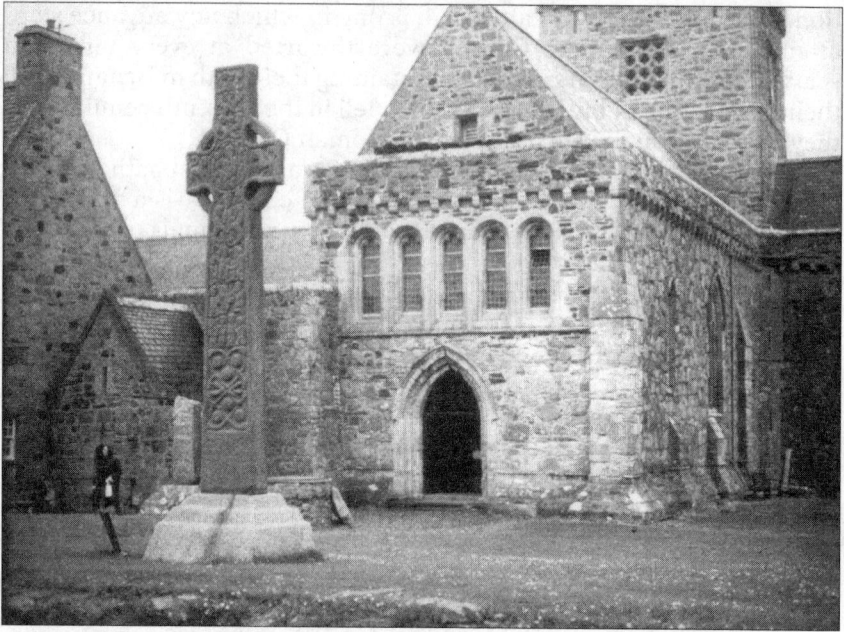

Picture 1   James Arrabito, Photographer

Iona Abbey marks the place of Columba's monastic institution

This reconstruction of the 13th Century Benedictine Abbey, that supplanted Columba's institution after six hundred years, preserves Columba's memory in maintaining the Apostolic Church ideal of pure, primitive Christianity. Notice the cross monument, reminiscent of Celtic symbolism.

Celtic Missionary Operations

Therefore the Irish *apostle* **Columba** set his sights on converting Scotland, by securing from Pictish King Bruide a beach-head for mission work on the lonely island of Iona, near Mull, off the north-west coast of Scotland, in 563 A.D. (See Picture 1). The apostle **Aidan**, called from Iona to convert the pagan Anglo-Saxons of England, followed the same strategy, by securing from King Oswald a mission base on the island of Lindisfarne, off the north-east coast of England, to begin work in the English kingdom of Northumbria, in 634. **Dinooth**, the apostle to Wales, was at the height of his teaching career in 597, having established a famous Celtic training college at Bangor, Northern Wales, that according to the first English historian Bede—subsequently boasted an enrollment of 3000 ministerial students, all of whom supported themselves by manual labor.[6] And what more can we say of **Maol Rubha** to the Hebrides, or Celtic pilgrims to Iceland.[7] But much more can be said of **Columbanus** the Celtic apostle to Europe, who set out in 585. To capture the impact of the Celtic missionary operations please consult the Map, Illustration 1.

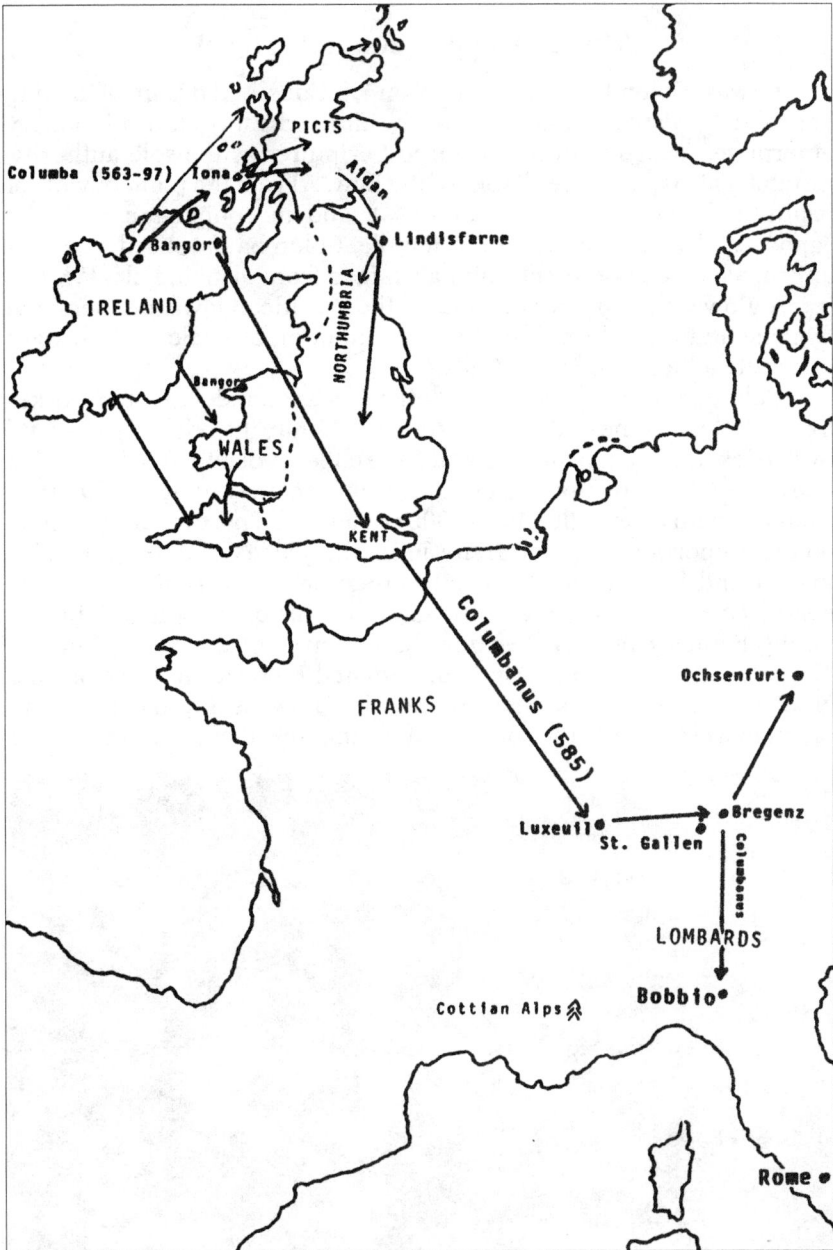

Illustration 1
Early Celtic Christian Expansion
Follow the missionaries: Columba from Iona to the Picts of Scotland; Aidan from Lindisfarne to Northumbria of England; and Columbanus from Bangor, Ireland, to Europe.

Celtic Leadership and Role Model

It was Columba, great-grandson of Conall, the son of a king baptized by Patrick, who vigorously initiated the Celtic missionary enterprise. Armed with the Inspired Scriptures as the sole authority, Columba also taught the "books of the Law."[8] From the point of view of healthful living (not ascetic practise), and in connection with the "apostles' doctrine" of the Body Temple, Columba practised vegetarianism, avoided condiments, and abstained from drinking ale. While a few followed Columba's example, the Levitical laws on personal hygiene and those forbidding the consumption of unclean flesh were generally adhered to by the Celts.[9]

Columba set the pace for his followers as an indefatigable worker for God. By the time of Columba, the Christianity introduced to Ireland by Patrick had taken firm root, and large colleges of ministerial training had resulted. The institute under the teaching of the renowned Finian of Clonard, with an enrollment of 3000 students at a particular time, took on the proportions of a university. From this place Columba gained his insight and love of the literal interpretation of the Bible as its own expositor. Here he became proficient in the art of copying and illuminating manuscripts that became the hallmark of the Celtic Church. Numerous Gaelic manuscripts, illuminated Lindisfarne Gospels, and New Testaments, were spread far and wide (now displayed in continental monasteries and the British Museum, see Picture 2). Columba

© L.L.T. Productions   Picture 2   James Arrabito, Photographer
"Old Latin" Itala Version of the Bible
Celtic Illuminated Bibles and Illustrated Celtic manuscripts found their way across Europe. A number of these are housed in a seventeenth century library at St. Gallen, Switzerland.

himself copied by hand 300 New Testaments. Besides that, he established over 300 churches, a third of which were church schools, generally designated "monasteries," but more like the schools of the prophets of the Old Testament. Columba's biographer Adamnan described Columba's industrious life with these words: "He could not pass the space of even a single hour without applying himself either to prayer, or reading, or writing, or else to some manual labor."[10] Such was the pattern he set for his missionary disciples to follow.

Celtic Model Institute of Iona, Scotland

Of course Columba's greatest accomplishment, was when he arrived on the island of Iona, where he ousted Druidic influence, and established a monastic community, not as a place of withdrawal, but as a model mission outpost, and a veritable island of culture in an ignorant world. And this mission outpost was maintained for six hundred years, until the Celts were driven out by Benedictine monks. The famous church historian Merle D'Aubigne says that Columba esteemed the cross of Christ higher than the royal blood which flowed in his veins, and that this "ocean rock" Iona, was justly named the "light of the western world."[11] From here the ten commandments were presented as "Christ's law," and from the "books of the Law" governing social, economic, and legal relationships, emanated laws governing Iona, to later enter the legislative halls of King Alfred the Great, and beyond. Light on health and healing came from the infirmary at Iona, where many who were sick or troubled in mind, went away healed. At Iona all the branches of learning then known were diligently cultivated, including astronomy.

Historian William Cathcart paid this tribute to Columba:

> Columba possessed a superior education. He was familiar with Latin and Greek, secular and ecclesiastical history, the principles of jurisprudence, the law of nations, the science of medicine, and the laws of mind. He was the greatest Irishman of the Celtic race in mental powers; and he founded in Iona the most learned school in the British Islands and probably in Western Europe for a long period.[12]

Celtic Church Transition, From 597

The year 597 is important for two reasons. First, it marked the death of Columba at Iona, aged 76, after thirty four years of ministry in Scotland, in which according to Bede, the eighth century British historian, he "turned the nation to faith in Christ by word and by example." On Saturday, June 9, Columba foretold his death while talking to his disciple Diermit: "This day is called the Sabbath, that is, the day of rest, and such it will truly be to me; for it will put an end to my labors."[13]

The second reason why 597 is important, is that it marked a turning point in the history of the Celtic Church—that is, the beginning of the end of the Celtic Church. Pope Gregory I sent a delegation of forty monks headed by archbishop Augustine to Canterbury, the metropolis of Kent (597), with the express purpose of bringing about the submission of the Celtic Church to the jurisdiction of archbishop Augustine, including subscribing to Papal practises. Soon after gaining the support of King Ethelbert of Kent these sentiments were presented to a delegation of Celtic bishops and leaders from Bangor, Wales. "But the bishops refused these things," says Bede, "nor would they recognize Augustine as their archbishop." The apostle Dinooth, as spokesman for the Celtic delegation, upheld the principle of love for one another, but further elaborated saying, "We know not, that any other obedience can be required of us towards him whom you call the pope or the father of fathers."[14]

Such refusal to submit to Roman demands drew forth the wrath of Augustine, who threatened, "If you will not unite with us in showing the Saxons the way of life, you shall receive from them the stroke of death."[15] Some time later King Ethelfrid of Northumbria waged war upon the Britons, but not until he slaughtered 1200 young men of the famous training college of Bangor, Wales, who were engaged in prayer at the time. And the venerable Bede of the Romish persuasion, did not denounce this dastardly act, but blithely commented on it as "divine judgment," in fulfillment of "Augustine's prophecy that the faithless Britons, who had rejected the offer of eternal salvation, would incur the punishment of temporal destruction."[16] The rest of the story is the gradual effacement of the Celtic Church in the British Isles no later than the early twelfth century.

Celtic Church Belief

While Bede's *History of the English Church and People* discusses Roman practises, he does not enumerate the "many other observances" or doctrines of the Celtic Church.[17] However, Bede does grant the Celtic Church "diligently followed whatever pure and devout customs that they learned in the *prophets, the Gospels, and the writings of the Apostles*"[18] (Italics supplied). Therefore the writings of the Apostles can be summarized as the "apostles' doctrine," a distinctive mark of the Apostolic Church (Acts 2:42). Thus the Celtic Church was steadfast in the "apostles' doctrine" of the Apostolic Church of the first century.

The Celtic believer was Saved by Faith, not by the merits of his deeds, but by the Grace of God (Ephesians 2:8, 9). The merits of Christ, imputed to the believer was vital to salvation. The relationship of the Law and the Gospel was understood. Adherence to the ten commandments did not save a person—they defined and exposed sin; then the law would drive the penitent to Christ to receive forgiveness, and be empowered to uphold the ten commandments, including the Sabbath commandment.[19] Confession of sin was not made to a priest. Celtic Christians believed in the High Priestly ministry of Christ to receive confession of sin direct.[20] There was no invocation of saints as intermediaries of salvation. In the formative years Celtic salvation was climaxed in adult Baptism—though triple immersion prevailed.[21] Celtic worship was simple, celebrating the Lord's Supper in remembrance of Christ's death.[22]

Other distinctive beliefs of the Celtic Church included conditional immortality, and the final glorification of righteous men, taking place only after the resurrection on the last day, at the Second Advent of Christ, at which time the wicked would be *annihilated* in hell fire, since eternal torment in hell was considered untenable, unbiblical, and unchristian.[23] The Second Advent was viewed to be near at hand—both Patrick and Columbanus emphasized this view.[24]

Impact of the Celtic Church on Europe

The Celtic Church was not only evangelical, but also evangelistic. It is no wonder then, that the Celtic Church would not be content to confine its endeavors to the British Isles, but would extend its mission to continental Europe. Armed with the Scriptures, and trained in the halls of learning at Bangor, north-east Ireland, Columbanus set out in the year 585 with twelve companions, bound for the land of the Franks—France. While Columbanus was to impress the pure Gospel on France, Germany, Switzerland, and Italy, perhaps more than anyone else who followed him, he also "proved to be the great avant-courier of the rebirth of civilization in Europe."[25]

As you read on, please consult the Map Illustration 1. In this way the story becomes more interesting and gripping.

The apostle Columbanus and his band of missionaries arrived in France. They accepted King Guntram's offer of an ancient half-ruined Roman fort at Anegray, and planted their first mission retreat. Before long multitudes thronged the mission outpost craving what the thirteen skilled Irish teachers could give them. Anegray now bursting at the seams, two more centers were located at Luxeuil and Fontaines, all within a radius of about twenty miles. This network of three mission settlements attracted more students, and more Irish missionaries to manage the three-pronged mission institute, on the cutting edge of early Medieval civilization in France—the renowned Luxeuil leading the way.

It is generally claimed that the papal legate Boniface from England was the apostle to Germany, but the facts are that the Celtic Irish missionaries preceded Boniface; and it turns out that Boniface (died 784) bitterly opposed the Celtic Church in Europe, as Augustine did in Britain.[26] The first known Celtic Irish missionary was Columbanus, who entered Germany, and left behind him a strong center in Ochsenfurt, and "Schottenkirche" in Regensburg, Germany. Centers were also established in Switzerland at Disentis and Ursanne by Columbanus and his men. He also wound up with a mission institute in Bregenz, Austria. Leaving Bregenz in the capable hands of his faithful co-worker, Gallus, Columbanus crossed the treacherous Alps, bound for Italy. The name of Gallus is connected with his mission college of St. Gallen, Switzerland, that was later forcefully taken over by Benedictine

Illustration 2
Waldensian Missionaries or Colporteurs Disguised as Peddlers

monks. A seventeenth century library at St. Gallen contains many old
Celtic manuscripts, including eighth century manuscripts of the New
Testament—mute testimony of a bygone age of primitive Apostolic
Christianity spread far and wide. Besides, in its heyday, St. Gallen was
the intellectual center of the German world.

We pick up the final acts of the apostle Columbanus, who was grate-fully received in the northern court of King Agilulf of the Lombards, who had established power over half of Italy. But his stay was brief, he wanted to establish an evangelical training center. The King recom-mended a ruined church at Bobbio. Columbanus' versatility in direct-ing the clearing of the forest, the construction of roads, the digging of wells, the erection of buildings, the domestication of wild animals, the production of crops, and acting as a physician—knew no bounds. The result of his labors, while beyond the age of seventy, was a Celtic train-ing center at Bobbio par excellence.

Bobbio, along with St. Gallen, became the chief book-producing center in Europe. When Columbanus died at the age of seventy two, in 615, every branch of knowledge known in his day was represented in his library at Bobbio. Columbanus himself is reputed to have twenty five extant manuscripts to his name. Needless to say, the training insti-tute at Bobbio was soon ranked the intellectual center of northern Italy. The memory of Columbanus was so stamped upon the history of the region, that the Roman Church eventually proclaimed him a saint, despite the Roman Church's efforts to destroy him when he was alive. Thus the Roman Church laid claim to Columbanus as a saint, in company with Patrick and Columba.[27]

THE WALDENSES

The welcome arrival of Columbanus by Agilulf, King of the Lombards, and his subsequent establishment of a prominent training center at Bobbio, made a profound contribution in swelling the growing evangelical faith of the archdiocese of northern Italy.

Forerunners of the Waldenses

In the fourth century Bishop Ambrose (died 397) not only forged an administrative independence from Rome, but also a spiritual independence in this archdiocese leaning emphatically toward evangelicalism. Contemporaries Jovinian and his followers likely taking "refuge in the Alpine valleys,"[28] and Vigilantius writing against Jerome from somewhere "between the Adriatic and the Alps of King Cotius" (according to Jerome), kept alive the evangelical teaching. Next Columbanus strengthened evangelicalism in the seventh century. By the ninth century the mantle of Ambrose and Vigilantius fell upon the bishop of Turin, northern Italy, named Claudius, who was accused of being infected with the "poison" of Vigilantius.[29] Because his jurisdic-tion included the Cottian Alps, Claudius earned the title, "Bishop of the Valleys," but in the tradition of his ancestors he gained the title, "Protestant of the ninth century." Finally, by the *eleventh century*, the independence of the Milan diocese came to an abrupt end, when Papal control was established under protest. Compare the effacement of the Celtic Church in Britain about the *same time*. Nevertheless, in the wake of the Papal takeover some protesters fled across the Alps, while others found refuge in the Cottian Alps—to become known as the **Waldenses,** who were out to restore the evangelical faith of the Apostolic Church.

The foregoing brief historical sketch describes the forerunners of the Italian branch of the Waldenses. They were united, or fused with the French branch of the Waldenses after Peter Waldo revitalized the Waldensian movement, and after the meeting in Bergamo, Italy, in 1218.

Peter Waldo Leans toward Christ-centered Faith of Apostolic Church

Waldo's contribution was not only evangelical but also evangelistic. The prosperous merchant, Peter Waldo of Lyons, France, abandoned his wealth in obedience to Christ (Matthew 19:21), procured a translation of the Holy Scriptures, and took to the streets, preaching repentance, in order to relive the 'life of the apostles' of the Apostolic Church.

But Waldo and his followers were upbraided for their *unauthorized preaching* of the pure Gospel, and for the distribution of the Scriptures—all of which ran against the grain of the Roman Church. During their condemnation at the Lateran Council (1179), it was reported that they were naked disciples who "follow a naked Christ."[30] The term naked can mean: without clothes—that is materially poor, and also without religious adornments, or extras, in the sense of *Christ only*, as imitators of Christ—*imitatio Christi*. Hence the Waldenses not only followed Christ, separated from the wealth of the world, but also as the very reference point of their faith, giving implicit heed to all his "commands" (Matthew 28:19, 20) and living out the tenets of the Sermon on the Mount, so well expressed in their ancient document—the *Noble Lesson* as follows:

> Now after the Apostles, were certain Teachers,
> Who taught the way of Jesus Christ our Saviour.
> And these are found even at this Day,
> But they are known to very few,
> Who have a great desire to teach
> the way of Jesus Christ.

Spiritual Gifts among Waldenses

The *Noble Lesson* stated that "all the popes which have been from Silvester to the present, and all Cardinals, Bishops, Abbots, and the like, have no power to absolve or pardon; Tis God alone who pardons, and no other." The Waldenses had pastors to shepherd the flock and receive confessions—believing God forgives. They called them "barbes," meaning originally "uncle," perhaps in contrast to the Roman Catholic priests, called "father." These barbes received their training from a college in the Angrogna valley, way up in the Pra del Tor of the Cottian Alps (See Picture 3). Their training included memorizing several gospels and epistles, the acquirement of some trade, the learning of languages and mathematics,

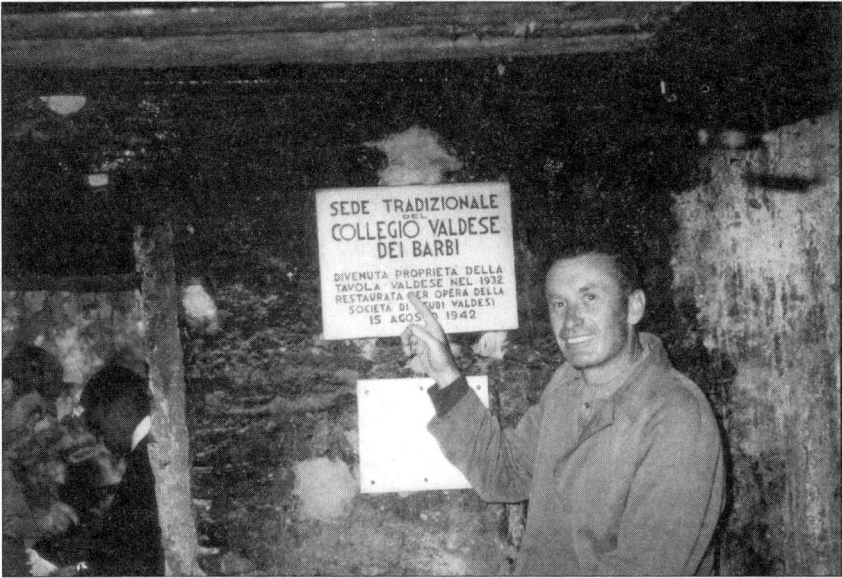

Picture 3
Waldensian College of the Barbes
The author, back in 1972, is seen in the restored Waldensian College, built entirely of stone, typical
of Waldensian dwellings. The College was remotely located in the Angrogna valley, way up in the
Pra del Tor (meadow of the tower) of the towering Cottian Alps.

and enough botany and rudimentary medicine and surgery, to bring the
healing touch to their ministry. Every barbe was required to serve several
years as a missionary. They went out two by two, an older man with a
younger man, usually in the guise of merchants, or peddlers, but as colporteurs, they secretly distributed the Scriptures. Clearly they gave evidence
of the Scriptural gifts of apostles, evangelists, and teachers (Ephesians
4:11), as they penetrated lands beyond Italy, such as: France, Germany,
Moravia, Bohemia, Austria, Switzerland, Hungary, Poland, Spain,
England, and even Bulgaria and Turkey. Thus these Waldensian missionaries exercised their Spiritual gifts and were Successful in Witness like the
Apostolic Church of the first century (See Illustration 3).

The "Noble Lesson" Contains the "apostles' doctrine" (Acts 2:42)

The *Noble Lesson*, the oldest extant document from the twelfth
century, takes the form of an anonymous poem of 479 lines, manuscript
copies of which are today at Cambridge, Dublin, Geneva, and
Grenoble. It was the equivalent of a confession of faith, and of an
evangelical heritage passed down from generation to generation. It is
even claimed that the "apostles' doctrine" (Acts 2:42) of the *Noble
Lesson* is a continuation of Claudius of Turin.[31] The *Noble Lesson*
upholds the ten commandments. It also points to the day of Judgment,
when Jesus returns, preceded by many Signs, but "no man living can
know the end." Nevertheless, the "end of this world approaches,"
continues the Noble Lesson, "there are already a thousand and one

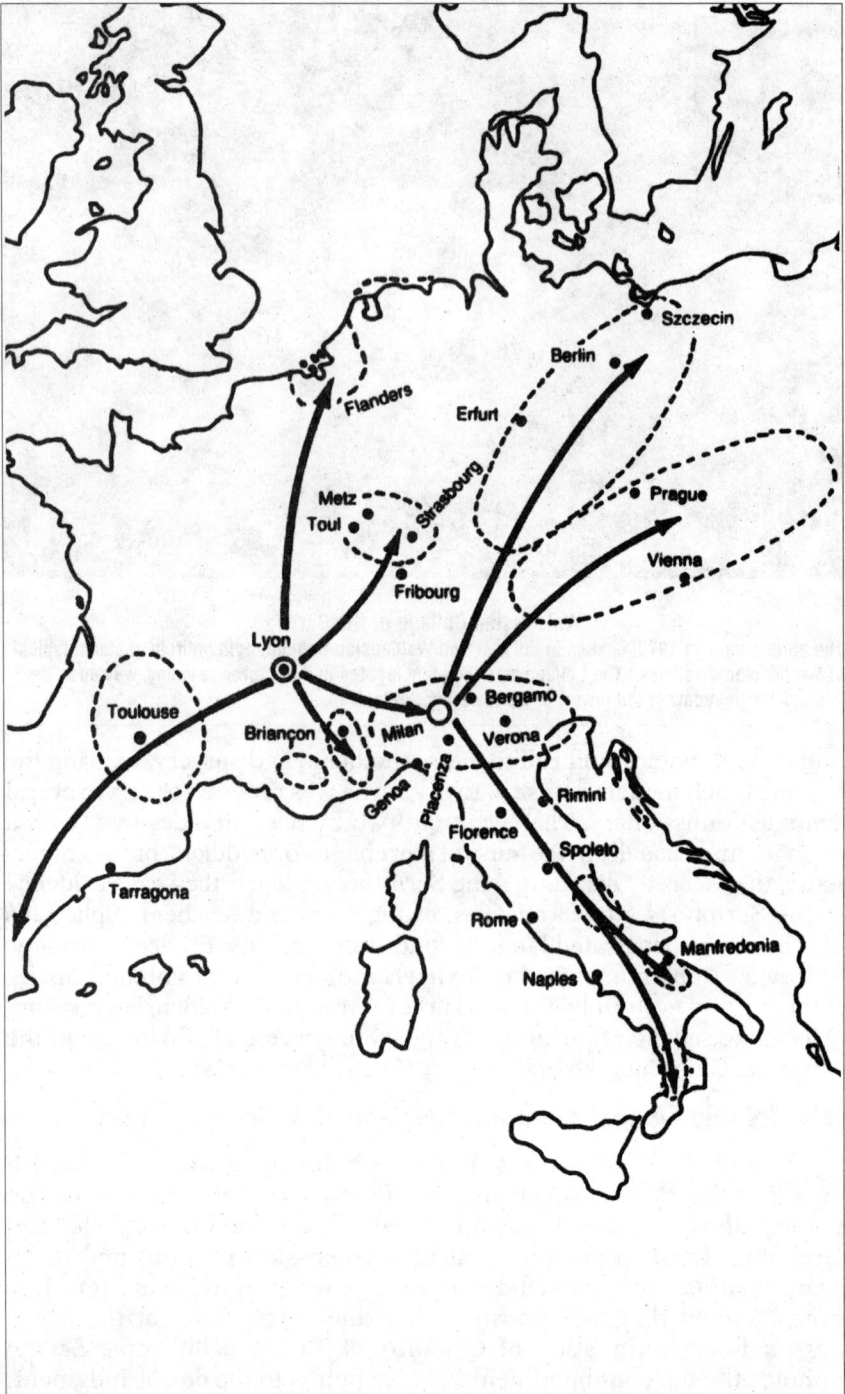

Courtesy Claudiana Editrice

Illustration - G. Tourn, *You are my Witnesses*, p. 60

Illustration 3
Pre-Reformation Waldensian Penetration

hundred years fully accomplished, since it was written thus, for we are in the last time."

Other Waldensian Beliefs

While the Waldenses in one of their treatises inveighed against purgatory, prayers for the dead, and invocation of departed saints, they tended to believe in the immortality of the soul. Hence the *Noble Lesson* portrays eternal torment for the wicked. Furthermore, while the *Noble Lesson* advocated "baptizing the nations," it was not stated whether it was administered to infants or adults.[32] What emerges from the scanty sources is that both forms of baptism were practised. Although the later articles of faith tabulated at Chamforans in 1532 supported baptism of "little children."[33] While these several beliefs, just mentioned, did not match the "apostles' doctrine" of the early Apostolic Church, there were others that did, some of which have already been noted.

Sabbatarian Waldenses

The Waldenses came under several names such as the Vaudois, meaning *valleys*, or Passagii (from Latin: *passagium*), meaning inhabitants of the passes.[34] Those classed as Waldenses in the broader sense: the Passagii and some among the "Waldensian Brethren," or Picards, of Bohemia, took the fourth commandment quite literally, and observed the seventh day of the week—Saturday.[35] Erasmus of Rotterdam reported that even as late as about the year 1500, Bohemians not only kept the seventh day scrupulously, but were also called Sabbatarians,[36] having restored the Sabbath of the Apostolic Church. For lack of historical information the extent and duration of Sabbath observance among Waldenses cannot be fully determined.

A Few Vegetarian Waldenses

On the "apostles' doctrine" of the Body Temple it was by no means universal among Waldenses. There were some Waldensian merchants in the twelfth century who often traveled from Switzerland into Suabia, Bavaria, and northern Italy. They lived on vegetables, rarely ate meat, and some of them never.[37]

Waldensian Identity with the True Church of the Apostles

In conclusion, it is to be noted that the Waldenses identified themselves with the metaphorical sun-clothed woman of Revelation, chapter 12—the True Church, separate from the scarlet woman of Revelation 17, the fallen church, according to their *Treatise on Antichrist*. Their connection with the Apostolic Church of the first century, noted for its primitive Christianity, is well expressed by one of their number, the great leader Henri Arnoud, who led the Waldenses back to their Alpine valleys after terrible persecution:

> The Vaudois are, in fact, descended from those refugees
> from Italy who, after St. Paul had there preached the

gospel, abandoned their beautiful country and fled, like
the *woman mentioned in the Apocalypse*, to these wild
mountains [Cottian Alps], where they have to this day
handed down the gospel from father to son in the same
purity and *simplicity as it was preached by St. Paul.*[38]

(Italics supplied).

THE ANABAPTISTS

At this juncture we recall the exciting adventure for the Lord, as
Columbanus, the Celtic apostle advanced with Gospel in hand, and
entered Switzerland. Reconnoitering in the region of Zurich in 610, he
met with opposition from the pagan Allemani or Suevi, and so he moved
on to establish other centers, and ended up in Bobbio, Italy. His compan-
ion Gallus, left behind, founded the famous mission institute at St. Gallen
for which he had labored for over twenty five years, until his death in 640.
But the work which he had commenced was carried forward by his disciples, who in turn established other centers, and made a great impact on
the region, lasting for many years to come, until the whole country was
brought under the control of the Roman Church.[39]

Free Church Concept

Nevertheless, the seed sown by Celtic Christianity, laid dormant in
the soil of Switzerland for centuries, buried beneath the mighty
avalanche of the Roman Church, until Huldreich Zwingli launched the
Reformation in Zurich. But while he advanced the Protestant Reformation, there arose a party in Zwingli's circle who advocated the *restoration of the Apostolic Church*, based on the restoration of primitive
Christianity—a FREE CHURCH, separate from city council, or state
control. This was an explosive innovation, since the Reformers relied
on a local prince, or city council to put their reforms in place. The
concept of a "free church" clashed with the Zurich Council, a rift
resulted, and Zwingli's circle of friends was broken—Dr. Balthasar
Hubmaier, Conrad Grebel, and Simon Stumf separated.[40]

Believer's Baptism

But the bombshell that really blew up in the face of the Zurich
Council, was when these three men and others, studied the great truth
of *believer's baptism* so prevalent in the Apostolic Church, and Grebel
carried out the first baptism (January 21, 1525), followed by a succession of baptisms. Hubmaier received baptism himself, and in turn
baptized 300 converts—the Anabaptist movement was now launched.
The Zurich Council was enraged at these developments, and passed
legislation November, 1526, that Anabaptists who practised believer's
baptism should be punished by DROWNING.[41]

Growth of the Anabaptists

Other Cantons in Switzerland followed the example of Zurich, and swiftly instituted legislation to suppress Anabaptism. The Council of St. Gallen decreed the penalty of imprisonment, or banishment, forbidding Anabaptists to administer believer's baptism by immersion. Before this decree went into effect, however, a large number were baptized in the Sitter River, resulting in a church membership of 800. At least 1500 new converts came to St. Gallen from nearby Appenzell. Many were imprisoned as a result of the decree, but still Anabaptism grew at St. Gallen—a leading growth point.[42] It has to be a strange coincidence that St. Gallen became a strong center of primitive Christianity in two ages, centuries apart, first—in the seventh century exhibiting Celtic Christianity, and second—in the sixteenth century displaying Anabaptist Christianity.

The Anabaptist movement spread like wild fire throughout Switzerland until the death of Zwingli (1531), when it was virtually extinguished by the state church, except for some small enclaves. As Anabaptism spread, so did the fires of persecution—Georg Blaurock, the first person baptized at the inauguration of the movement, was burned at the stake in 1529.

Anabaptist Evangelism

The Swiss story was repeated elsewhere. Spirit endowed evangelists, (Ephesians 4:11), like the charismatic Hans Hut, penetrated Austria and Moravia. His spirited efforts earned him the epithet "Apostle of Austria." He evangelized, baptized converts, and set the pace, by immediately appointing new converts to evangelize—thus putting into practise the concept of a priesthood of believers—men and women of all ages sharing their faith. It was like a page out of the book of Acts (Acts 2:47), making the Anabaptist movement so Successful in Witness, like the Apostolic Church.

Persecution of Anabaptists

But, matching the dynamic spread of Anabaptism was the suppression and persecution of Anabaptists. Within days after the memorable Protest of the Princes at the Diet of Speier (1529), the Diet, with the concurrence of the Evangelicals, enacted an imperial decree to exterminate Anabaptists. As a result thousands of Anabaptists were slain in Austria under Papal persecution, let alone Protestant. Therefore, the Anabaptist movement was crushed in Austria, practically disappeared in South Germany, and was eventually consolidated in the Netherlands by Menno Simons—founder of the Mennonites.

Anabaptists Believe in Soul-Sleep

Even in England persecution of Anabaptists was rife. In 1575 two Dutch Anabaptist refugees were burned at the stake for their belief in "soul-sleep" similar to the Apostolic Church, among other beliefs. Again in 1611 two English Anabaptists, each met a martyr's death by burning for his belief in soul-sleep under the authority of King James I, Defender of the Faith, and by whose authority the King James Version of the Scriptures came out in the same year. The "state of man in death" must have been a volatile issue at this time, because the one Anabaptist martyr, Edward Wightman, was thrice charged specifically for the heresy of soul-sleep, and in the same year, 1611, a work opposing the mortality of the soul appeared. The work, written by John Jackson, was entitled *The Soule is Immortal; or Discourse Defending the Immortality of the Soule; Against Anabaptists* [such as Legatt and Wightman], *Atheists, etc.*[43]

Martin Luther believes in Soul-sleep

Isn't it strange that Martin Luther was *not bitterly persecuted* for his outright declaration, among others, that *"the soul is immortal"* [*animam esse immortalem*], is one of the pope's "monstrous opinions to be found in the Roman dunghill of decretals."[44] Neither was he persecuted for his constant belief in soul-sleep: a total suspension of thought and consciousness, totally oblivious to the passing of time or events,—all of this during the interval between death and the final day of resurrection, at which time both body and soul will be united again. Had Luther made soul-sleep part of his Reformation package, he might have invited persecution. He delicately illustrated his conviction in these words:

> We shall sleep, until He comes and knocks on the little grave and says, Doctor Martin, get up! Then I shall rise in a moment and be happy with Him forever.[45]

"A Brief Confession and Declaration of Faith"

Back to the Anabaptist saga, English Baptists in 1660 presented to King Charles II: "A Brief Confession and Declaration of Faith set forth by many of us falsely called Anabaptists." The Confession of Faith stated it was "owned and approved by more than 20,000," and that all twenty five articles were believed to be the "apostolical way." Article XXII stated that it was not until the Second Coming that the Righteous would enter the eternal kingdom. Obviously the Righteous were in a state of insensibility until then. As for the wicked they "perish for ever, like his own dung; they which have seen him, shall say, where is he?"[46]

Sabbatarian Anabaptists

Luther was not enamored with Sabbatarian Anabaptists, whom he identified as living in Austria and Moravia.[47] And yet, were they not living up to *his own definition* of the True Church: "Where God's Word is purely taught there is the true church?"

Dr. Hubmaier, Anabaptist theologian, with twenty four works to his name—including monumental, incisive tracts against infant baptism and religious intolerance, settled in 1526, in Nikolsburg, Moravia, not too far north of Vienna. The region belonged to the princes of Liechtenstein. Here the tolerant, protector of the Anabaptists, Prince Leonhard von Liechtenstein and his brother were baptized by Hubmaier. An estimated 12,000 Anabaptists gathered in Nikolsburg under Hubmaier's influence, before his death by burning in 1528.[48] But this large gathering of Anabaptists was divided, a number of whom were Sabbatarians, like the Apostolic Church, and even Prince Leonhard "held to" or favored the Sabbatarian Anabaptists.[49] (See Illustration 4).

Courtesy Herald Press Illustration.

W. Pipkin, *Balthasar Hubmaier Theologian of Anabaptism*, Frontispiece

Illustration 4

Dr. Balthasar Hubmaier, Anabaptist Theologian

The only known portrait, from an old woodcut. Hubmaier was burned at the stake primarily for his belief and practice of believer's baptism.

Anabaptists and the Second Coming

The division at Nikolsburg was also of another nature. The evangelist Hans Hut had preached that the Second Coming would take place May 15, 1527 (second anniversary of the battle of Frankenhausen), and when that failed, he set on the date of Whitsunday, 1529. Nevertheless, Hubmaier opposed Hut and taught his followers *not* to look for the immediate Second Coming and the setting up of the millennial kingdom.[50]

The Gospel Economy

But the divisive teaching of Hut that really split the Nikolsburg church was the doctrine of Christian communalism. Hubmaier opposed Hut, and was firm on the Gospel economy practised by the Apostolic Church, that meant Christian believers should hold all property, subject only to the needs of the poorer believers of the church for distribution (Acts 2:44, 45). Hubmaier's teaching was generally held as an Anabaptist tenet of faith. But Hut's teaching brought about a separation and emigration from Nikolsburg of the communalistic element. It was further fostered and organized by Jacob Hutter in Austerlitz—a town about thirty miles north of Nikolsburg. This colony of Anabaptists living communally was greatly welcomed, and it thrived economically in agriculture and industry, and grew to great proportions, as high as 70,000. It continued in peace and prosperity until 1535, when King Ferdinand I, in reaction to the debacle of Munster, ordered that all Anabaptists in Moravia be rooted out.[51] Anabaptists then fled and took refuge in Bohemia and Hungary, others made their way into southern Russia. By 1874 these Hutterian Anabaptists left Russia and migrated in a body to South Dakota, U.S.A., to continue their Christian communalism, first practised in 1529.[52]

Genuine Christianity

The Anabaptists were intent on restoring the Apostolic Church, which in essence meant a restoration of genuine primitive Christianity that marked that age. The expectations were high, it was not an "easy believism," but a genuine commitment to Christ. The believer was expected to give evidence: of true repentance (Acts 2:38) and the regenerated changed life. He was expected to separate from the "abominable" lifestyle of the pleasure-loving, wealthy, proud, and violent world (1 John 2:15–17), refusing: to participate in the magistry, to take oaths, and to take up the sword in warfare—all according to the Schleitheim Confession (1527). He was expected to take up his cross to follow Christ (Matthew 10:38) in self-denial and suffering, to learn of Christ (Matthew 11:28–30), to observe his teachings (Matthew 28:19, 20), and to adopt the Sermon on the Mount, as a literal code for all Christians. Upon a personal confession of faith the believer would be baptized into the corporate body of the church (1 Corinthias 12:13), and subscribe to its discipline if the need should arise (Matthew 18:15–18). Having entered the community of believers the reborn Anabaptist Christian would have a new attitude towards property (Acts 2:44, 45). He would live in peace with his fellow men—dubbed "the quiet in the land;" where simplicity, religious fervor, brotherly love, industry, and temperance, marked their community—a priesthood of believers, and a light to the world.

On that beautiful note we conclude this chapter, and spring into the nineteenth century to consider the Christian developments of that age found in Chapter 3.

But the nineteenth century, believe it or not, presents an age in which the "apostles' doctrine" (Acts 2:42) of the Second Advent comes under fire, both in the British Isles and America. Spurious interpretations of the Second Advent and the Signs of Christ's Second Coming arise. An attempt is made to restore the Apostolic Church in England, complete with a restoration of all Spiritual Gifts—notably tongues, prophecy, and healing. Finally there emerges from an Advent movement in America, a Restoration of the Apostolic Church of the Last Days. Such is the theme of the following chapters, to engage the interest of the reader, as you move into Chapter 3 with great anticipation.

Harry Anderson, Artist

Picture 4

Albury Park Prophetic Conference, 1826

This historic meeting of about twenty prominent ministers and laymen, convened to study Bible Prophecies, spearheaded the Great Second Advent Awakening. The standing figure is that of Henry Drummond, who became an "apostle" of the Catholic Apostolic Church. On the extreme right, seated, is Joseph Wolff, famous itinerant missionary, who preached the Second Advent to take place in 1847. A key figure, at the conference is Edward Irving, second to Wolff's right, a powerful Advent preacher, who fostered the restoration of charismatic gifts, resulting in the establishment of the Catholic Apostolic Church. Second to Irving's right is Daniel Wilson, who became Bishop of India.

Chapter 3

THE GREAT SECOND ADVENT AWAKENING

An unprecedented religious awakening during the first half of the nineteenth century captivated the world. It was spear-headed in Great Britain and spread to continental Europe, reaching Asia and North Africa. It was ignited in South America and exploded in North America. The thrust of the religious awakening was directed toward the imminence of the Second Coming of Christ. It was a great Second Advent Awakening, a sudden awareness and realization that the Second Advent was near at hand, spurred on by an earnest, intense searching of the Prophetic Scriptures.

Prophetic Awakening through Conferences, Periodicals and Books

But, let us now narrow the field, and turn back the clock, and through our imagination open a door in this era. We peek into the library of the palatial Villa at Albury Park, Surrey, England. The Villa was made available by the rich banker and parliamentarian Henry Drummond, who was later designated an apostle in Edward Irving's Catholic Apostolic Church. We view an August assemblage of twenty various church ministers and laymen, by invitation of Drummond. This was the nucleus of a group, destined to play an important role in the Advent Awakening. It comprised prime movers like Joseph Wolff, famous itinerant missionary and linguist; William Cuninghame, with twenty one works to his name; Daniel Wilson, later Bishop of Calcutta, India; and Edward Irving, whose advent preaching held thousands spell-bound, who also helped to launch the voluminous prophetic periodical of the day—*The Morning Watch* (financed by Drummond from 1829–1833). Such was the assemblage of the first Prophetic Conference, convened for six days—most likely the first of its kind in Redemptive history. What a momentous occasion, dated 1826![1]

Besides the Prophetic Conferences held at Albury Manor (1826–1830), located about thirty miles south-west of London, Lady Theodosia Viscountess Powerscourt in 1831 offered her mansion for Prophetic Conferences, located about fifteen miles south of Dublin, Ireland. She often filled her mansion with prominent ministers of every persuasion from England, Ireland, and Scotland—including Edward Irving and John Darby of the Plymouth Brethren. Following the lead of Great Britain, Ireland also launched a prophetic periodical, supported by at least a hundred clergymen, entitled *The Christian Herald* in 1830.[2]

Prophetic Conferences like those of England and Ireland also arose in Scotland and France. In addition, in that notable year 1826, James Frere launched the first Society for the Investigation of Prophecy that lasted for twenty two years—and others were to follow the lead.[3]

During the first half of the nineteenth century at least ten prophetic periodicals and over a hundred and fifty books spread over the land like the leaves of autumn, proclaiming the nearness of the pre-millennial Second Advent of Christ, as never before.

Living in the Time of the End

The amazing significance of the Advent Awakening as outlined above, is that Christians believed they were living in the time of the end. They saw themselves in the midst of prophecy fulfilling all around them, as expressed by Joseph Wolff and others, while commenting on the text that reads:

> But you, Daniel, shut up the words, and seal the book
> until the time of the end; many shall run to and fro, and
> knowledge shall increase. Daniel 12:4.
>
> *The New King James Version*

The first time the expression "time of the end" is used in Daniel is at Daniel 8, verse 17: "Understand, son of man, that the vision *refers* to the time of the end." At verse 26 Daniel is told: "Therefore seal up the vision, For it *refers* to many days in the future."

Now, the "vision" in the "book" of Daniel that was to be sealed in Daniel's day (Daniel 8:17, 26; 12:4) was to be unsealed or revealed, and "knowledge shall increase" concerning it, in the "time of the end." The specific vision referred to in this context is at Daniel 8, verse 14: "For two thousand three hundred days; then the sanctuary shall be cleansed" (NKJV).

According to the statement of Daniel 12, verse 4, quoted above, the prophecies of Daniel, and more specifically from Chapter 8 to Chapter 12 will be shut up, and sealed, meaning these prophecies would not be comprehended until the "time of the end." And eventually at the "time of the end" the prophecies would be comprehended or unsealed, and "knowledge shall increase" with regard to Daniel's prophecies. Joseph Wolff and others believed that they were actually living in the "time of the end" as evidenced by the great Advent Awakening, brought on by an increased study, and upsurge of interest and knowledge of the prophecies.[4]

Time of the End: from 1798

They believed that they had entered into the last lap of historic time, that commenced from the cataclysmic collapse of the Roman Papacy in 1798.

At that time, 1798, Pope Pius VI was deposed and the Vatican was plundered by General Berthier, by order of the French Directory. Pius VI was exiled to Valence, southern France, where he died the next year. The Roman Papacy, identified as the Little Horn Antichrist of Daniel, Chapter 7, had concluded its 1,260 year dominance over the consciences of men according to Daniel 7, verse 25: "Then the saints

shall be given into his hand for a time and times and half a time"
(NKJV).

The expression "a time and times and half a time" is found again at
Revelation, Chapter 12, verse 14, and is equated in the same context
with Revelation, Chapter 12, verse 6: "one thousand two hundred and
sixty days" (NKJV). That is 1,260 prophetic, symbolic days, was interpreted as 1,260 literal years, based upon the *day for a year principle*
(enunciated at Numbers 14:34; Ezekiel 4:6).

The *deposition* of Pope Pius VI in 1798 concluded the 1,260 year
period of Papal dominance and supremacy, since the *elevation* of the
Pope in 538. The Pope's *elevation* had been brought about by the eastern
Roman Emperor Justinian, who by decree pronounced him, "universal
head of the church." The period of Papal dominance was therefore
calculated from the Justinian era through the French Revolution: that
is 538 + 1,260= 1798.

Thus, with the passing of the event of 1798, one of the clearest
characteristics of prophecy was evident—that history is the true and
final interpreter of prophecy, so well defined by Jesus who said, "And
now I have told you before it comes, that when it does come to pass, you
may believe" (John 14:29, NKJV). Certainly when the event came to
pass *many believed*, and this amazing fulfillment of prophecy more than
any other, catapulted the Christian world into the "time of the end" and
precipitated the great Advent Awakening.

Apart from the universal recognition of the Papal collapse by the
Protestant world,[5] the sombre reality of it trickled down into the Catholic world. Leopold Ranke, famous historian of the monumental work,
The History of the Popes penned the fateful words: It "now seemed that
the papal power had been brought to a final close."[6] Nevertheless, that
was not the case, prophecy envisages a resurgence of Papal power, and
Adam Clarke, noted Methodist Bible Commentator of the Advent
Awakening unhesitatingly referred to Revelation 13, verse 3, when he
wrote:

> In 1798 the French republican army under General
> Berthier took possession of the city of Rome, and
> entirely superseded the whole papal power. This was a
> deadly wound, though at present it appears to be
> healed; but it is but *skinned over*, and a dreadful
> cicatrice remains.[7]

Time of the End introduces Pre-Advent Judgment Scene

After the striking fulfillment of Daniel, Chapter 7, concerning the
collapse of the Roman Papacy in 1798, and the entrance into the "time
of the end," the prophetic spotlight of enquiry was focused on further
events before the end of time. Daniel 7, verses 9 to 14 portrays a
Pre-Advent Judgment scene depicting the Ancient of Days seated before
an innumerable company of angels, and the books of record are
opened. The Judgment convened to judge against the Papal Little Horn,

and take away its Dominion (Daniel 7:26). But *also* "judgment was made *in favor* of the saints of the Most High, and the time came for the saints to possess the kingdom" and it "shall be given to the people, the saints of the Most High" (Daniel 7:22, 27, NKJV).

The grand consummation of the ages in the Second Coming of Christ and the establishment of His Kingdom of Saints, follows after the Pre-Advent Judgment. Notice how Daniel describes these events:

> I was watching in the night visions,
> And behold, One like the Son of Man,
> Coming with the clouds of heaven!
> He came to the Ancient of Days,
> And they brought Him near before Him.
> Then to Him was given dominion and
> glory and a kingdom,
> That all peoples nations and languages
> should serve Him. Daniel 7:13, 14.
>
> *The New King James Version*

William Cuninghame (1776–1849), Esquire of Lainshaw estate, a frequent participant in the Albury Prophetic Conferences, as early as 1807, set the pace for prophetic studies. He recognized the Pre-Advent Judgment scene, following the 1,260 years of Papal Dominance, as outlined above. He noted the judgment taking away Papal power and instituting Christ's Kingdom. He outlined the Second Advent as "one like the Son of Man Coming with the clouds of heaven!"[8] (Daniel 7:13).

The Hour of Judgment has Come

Cuninghame believed Daniel's Pre-Advent Judgment truth was for his day and age, and related it to the first angel's message of John the Revelator, recorded at Revelation, Chapter 14, verses 6 and 7:

Then I saw another angel flying in the midst of heaven, having the everlasting gospel to preach to those who dwell on the face of the earth—to every nation, tribe, tongue, and people—

Saying with a loud voice, 'Fear God and give glory to Him, for the hour of His judgment has come; and worship Him who made heaven and earth, the sea and springs of water.'

The New King James Version

Here are the exact words of Cuninghame, who made this remarkable relationship of the Pre-Advent Judgment message of Daniel with Revelation's message announcing "the hour of His judgment has come":

> The hour of God's judgment is a time well known, and exactly defined in the chronological prophecies of Daniel and John. It is the period of the judgment mentioned in Daniel 7: 26, when the little horn, or the papacy, is deprived of its power. It is likewise the time of the seventh trumpet....[9]

Judgment Hour Message Related to Universal Gospel Proclamation

During this great Advent Awakening one of the Signs of the End found in Jesus prophetic discourse, that made an impact, was: "This gospel of the kingdom will be preached in all the world as a witness to all the nations, and then the end will come" (Matthew 24:14, NKJV). Cuninghame also matched this sign in fulfillment, with the first angel's message of Revelation as follows:

> Of this end, our Lord's words lead us to see that the immediate forerunner is to be an universal promulgation of the gospel, typified, also, by the flight of the Apocalyptical angel, chapter 14:6 having the everlasting gospel to preach to all nations.[10]

The relationship of Daniel 7:22, 26, regarding the Pre-Advent Judgment with Revelation 14:6, 7, and Matthew 24:14, regarding universal gospel proclamation was forging a chain of prophetic truth that was stretching across the land and beyond. Yet another link was added, as the Advent Awakening gained momentum, and that link was Revelation, Chapter 3, verse 7: "And to the angel of the church in Philadelphia write" (NKJV).

Philadelphian Age Related to Universal Gospel Proclamation

The messages to the seven churches of Revelation, Chapters two and three, were understood to be a prophetic forecast of the condition of the Christian Church from its inception to its consummation at the Second Advent, stretching across the entire span of Redemptive history from the year of our Lord Jesus Christ. The sixth phase of the Christian Church, namely that of Philadelphia (Revelation 3:7–13), was fully identified with the Advent Awakening of the early nineteenth century.[11] As the word Philadelphia implies, it was indeed an age of "brotherly love." An age to prepare people to meet their soon coming Lord—"all them also that love His appearing" (2 Timothy 4:8, AV). It was the all absorbing love of the Second Advent that stepped across denominational lines, and unified the various denominations.

The Philadelphian age of brotherly love meant the extension of the Gospel to all mankind (Matthew 24:14; Revelation 14:6, 7): to Jews and Gentile heathen brothers. To prepare them all to meet their Lord. Therefore it was in the Providence of God that the "time of the end" ushered in a Protestant Missions Movement of great proportions.

William Carey was the first missionary to leave England for India, and Robert Moffat and David Livingstone penetrated southern Africa. German missionaries Krapf and Rebmann entered East Africa. And so the list of missionaries grew, and denominational mission societies multiplied. One country after another, including America, sent missionaries to the far flung ends of the earth, like China and the Pacific Islands. The Gospel was to go to "every nation, tribe, tongue"—that meant translation of the Bible, which William Carey soon gave attention to, followed likewise by a host of other missionaries—grappling with strange sounding dialects and tongue twisters. That, brought about the organization in 1804 of the British and Foreign Bible Society, followed by other societies, to produce Bibles and portions of the Bible in the vernacular tongues.

Such was the great Advent Awakening that broke down racial and class barriers—high and low, rich and poor, clergy and laity united on the one sweet theme of the "blessed hope" (Titus 2:13) and searched the Scriptures systematically.

Prophetic Structure of Daniel

It was soon discovered that the prophetic books of Daniel and Revelation were not imponderable mysteries. There was structure, order, and progression. Both books contained several series of often parallel outline prophecies, that unfold an unbroken sequence of events leading up to the establishment of the eternal kingdom of God. Each distinct series reveals a *repetition* and further *enlargement* of certain parts of a previous series. In fact, as far back as the fourth century, Victorinus, a bishop near modern Vienna, Austria, produced the earliest systematic commentary on Revelation, and was the first to establish the fundamental principle of *repetition*. The Revelation is not to be regarded as one continuous and progressive line of prophecy, but rather that it presents a sequence of events, and returns to parallel or repeat that sequence with different symbolic language, and with further *enlargement*.[12] The following Prophetic Structure is an illustration current in Cuninghame's day and nowadays, of the principle of *repetition* and *enlargement* in Daniel:

PROPHETIC STRUCTURE

Outline Prophecy	Repetition & Enlargement	Repetition & Enlargement
Daniel 2:	Daniel 7:	Daniel 8:
v.38, Gold = Babylon	v.4, Lion = Babylon	
v.39, Silver = Medo-Persia	v.5, Bear = Medo-Persia	v. 3 Ram = Medo-Persia
v.39, Brass = Greece	v.6, Leopard = Greece	v. 5 He-goat = Greece
v.40, Iron = Rome	v.7, Beast = Rome	vs. 8& 9 Initial Little Horn = Rome
	v.8, Little Horn = Papacy	vs. 9 to 12 Great Little Horn = Papacy
vs. 44 & 45 Stone = Kingdom of Second Advent	vs. 9 to 14, Pre-Advent Judgment and Kingdom of Second Advent	v.14 Cleansing of Sanctuary

Prophetic Structure of Revelation

On the principle of *repetition* and *enlargement* regarding the Prophetic Structure of the book of Revelation, Cuninghame and colleagues observed the **Seven Churches** as the historic phases of the Christian Church, from the apostolic period to the end of time at the Second Advent (Revelation 2 and 3). The **Seven Seals** repeated the same span of time, and by means of repetition and enlargement, it traced the history of the Christian Church from purity through stages of apostasy and persecution (Revelation 5 and 6). The Sixth Seal presaged the Second Advent.

The **Seven Trumpets** (Revelation 8 and 9) also spanned the early centuries of the Christian era to the end of time at the Second Advent, and represented the incursions upon the Roman empire, West and East. The Fifth and Sixth Trumpets find their fulfillment in the rise of the Mohammedan hordes of the Saracens and Turks, timed respectively to 150 years (Revelation 9:5, 10) and 391 years (Revelation 9:15), the latter period ending in 1697. When the Seventh Trumpet sounded, "the mystery of God should be finished" (Revelation 10:7).

Such was the passing parade of fulfilling prophecy, and it is no wonder, that Cuninghame's book, *Dissertation on the Seals and Trumpets* (1813), excited widespread interest while going through four editions.[13]

Introducing Daniel's 2,300 Day Prophecy

Cuninghame, dubbed the "learned layman" (later a minister) was one of the most prolific writers of prophecy during the great Advent Awakening. He serves the purpose well, as the spokesman of the Awakening, relating in-depth insights of prophecy, whose greatest concern was the pursuit of truth. His interpretation of the Papal Little Horn Antichrist of Daniel, Chapter 7, followed by the Pre-Advent Judgment in the same chapter, made its mark. (See illustration of Prophetic Structure of Daniel). But his parallel interpretation of the Papal Horn of Daniel 8 was all the more impressive, because he showed the historical fulfillment of that Papal Power that cast "the truth to the ground; and it practised and prospered" (Daniel 8:12).[14] Still more impressive was Cuninghame's scholarly defense of the integrity of the Number 2,300 (according to the original Septuagint rendering and Hebrew text),[15] a prophetic highlight found at Daniel Chapter 8, verse 14:

> Unto two thousand and three hundred days;
> then shall the sanctuary be cleansed.
> *Authorized King James Version*

Cuninghame and his colleagues consistently applied the day for a year principle to the 2,300 prophetic days, just like they had done for the 1,260 prophetic days. Thus the symbolic 2,300 days meant 2,300 *literal years*.

The immediate context of the 2,300 day prophecy does not reveal the time of commencement of the period, or its meaning. It does, however, indicate that the prophecy is no short period, but one that extends to the "time of the end," an expression used for the first time in Daniel (Daniel 8:17). In fact Chapter 8 concludes by telling Daniel the prophet: "The vision of the evenings and mornings which was told is true; Therefore seal up the vision, For it refers to many days in the future" (Daniel 8:26, NKJV). It's no wonder that Daniel was overcome by such words—he collapsed and became ill. In utter disappointment he concluded: "I was astonished by the vision, but no one understood it" (Daniel 8:27, NKJV).

The first part of Daniel Chapter 9, shows how perturbed Daniel was, over not understanding the vision of the 2,300 days (or evening-mornings constituting days).[16] He pondered over the seventy years Babylonian captivity of Israel according to the prophet Jeremiah (Daniel 9:2; See Jeremiah 25:12) thinking it may throw light on the 2,300 day prophecy. Daniel figured that the captivity in Babylon was nearly over—he continued to ponder and pray earnestly. Then all of a sudden Daniel records:

> 'While I was speaking, praying, and confessing my sin
> and the sin of my people Israel … the man Gabriel,
> whom I had seen in the vision at the beginning …,' said,
> 'I have come to tell you, for you are greatly beloved;
> therefore consider the matter, and understand the
> vision' (Daniel 9:20–23, NKJV).

Threefold Linkage of Daniel 8 & 9

These three verses of Daniel 9:20 to 23 form an important bridge or linkage with Daniel 8 regarding the vision of the 2,300 days (Daniel 8:14, 26). (1) The angel Gabriel was told to help Daniel to *understand the vision*" of the 2,300 days in the context of Daniel 8 (Daniel 8:16). Now, in the context of Daniel 9 the prophet says Gabriel again appeared, whom he "had seen in the vision at the beginning"—thereby linking chapter 9 with chapter 8. (2) Furthermore, the prophet concluded chapter 8 stating that he was "astonished at the vision, but none *understood* it" (Daniel 8:27). Now in the context of Daniel 9 Gabriel encourages the prophet Daniel to "*understand* the matter and consider the vision" of the 2,300 days, obviously given at the beginning. (3) Then having reminded Daniel to consider that vision, Gabriel immediately links it with the "70 weeks of years" (RSV) when he declared:

> Seventy weeks are determined upon thy people and
> upon thy holy city, to finish the transgression, and to
> make an end of sins… (Daniel 9:24).

Just as Jesus said one should forgive his brother up to "seventy times seven," so God was granting His chosen people, Israel, a probationary period, "to make an end of sins," up to "seventy weeks," or seventy times seven, amounting to 490 years.

Just as Daniel was praying and mulling over the continuous time unit of seventy years Babylonian captivity, his mind was bombarded with the seventy consecutive weeks of years apportioned to literal Israel only, designed to run its full course without interruption.

Since Daniel had pondered the seventy years prophecy, Gabriel told him the seventy *years* is to be multiplied seven times, obviously suggesting 490 *years*—*"seventy weeks of years" (RSV). Weeks of years were well known to the Jews and to other ancient nations.*

490 Year Prophecy Linked With 2,300 Year Prophecy

"Seventy weeks are *determined* upon thy people," said Gabriel. The Hebrew word translated *determined* here is unique, and is not found anywhere else in Scripture. It has the literal connotation of "cutting off" or severing from a larger portion.[17] Thereby it is suggesting that the 490 year period is cut off, or severed from the larger portion of the 2,300 year period. The Septuagint (Theodotian) uses the word "to shorten," and the Latin Vulgate uses the word *abbreviare*, meaning "to cut short," or abbreviate. Such concurrence of the different versions of the Scriptures makes it absolutely clear, that the 490 years is a lesser epoch linked as a segment within the larger epoch of the 2,300 years, and that these epochs must have a synchronous commencement.

Synchronous Commencement of 490 Years and 2,300 Years

The study of Daniel 8 and 9 as outlined above, led men like John A. Brown to set the pace of the great Advent Awakening by publicizing in *The Christian Observer* of 1810, the synchronous commencement of the two epochs—the 2,300 years with the 490 years.[18] He was of the same mind eighteen years later.[19] It was the concensus of Advent teaching, as stated by the editor of *The Morning Watch*, 1832: "Both these numbers must have the same commencement."[20]

Commencement of 490 Years and 2,300 Years: 457 B.C.

The big question now is, what is the date of commencement to set in motion the 490 years with the 2,300 years. One does not have to beat the bushes to find out. Because the very next verse after the announcement of the "seventy weeks of years" gives the clue:

> Know therefore and understand,
> That *from* the going forth of the command
> To restore and build Jerusalem
> Until Messiah the Prince,
> There shall be seven weeks and sixty two weeks.
>
> Daniel 9:25 (Italics supplied)
> *The New King James Version*

*Both the 490 year prophecy and the 2,300 year prophecy begin in
tandem "from* the going forth of the command to restore and build
Jerusalem." The command, or decree is found in the book of Ezra,
Chapter 7, verses 12 through 26 written in Aramaic, the diplomatic
language of the day, and suggesting that it was a transcript of the decree
(verse 11). The content of the decree incorporated the restoration of
religious and civil authority, granting autonomy for the Jewish nation
under Persian sovereignty. The *introduction* to the text of the decree is
given by the historic king of Persia, Artaxerxes I, Longimanus
(465—423 B.C.), as follows:

> Artaxerxes, king of kings,
> To Ezra the priest, a scribe of the Law
> of the God of heaven:
> Perfect peace, and so forth.
> I *issue a decree* that all of those of the
> people of Israel and the priests and Levites
> in my realm, who volunteer to
> go up to Jerusalem, may go with you.
>
> Ezra 7:12,13 (Italics supplied)
> *The New King James Version*

"The command to restore and build Jerusalem" was given "in the
seventh year of Artaxerxes the king" during the fall, or fifth month of the
Jewish year (Ezra 7:7, 8). And the *seventh* year of the king was 457 B.C.,
at which time the *decree* was issued to go into effect.

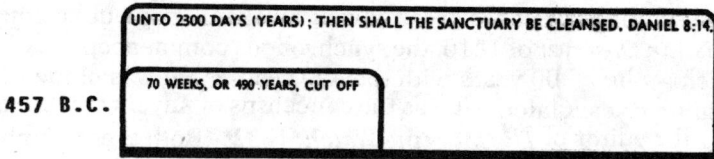

Illustration 5
Synchronous Commencement of 490 years and 2,300 years from 457 B.C.

Hence the commencement of the 490 years and the 2,300 years
from 457 B.C. was declared by John A. Brown as "one of the most
remarkable and distinguished points of time in the whole Scripture
chronology."[21] (See Illustration 5).

69 Weeks Until Messiah: 27 A.D.

Daniel 9, verse 25, that supplied the commencement of the 490
years *"from* the going forth of the command to restore and build Jerusalem" in 457 B.C., continues to disclose a great event along the path of
the 490 years. It measures off from the starting point "seven weeks and
sixty two weeks." That is 69 weeks of years, or 483 years *"until* Messiah
the Prince " (Daniel 9:25). By simple mathematics deduct 457 from 483
and the result is 26. Allow one extra year for the conversion from B.C. to

A.D. and we arrive at the year 27 A.D. *"until* Messiah the Prince." (Now follow Illustration 6).

"SEVENTY WEEKS ARE DETERMINED UPON THY PEOPLE" 490 YEARS

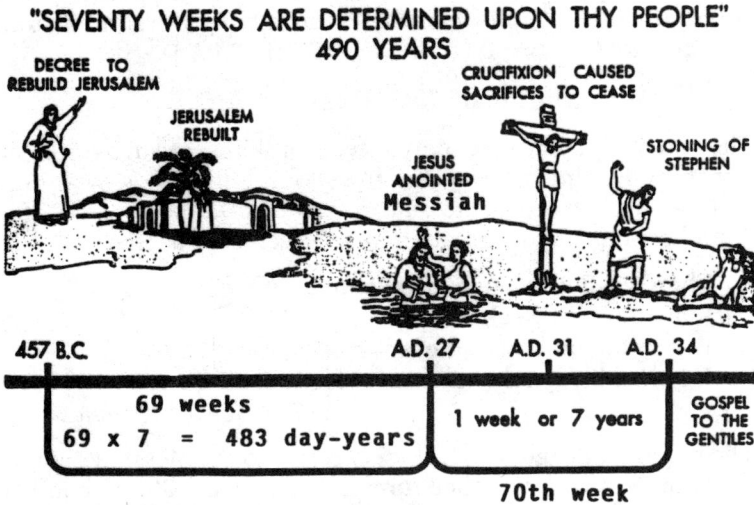

Illustration 6
"Seventy Weeks of Years are determined Concerning your people" (RSV)
Seventy weeks of years suggests 70 x 7 = 490 years. The expression weeks of years was well known among ancient nations, so God's people, Israel, recognized the seventy weeks prophecy applied to them (Daniel 9:24).

The sixty nine weeks of the "seventy weeks of years" introduces the reader to the Messiah, the Anointed One, or Christ (according to the Septuagint) in 27 A.D. This historic date coincides with the "fifteenth year of the reign of Tiberius Caesar" (Luke 3:1), emperor of the Roman empire. Luke says that on this date John was "preaching a baptism of repentance" and "it came to pass that Jesus also was *baptized*" (Luke 3:3, 21, NKJV; Italics supplied). The baptism of Christ constituted His anointing by God when His voice declared, "This is my beloved Son," and Andrew called out, "We have found the Messias, which is, being interpreted, the Christ" (John 1:41).

The baptism of Christ, the Messiah, marked the beginning of His ministry for the salvation of mankind: "Behold the Lamb of God, which taketh away the sin of the world" (John 1:29). Christ's baptism marked the fantastic event "until Messiah the Prince." Heaven's zero hour had struck with astonishing precision, and Jesus proclaimed, "The time is fulfilled" (Mark 1:15) referring to the fulfillment of the event after sixty nine weeks of years.

70 Weeks to End 34 A.D.

If the year 27 A.D. marks the end of 69 weeks or 483 years, then 34 A.D. would mark the end of the 70 weeks, or 490 years (simply 27 + 1 week or 7 years = 34). The stoning of Stephen took place in 34 A.D., signifying Israel had totally rejected the appeal of God "to make an end of sins." By rejecting the pleas of God, Israel's probation was over, she had forfeited her right as God's chosen people, and Paul who consented to the stoning of Stephen, became the apostle to the Gentile world. Israel had filled her cup of iniquity by crucifying Christ and stoning Stephen, and so God turned to the Gentiles in 34 A.D.

Middle of 70th Week: 31 A.D.

The conclusion of the seventy weeks, or 490 years in 34 A.D., may be important. But an event during the seventieth week is most important. After focussing on the Messiah by name at Daniel 9, verses 25 and 26, Daniel concludes this great chapter at verse 27 declaring:

> Then he shall confirm a covenant with
> many for one week;
> But in the middle of the week
> He shall bring an end to sacrifice and offering.
>
> *The New King James Version*

The personal pronoun "He" (v.27) refers to the Messiah addressed in the two previous verses (See Appendix B). "He," Christ, confirmed the covenant, relative to the seventy weeks, or 490 years apportioned to Israel, for one last week of years—7 years. But in the middle of the seventieth week of 7 years "He shall bring an end to sacrifice and offering." That is He would bring the sacrificial system to an end.

The last prophetic seventieth week of 7 years, stretches from 27 A.D. to 34 A.D. The middle of that period would be 31 A.D., the most important date to all Christendom, since Christ was violently "cut off" by a vicious and vicarious death—Crucifixion (Daniel 9:26; Isaiah 53:8). Said Paul, "Christ our passover is sacrificed for us" (1 Corinthians 5:7). Matthew describes how Christ "shall bring an end to sacrifice and offering:"

> Jesus, when He had cried out again with
> a loud voice, yielded up His spirit.
> And behold, the *veil of the temple was torn*
> in two from top to bottom; and the earth
> quaked, and the rocks were split.
> Matthew 27:50, 51
>
> (Italics supplied)
> *The New King James Version*

Christ's Crucifixion Ends the Sacrificial System: 31 A.D.

At the very moment of Christ's expiry on the cross "the *veil of the temple was torn* in two from top to bottom," signifying that the sacrificial system was wrapped up (See Picture 5). The Veil or curtain that separated the two apartments, the Holy apartment from the Most Holy apartment, was ripped in two. That meant the Presence of God, the Shekinah Glory, vanished from the Most Holy place, where the veil was

Picture 5
The Rent Veil
The moment Jesus expired on the Cross, the "veil of the temple was torn in two from top to bottom." It signified the end of the sacrificial system—Christ having brought "an end to sacrifice" (Daniel 9:27 NKJV).

designed to shield His Presence from human eyes. For no man could look upon God's Presence and live. But now, with the curtain ripped in two, human eyes could peer into the Most Holy apartment devoid of God's Presence.

Since God's Presence disappeared, there was no efficacy in the sacrificial system. Type had met Antitype in Christ's sacrifice. Jesus' words were fulfilled, "Behold, your house is left unto you desolate" (Matthew 23:38).

Writers in the Advent Awakening from the time of chronologist Dr. William Hales in 1812 until 1832, expressed with either major or minor emphasis, the sentiments of the 70 weeks prophecy as outlined above. There was general unanimity on the climactic prophetic seventieth week of years, pinpointing the commencement of (1) Christ's Ministry; (2) His Crucifixion around 31 A.D. or 33 A.D.; and (3) the end of the 70 weeks prophecy with the stoning of Stephen, 33/34 A.D. or 37 A.D.[22]

Please review the events of the seventy weeks back at Illustration 6.

2,300 Year Prophecy Ends 1844 A.D.

The synchronous commencement of the 490 year prophecy with the 2,300 year prophecy has already been ascertained as outlined above. It was discovered that the two epochs commenced in 457 B.C.

By advancing 2,300 years from 457 B.C. the terminus of the prophecy would be the year 1844 A.D. The calculation is simple:

2,300–457 = 1843. Add 1 year for the conversion from B.C. to A.D.: 1843 + 1 = 1844. (See Illustration 7).

From the year 1810 John A. Brown terminated the 2,300 year prophecy in the year 1843, citing this year as "one of the most memorable periods in Scripture history."[23] By 1832, just a few years before the termination, the 2,300 year prophecy was a hot subject preached far and wide.[24] Nevertheless, throughout this period of proclamation, close scrutiny of the subject, resulted in various terminal dates being advocated: 1843, 1844 and 1847.[25]

Meaning of 2,300 Year Prophecy and Cleansing of the Sanctuary

Just as varied were the *meanings* attached to the text which read:

Unto two thousand and three hundred days;
then shall the sanctuary be cleansed (Daniel 8:14).
Authorized King James Version

One meaning attached to the 2,300 year prophecy was succinctly stated in *The Morning Watch*, 1832:

The first number given is 2,300 years
(viii. 14) which includes the *time of
both advents*; the second number given is
490 years, or 70 weeks (ix. 24), which includes
the time of the *First Advent only*.[26]

(Italics supplied)

It was clear to commentators of the Advent Awakening in England that at the termination of the 2,300 year prophecy "shall the sanctuary be cleansed." But the interpretation of the cleansing took on various shades of meaning:

(1) The Scottish minister and author of a dozen works, Archibald Mason, who received a Doctorate of Divinity from the United States,

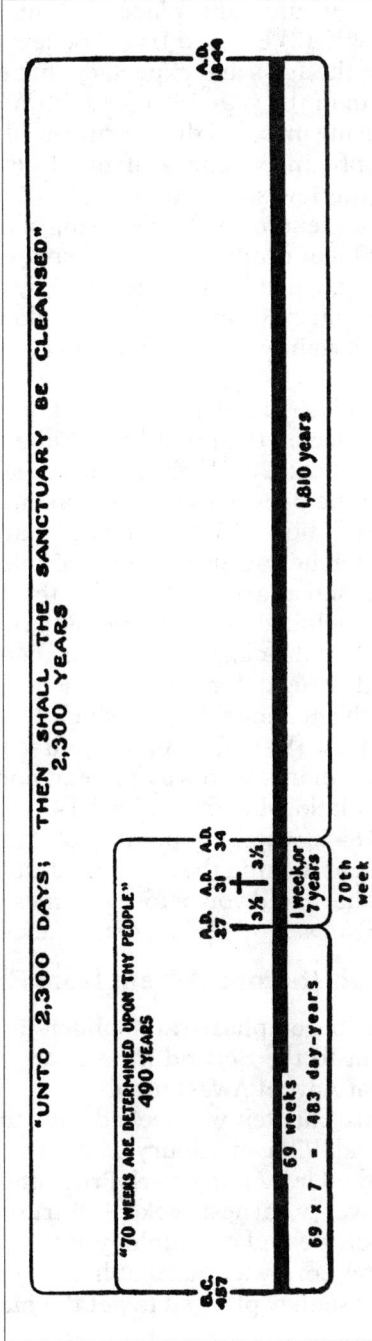

Illustration 7

Terminus of 2,300 Years in 1844 A.D.

believed the cleansing meant—the Christian Church as the sanctuary and the nations would be delivered entirely from the abominations of Popery,[27] and Armageddon would take place[28]. Cuninghame held similar views of the cleansing[29]. (2) Edward Irving believed the cleansing meant the conversion of the Jews and expected "that true worship will be restored in Jerusalem in the year 1847."[30] John A. Brown held similar views, that the cleansing involved the overthrow of the Mohammedan abomination in the precincts of Jerusalem and Palestine, and included the restoration of the Jewish kingdom.[31]

Such is a sampling on the meaning of the cleansing of the sanctuary at the conclusion of the 2,300 year prophecy. Some were quite dogmatic about it. But Cuninghame, who held his particular view, was cautious with regard to unfulfilled prophecy, when he wrote: "It does not appear to me that we can arrive at certainty on this till the event shall make it clear."[32]

Cuninghame came very close to the *true* meaning of the cleansing of the sanctuary when he dilated on the Pre-Advent Judgment found in Daniel, Chapter 7, verses 9–14, 22, 26. He matched Daniel 7:26 on the Pre-Advent Judgment which he believed was now taking place in the nineteenth century, with Revelation 14:7 announcing that "the hour of God's judgment was come."[33] If he had also matched Daniel 8:14 on the *timing* of the cleansing of the sanctuary in 1844 with "the *hour* of God's judgment," he would have concluded that the *time* 1844 coincided with the *hour of judgment*. Therefore the cleansing of the sanctuary in 1844 would *mean* the hour had struck, for the commencement of the heavenly sanctuary's Pre-Advent Judgment, at which time mankind's "books were opened" for review (Daniel 7:10). Of course this relationship never occurred to Cuninghame who was so near, and yet so far.

The recognition of the relationship of Daniel 8:14 with Revelation 14:7 only happened after 1844, when the passing of "the event shall make it clear." Thus, is brought to mind the advice of Jesus concerning prophetic interpretation: "I have told you before it comes to pass, that, *when it is come to pass, ye might believe*" (John 14:29; Italics supplied).

Heroic Preachers of the Second Advent from England

Having briefly related the emphasis and understanding of the prophetic message pertinent to the Second Advent, we consider the messengers during the Great Advent Awakening.

At the beginning of this chapter we peeked into the library of banker Drummond's palatial Villa at Albury Park. Once again we consider the motivation of the First Albury Park Prophetic Conference in 1826. The gathering of twenty earnest seekers of truth produced a unity on major points of doctrine and eschatology, that galvanized the conviction that the day of the Lord was "hard at hand, yea even at the very door." That being the case they pledged to get the message out as expressed by Edward Irving:

All agreeing that in view of these things,
there was required of us the greatest vigilance
at our several posts, and the most fearless
constancy in affectionately warning and
preaching righteousness to all.[34]

After receiving their marching orders to prepare a people to meet their Lord, the delegates marched into the Second Albury Park Prophetic Conference in 1827 with a larger contingent. The session gave further attention to the events of the "time of the end," and the Second Advent was set for 1847.[35]

One of the participants in the early Albury Park Prophetic Conferences was **Daniel Wilson D.D.**, Bishop of Calcutta, India, with many works to his name. Wilson is also noted for his powerful preaching in London with emphasis on prophecy. But his treatise from India (1836) demonstrated the spread of the Advent message in distant lands, relative to the cleansing of the sanctuary in 1847 followed by the Second Advent.[36]

Another outstanding participant in the Albury Park Prophetic Conferences was the converted Jew **Joseph Wolff**, whose knowledge of Hebrew was often appealed to in settling Biblical questions. Besides Hebrew, Wolff had knowledge of a dozen languages with proficiency in about six. Equipped with language ability he became the most famous linguist and itinerant evangelist and missionary of his day, penetrating lands far and wide. The versatility of Wolff knew no bounds—he was equally at ease preaching to English nobility, or addressing pashas, sheiks, shas, kings and queens, American Presidents, the joint session of the United States Congress, including the legislatures of New Jersey and Pennsylvania.

An indefatigable worker, Wolff set out in 1821 on his world-wide missionary venture, initially financed by the banker Drummond, who equipped him with a printing press, so that he could print literature, besides distributing tracts and Bibles. This modern Apostle to the Gentiles, faced trials and perils comparable to Paul (2 Corinthians 11:23–27)—he was beaten, starved, sold into slavery, thrice condemned to death, attacked with cholera, and "almost every Asiatic fever in existence." Yet he pressed on undaunted, traversing four continents until he died in 1862, while contemplating still another difficult missionary venture.

Wolff's preaching itinerary included the British Isles, the Mediterranean islands, Holland, Germany, Italy, Egypt and Abyssinia, the Crimea and Georgia, the lands of the Ottoman empire and the Middle-East, and the Asian countries of Afghanistan, Cashmere, Hindustan and India, and finally the United States. Suffice it to say that Wolff preached to Jews, Turks, Parsis, Hindus, Chaldeans, Armenians, and Syrians, and the list goes on.

Dr. Wolff, the intrepid herald of the Second Advent promulgated the "blessed hope" more widely than any other individual of his times.

The tenor of his message included the Signs of Matthew 24 and other prophecies of Daniel and the Revelation prior to the Second Coming. He proclaimed, without equivocation, in all his travels, the Second Advent in 1847, when the sanctuary at Jerusalem would be cleansed, and Jesus would commence His reign at Jerusalem.[37] An occasion to be remembered, was when Wolff addressed the American Congress, and with warm affection left a message ringing in the Congressmen's ears: "Behold He comes in clouds."

Prince of preachers in the British Advent Awakening, **Edward Irving** was a man of great piety, tall, dark and handsome, he presented a pleasing personality—all of which augured well for a powerful ministry. The first shaft of truth on the Second Advent penetrated his heart when he preached on the Second Coming, Christmas Day, 1825. He became aware that he was living in the "time of the end," stating that the end was "close at hand, both by the signs of the times, and from the prophetic numbers expressly given to guide."[38]

When Irving started out with his Advent preaching he expressed shock at what he called: "the erroneousness of the opinion amongst us that He [Christ] is not to come till the end of the millennium."[39] Irving could not go along with the doctrine of a temporal millennium of peace and righteousness before the Second Coming of Christ, that would tend to lull mankind into complacency, and put off the day of salvation. Besides, he found the Scriptures did not support a *post-millennial* Second Advent, but rather a *pre-millennial* Second Advent. Furthermore, when he began fervently to preach in London Christ's *pre-millennial* Advent, he found himself insulated from most of his colleagues in the ministry.[40] But soon, as a result of Irving's strong lead, a great revival of *pre-millennialism* swept over Britain, joined by men like J.H. Frere and Cuninghame.

The literal, personal, *pre-millennial* Coming of Christ was held by the *apostolic church*, taught by Christ and His apostles. This was one aspect in the restoration of the Apostolic Church in the nineteenth century, but the next chapter will show how this was not maintained in its entirety.

Irving's pre-millennial Advent preaching was well received in London, where a thousand souls packed his new church in Regent Square, week by week (1827). Next, his preaching tours rocked Scotland—where the largest churches were overcrowded, and open-air audiences ranged from 10,000 to 12,000 eager and enthusiastic souls. On that high note we must leave Irving. In the next chapter another phase of his ministry will be addressed.

Heroic Preachers of the Second Advent in Europe

As has been outlined, the Great Advent Awakening in England was brought about by the Divine hand of God. So, likewise in Europe, one can trace the leading of the Holy Spirit, in awakening in men, an awareness that they were living in the "time of the end," and that the Second Coming was very near. Such was the experience of the French-Swiss evangelical professor, **Francois Gaussen**, whose attention happened to be drawn to Daniel, Chapter two, after reading Rollin's *Ancient History*. He was amazed to find that the details of the prophecy had exact fulfillment in the events of ancient history—testifying to the authenticity and the Divine inspiration of the Scriptures. This touched off an intense study of the prophecies, resulting in an awareness that Jesus was soon to come, and that he must declare the imminence of the Second Advent.

Apart from the spirit of rationalism that pervaded all Europe, Gaussen encountered many obstacles before he could present the Advent message. A formidable obstacle to him, was the opposition of the majority of the Geneva clergy, banded together as the Venerable Company of Pastors, who eventually suspended him from the ministry. Nevertheless, his cause received aid from England, when Robert Haldane promoted the renewal of the evangelical faith. In addition banker Drummond provided asylum for ministers ejected by the Company, and encouraged them to form a separate body. Drummond went a step further, by organizing and financing the Continental Society for the Diffusion of Religious Knowledge and the training of missionary students. Gaussen, in company with the celebrated Swiss church historian Merle D'Aubigne, followed suit, by organizing the Evangelical Society to distribute Bibles and tracts, to foster foreign missions, and to establish a School of Theology in Geneva.

Soon after Gaussen was deposed by the Consistory, he became a professor in the School of Theology in 1834. Looking for a way to reach adult minds, his Sunday School lessons on *Daniel the Prophet* , directed to the children, constituted a breakthrough to the parents' minds as they attended his lectures too. Other adults of rank and learning, including visitors, swelled the audience. Next, he published the lessons, explaining the prophecy of Daniel 2 ending with the Second Advent, and identifying the Papal Little Horn of Daniel 7. He applied the day for a year principle to all prophetic periods, including the cleansing of the sanctuary after 2,300 years in 1846–47. Gaussen's teaching, preaching, and publishing continued for twenty five years—a heroic messenger of the Second Advent in Europe.

Although not specifically connected with the nineteenth century Great Advent Awakening, mention ought to be made of the Lutheran minister **Johann Bengel** of Wurtemberg, Germany, who published his *Explanation of the Revelation of John*, with strong Protestant Historicist interpretation in 1740. This book and others ran through several editions and were translated into a number of European languages. An outstanding champion of pre-millennialism, Bengel advocated preparation for the Second Advent. And all of this started to bombard his mind, while preparing a sermon one day from Revelation 21.

Bengel's influence extended beyond his death, and spilled over into the nineteenth century, gaining a large group of followers in Germany and among German colonists in Russia. These followers also rounded out their Advent beliefs by assimilating the writings of English authors such as: Lewis Way, W. Noel, Henry Drummond, and Edward Irving.[41]

In **Sweden** the Advent Awakening took a phenomenal turn, inspired and imbued by the Holy Spirit alone, much like the Apostolic Church. In spite of a hundred year old royal decree from Stockholm prohibiting religious meetings in private homes and enforced by stiff penalties, the Holy Spirit prevailed upon little children, unable to read or write, together with teen-age youth, to proclaim the Second Coming.[42] The severity of the punishment meted out to some young preachers was evident in the case of two teen-age youth: Ole Boqvist and Erik Walbom. Their bare backs were beaten with birch rods until blood was drawn. With bleeding wounds they were cast into the prison in Orebro, where they were tortured by powerful streams of cold water. After their release they were asked, "Will you cease preaching this doctrine?" Their reply was, "We will preach the preaching that the Lord bids us." And they continued the next year or two preaching until 1844.[43] Boqvist's later testimony was:

> When we were brought before the governor for examination, he demanded by what authority we were sent to preach. We referred him to Joel 2 and Revelation 14:6–8, and told him further that the Spirit of God came upon us with such power that we could not resist it.[44]

Child preachers, some ranging from six to ten years, others older, centered their preaching among Pietist peasantry in several provinces of southern Sweden from December 1841 to 1843. Their influence was extensive. A contemporary Swedish Newspaper reported:

> The girl from Swenarum, daughter of a poor peasant, preached twice a day, and had always two or three hundred listeners daily. The 6th and 7th of this February, which days she declared to be the last when she would preach publicly, she was visited by about 3,000 to 4,000 people.[45]

The unbiased, objective records of Bishop J.A. Butsch, of Skara, and the eminent, knighted physician, Dr. S.E. Skoldberg, testify to the sanity, simplicity, humility, and orthodoxy of these child preachers, who received their messages through *visions*, while oblivious to their surroundings, preaching in changed tone of voice and manner, far beyond their years, similar to adults. They preached reform and separation from sin—such as card-playing, drunkenness, dancing, and frivolity. Their call to repentance resulted in seventy distillers in one area alone, giving up distilling within a fortnight.[46]

Dr. Skoldberg compiled an eye-witness report and examination of the supernatural physical phenomena of the Swedish child preachers. He tried to discontinue the witness of thirteen year old Mary Swensdotter, by compressing her nostrils and lips. He found it absolutely impossible to silence her—she went right on until she had finished. Prior to the presentation of the message the child preachers were in a stunned condition for some time, some were wholly motionless, the "breath cannot be observed, although they doubtless must breathe." Then, from this dormant condition, at the propitious moment, not of their choosing, but "impelled by an inexplainable urge," testifies Dr. Skoldberg: "the message gushes from their breast like a bubbling spring—I repent of all my harsh opinions and stand in amazement of them."[47]

The child preachers exhibited no emotional or fanatical excitement. They spoke in the language of the people, clear, forceful and with "boldness" akin to those who were "filled with the Holy Ghost" in Apostolic times (Acts 4:31). They expounded the first angel's message: "Fear God, and give glory to Him; for the hour of His judgment is come" (Revelation 14:7).[48] Despite denunciation from the Lutheran ministry, the child preachers claimed their ministry was in fulfillment of Joel 2: "And it shall come to pass in the last days, saith God, I will pour out my Spirit upon all flesh; and your *sons and your daughters shall prophesy, and your young men shall see visions*, and your old men shall dream dreams" (Italics supplied). The claim of fulfillment was verified by a Stockholm Newspaper reporter who described "their preaching as a great miracle from God"[49] (See Picture 6).

© Pacific Press Pub. Association　　　　　Picture 6
Spirit Endowed Swedish Child Preachers
In fulfillment of Joel 2, Swedish child preachers miraculously proclaimed the Second Advent with "boldness," akin to those who were "filled with the Holy Ghost" in Apostolic times (Acts 4:31).

Heroic Roman Catholic Writer of the Second Advent

Manuel de Lacunza, a Chilean Jesuit priest, was exiled from his native land at the time of the expulsion of his order. He retired to Imola, near Bologna, in central Italy, and lived the life of a recluse for thirty years, consulting the Church Fathers and the entire Patrology. Combined with this concerted study, he gave more and still more attention to the Holy Scriptures, until they became his all consuming activity. The result was his *opus magnum—The Coming of the Messiah in Glory and Majesty*. This magnificent, rather ponderous tome, appeared in manuscript form about 1791. Fearing that his Spanish treatise might be placed on the Index of Prohibited Books, Lacunza wrote under the pseudonym Juan Josafat Ben-Ezra, purportedly a Christian Hebrew. Nevertheless, the manuscript was copied and made its rounds in Spain and South America—from North to South. It was translated into Latin and Italian. Such was the great interest generated in the Roman Catholic world, and Lacunza collapsed and died on the river bank, near Imola, in 1801, before seeing his book printed.[50]

Apparently the first printing of Lacunza's book was the Spanish Cadiz edition of 1812. And when a copy of this edition fell into the hands of Edward Irving in 1826, he translated it into English, and the book took a flying leap into the Protestant world. An abridged English edition came out from Dublin in 1833, thereby extending its influence far and wide. But a Spanish edition of 1500 copies printed in London in 1816, bound for Argentina, set the pace for further printings in Spanish, and in Latin, Italian, French, and German, destined to be read half way round the Catholic world of South America and Europe—especially impacting the clergy, and drawing forth both rejection and joyful acceptance.[51]

The theme of Lacunza's one, and only book, was the *two* Advents of Christ—the first in obscure humility, the second in Glory and Majesty. These objectives and goals were backed by the prophetic Word of God. Above all he forged ahead with the fundamental truth of a personal Pre-millennial Second Advent of Christ, the Messiah, soon to take place. He dispensed with the Augustinian view of the setting up of the Stone Kingdom of Daniel, Chapter 2, at the First Coming of Christ with the introduction of the millennium in the early centuries. Instead, he placed the Stone Kingdom at the Second Coming of Christ, at which time the millennium would commence. Furthermore, Lacunza rejected the Riberan view of an individual Antichrist as a Jew from the tribe of Dan. Instead, he maintained that the Antichrist was within the Christian Church Temple (2 Thessalonians 2) in embryo in Paul's day. It was destined to come to great fruition in the *future* through a "moral body" of apostasy "under the metaphor of a beast with two horns" (Revelation 13:11)—"Yes, my friend, our priesthood!"[52]

It is obvious that such teachings would eventually get Lacunza into trouble with the Papacy. His book was placed on the Index of Prohibited Books by Pope Leo XII and its publication was banned. The main reasons for banning, was that:

(1) Lacunza elevated the Scriptures above Tradition;
(2) he wrote his book in the vulgar tongue Spanish, instead of Latin;

(3) he committed the most egregious sin, by identifying the Antichrist as the Roman Catholic priesthood prefigured in Revelation 13 and 17.[53]

In spite of the ban, Lacunza's book was published in English by Irving and in other languages, to continue to make its mark. However, there were some elements of the book's theme that were unsavory, to be discussed in the next chapter.

Conclusion

The great Second Advent Awakening in the British Isles gathered momentum, and peaked during the decade 1825 to 1835. Confidence in the "Protestant Continuous Historic Scheme of Interpretation" of Prophecy was enhanced by the universal recognition of the collapse of the Papacy in 1798, fulfilling the 1,260 *year* Dominance of the Papacy, as an accurate and clear interpretation of Daniel, Chapter 7. The principle of interpreting a symbolic day to mean a literal year was applied as the yardstick for *all* prophetic time periods; including the 70 weeks as a smaller epoch within the larger epoch of the 2,300 days, commencing together in tandem. This was a new emphasis, with divergent opinions regarding the *close* of the 2,300 day-years in 1843, 1844, or 1847, besides a few differences as to what *event* would transpire at the termination. In time the growing diversity of opinion in this and other areas, led to increasing friction, variance, loss of cohesion, and distrust of the historic expositions and their expositors.[54] The result was that interest began to wane and dry up, *before* they could realize or even check out the terminal events, set for the close of the 2,300 day-years (Daniel 8:14).

Besides the flagging fervor of the Advent Awakening, their solid interpretation of the Papal Apostasy, prefigured in 2 Thessalonians 2, and Revelation 11, 13, and 17, was vehemently attacked, almost from the word go. The Futurist attack included a broadside against the day for a year principle. The attack on the Advent Awakening was compounded by the odious atmosphere created by the "tongues phenomenon," the "secret rapture," and a "two-stage" Second Advent—all of which will be addressed in the next chapter. Suffice it to say, that such conflicts and confusion brought the two great prophetic periodicals to an end: *The Morning Watch* in 1833,[55] and *The Christian Herald* in 1835.[56]

Nevertheless, may it be acknowledged that the great Advent Awakening restored the fundamental belief of the Apostolic Church: the visible, literal, personal, pre-millennial Second Advent of Christ. Cuninghame contended that the time had arrived for a revival of the "primitive doctrine of the personal Advent of the Messiah."[57] Concurrent with the Second Advent as a single glorious event, Advent believers taught the translation of the living saints, and the resurrection of the dead saints, to meet the Lord in the air. Next, the wicked were to be destroyed with the Antichrist power. The Second Advent introduced the millennium and the establishment of God's kingdom. The approach of the Second Advent was to be heralded by the fulfillment of the prophecies.[58] Such were the cardinal truths surrounding the Second Advent that were brought to the forefront of the Advent Awakening in the British Isles.

Chapter 4

FROM ENGLAND'S SECOND ADVENT AWAKENING -

EMERGES THE
CATHOLIC APOSTOLIC CHURCH

The Parable of the Sower illustrates well the strange turn of events that took place during the great Advent Awakening in the British Isles. Here are Christ's words recorded at Matthew 13:

v. 3. Behold, a sower went out to sow.

v. 4. And as he sowed, some seed fell by the wayside; and the birds came and devoured them.

v.19. When anyone hears the word of the kingdom, and does not understand it, then the wicked one comes and snatches away what was sown in his heart. This is he who received seed by the wayside.

The New King James Version

No sooner had the great truths of salvation by grace through faith in Christ, and the full identification of the Papal Apostasy, been established by the Protestant Reformation, than the Roman Catholic Counter Reformation, like the "birds" representing the "wicked one" in the Parable, "snatched away what was sown." The Council of Trent (1545–1563) condemned Luther's teachings, and the astute Jesuit scholar Ribera (ca. 1590) nullified the prophetic identification of the Papal Antichrist, by deflecting the Antichrist into a miniscule period of time, way into the distant indefinite *future*. Therefore by subterfuge and deceit Ribera became the founder and father of *Futurism*.

Similar to the snatching away of the seeds of truth sown by the Protestant Reformation, was the situation that prevailed at the time of the great Advent Awakening. But in point of time, more precise—it was absolutely immediate. The Advent Awakening in the British Isles gained momentum and peaked during the period 1825 to 1835. No sooner had it entered into its peak period, than birds "came and snatched away what was sown," converging on the years 1826–1827. Those who snatched away the Apostolic truth of the visible, literal, personal, Pre-millennial Second Advent of Christ were Maitland and his cohorts, Lacunza, Stewart and Irving, and Darby. These individuals endeavored to remove the landmarks of the Advent Awakening either intentionally, or inadvertently, as the following story will show.

1826: Dr. Samuel R. Maitland

The momentous year of the great Advent Awakening, had dawned in 1826. The year in which, about twenty students of prophecy, among the clergy and laity of different churches, converged on the Albury Park mansion, to consult with one another, and consolidate their views on "the system of prophetic visions and numbers of Daniel and the Apocalypse." Unanimity was achieved on the day for a year principle of interpretation of the prophetic "numbers," such as the 1,260 day-years (Daniel 7:25; Revelation 11:2, 3; 13:5), culminating in the collapse of the Papal Apostasy at the time of the French Revolution.[1] Moreover, the day for a year principle "had received the sanction of almost all the Protestant writers, or commentators, of any note, for the last two hundred years." The key that unlocks the mystery of the prophetic "numbers" is found at Ezekiel 4, verse 6, where "it is expressly said, that a 'day' is to be taken 'for a year.'"[2]

Nevertheless, during that momentous year 1826, these students of Prophecy met with a frontal attack led by Dr. Samuel R. Maitland, Librarian to the Archbishop of Canterbury. His first volley was a seventy two page pamphlet entitled, *An Enquiry into the Grounds on which the Prophetic Period of Daniel and St. John, Has been Supposed to Consist of 1,260 Years*. This was followed by *A Second Enquiry* (1829) shooting holes into the prophetic fabric of the 1,260 days representing years, as held by writers and commentators of the Advent Awakening. In rapid succession followed his next round, *An Attempt to Elucidate the Prophecies Concerning Antichrist* (1830). For over ten years Maitland assailed the Protestant application of the Little Horn (Daniel 7), and Revelation's Beast and Babylon to the Roman Papacy—the Antichrist.[3] Like Ribera, Maitland opted for an *individual infidel Antichrist*, or "Man of Sin" (2 Thessalonians 2), who was yet to arise *outside the church of God*, "and sit for 1,260 literal days in a literal temple, of brick or stone, proclaiming himself to be God."[4] With the precision of a sharp shooter, and due to his legal training, Maitland fired volley after volley as it were, against all and sundry—against the prophetic periodical *The Morning Watch*, with personal attacks against Faber, Digby, Cuninghame, to name a few. All of this initiated a "paper war" unprecedented, since Reformation times, that continued half way through the nineteenth century.[5]

Maitland was out to demolish the Protestant citadel, so he brought in his "heavy artillery," so to speak, from the Established Church of England. Those "big guns" included Dr. James Todd, Fellow of Trinity College, Dublin, whose writings were a series of negations of the whole Protestant Church. Another "big gun" to enter the fray, was Dr. John H. Newman, the famous High Church Anglican convert to Roman Catholicism—a prime mover of the Oxford Tracterian Movement.[6] Launched in 1833 from London, the objective of the Oxford Tracts was to "unprotestantize the Church of England."[7] This "left Protestantism consequently all open to the charge of unjustifiable schism; and the Papacy all open to the Catholic desires, and aspirations of the Tractators for re-union."[8] Thus, "a Romeward movement was already arising, destined to sweep away the Old Protestant landmarks, as with a flood."[9]

1826: Influence of Manuel de Lacunza's Book

The Scottish Presbyterian minister Edward Irving played an important role in the course of the great Advent Awakening in the British Isles during those peak years 1825 to 1835. In the year 1826, while Irving was feeling painfully insulated from his brethren in the ministry, over his recognition of the great truth of the Pre-millennial Second Advent of Christ, an elaborate treatise, *The Coming of the Messiah in Glory and Majesty*, was placed in his hands. He was thrilled to discover that the author, Manuel de Lacunza, was a Jesuit priest from Chile, presenting a Pre-millennial Advent (though futuristic). Immediately his state of insulation disappeared, his heart was cheered, and a state of kinship was established.[10] He was so enamored with Lacunza's book, that he promptly translated it from Spanish into English. The sentiments of Lacunza's book exerted a profound influence, through Irving, on the Albury Park Prophetic Conference of 1826. Even more profound was the influence it had on the Protestant English reading public, after it was printed in 1827 with Irving's virtual endorsement.[11]

It must be remembered that when Irving translated Lacunza's book he was a "Historicist" pre-millennialist, whilst Lacunza was a "Futurist" pre-millennialist. In a lengthy "Preliminary Discourse" by Irving, written like a preface to the actual translated English text of Lacunza's book, Irving elaborated on the Futuristic elements of the book.

Irving, in his Preliminary Discourse to Lacunza's book, gave an honest appraisal by stating: "I confess, however, I am tempted to break a spear with my master upon the subject of Prophetic Interpretation, because here the case is completely altered, for as much as he appears directly as an antagonist."[12] The root of the problem regarding Prophetic Interpretation, Irving indicated, was that Lacunza "our author, does not seem to have known the method of *synchronism* first laid down by Mede."[13] That is, parallel prophecies like Revelation's Seven Churches, Seven Seals, and Seven Trumpets, each have the same starting point from the earliest centuries of the Christian era and run through to the consummation. While Lacunza taught the Seven Churches were prophetic, commencing from the earliest centuries and reaching to the consummation, he was "rooted in the idea that the rest of the Apocalypse was but a thick-coming *series of signs* ushering in that glorious possession."[14]

The reason why the *rest* of the Apocalypse or Revelation, was a "thick-coming series of signs," was that Lacunza compacted the signs contained in Revelation from chapter four to chapter nineteen, and packaged them to evolve "with a rapidity of succession" in a miniscule period of $3\frac{1}{2}$ years, placed way into the future, just prior to the Second Advent. He also packed into this period of "Antichristian tribulation" the series of signs in Matthew, Chapter 24.[15]

Bearing this Futuristic view in mind, Irving observed that to sever chapters 4 through 19, and place their fulfillment way into the future, would introduce a vast **gap** of time. It would "interpose seventeen hundred years, during which no part of it hath been confirmed," or "accomplished," or fulfilled. Such a view, Irving concluded: "is like no other prophecy that the Spirit of God ever indited."[16]

Of course Lacunza's view simply gave credence to what Ribera concocted, and dished up for Catholic consumption way back, about 1590. But Lacunza was perhaps more convincing in his presentation, as is borne out by Irving in his "Preliminary Discourse." Irving acknowledged that Lacunza: "perceived not the *symbolical meaning of this period 'time, times, and half a time', but interpreted it literally*, to mean three years and a half, or forty and two months, or 1,260 days—which led him into his whole *theory* of this vision" (Italics supplied).[17] Irving then followed up with this astounding statement regarding the miniscule period of "Antichristian trouble" incorporating Daniel's numbers, "which precedes the coming of the Lord":

> I *confess* that upon this sytem he hath made out *such a strong case*, derived and deducted from all the Scriptures, that though he hath not shaken me in the least out of *our interpretation of these numbers*, he hath sometimes awakened in my mind the *suspicion of a possibility*, that when the time of that last great *Antichristian trouble* shall arrive, these *numbers* may be found to have a *literal application* without prejudice to that *symbolical* one which they have already had.[18]
>
> (Italics supplied)

Suffice it to say, that Lacunza had made "such a strong case," even beyond the "suspicion of a possibility," that he actually convinced Irving himself, who in later years became a Futurist. Even Joseph Wolff, the renowned itinerant world missionary, who promoted the reading of Lacunza's book in Italy,[19] may have been influenced by Lacunza's book, since in later years he too, looked for a futuristic Antichrist.[20] And who knows how many of England's Protestants were convinced of Lacunza's views, after reading his book in English, virtually endorsed by the great Protestant preacher Edward Irving? Even though Irving's "Preliminary Discourse" pointed out the errors of Lacunza, the latter pages being Lacunza's work, would make an impact upon the reader's mind. The entire book therefore conveyed a mixed message, and therefore Irving's translation of Lacunza's book inadvertently snatched away the seeds of truth, and replaced them with error. Irving really "shot himself in the foot." And the strange thing of it all, was that Irving's colleagues in the Advent Awakening, did not sense the danger of a Protestant giving credence to a Roman Catholic author, Lacunza, and his erroneous views. They did not advise Irving against translating and publishing Lacunza's book. However, John A. Brown did express regret, in one of his books, that Lacunza's view of Antichrist was retained in the English translation done by Irving.[21]

Another far-reaching error that Lacunza's book presented, was a Partial Resurrection of the dead saints at the Second Advent. With reference to the description of the Second Coming at 1 Thessalonians, Chapter four, Lacunza stated: "that the Apostle in this place is speaking of the resurrection of the dead *who are in Christ*, or of those who sleep in Jesus, and not a single word does he speak of the other infinite multitude; doubtless for this very reason that their time is not yet come."[22]

The former saints, the dead "who are in Christ," Lacunza declared are: "this privileged class, great saints, saints of extraordinary sanctity" who have profited "above all, in the sacrament of his body and blood." The latter saints, the "other infinite multitude," are resurrected apparently later.[23] Obviously, according to this view there are two classes of saints, one of which is more holy than the other—separated on the basis of their worthiness, and not on the basis of the merits of Christ. Watch for an interesting resemblance to Lacunza's view when we discuss the revelation of Margaret MacDonald.

1827: James H. Stewart's Call for the Outpouring of the Holy Spirit

English theologian and writer James H. Stewart attended the historic Albury Park Prophetic Conference in 1826. He came away from that Conference all fired up with the urgency to prepare a people to meet their God. Much like Irving, Stewart sensed that religion throughout England was at a low ebb. Whereupon he published a tract that was widely circulated to arrest the situation, and organized a brotherhood for the purpose in 1827. His tract urged people to put away their differences, and to unite in prayer, calling upon God for an extensive outpouring of the Holy Spirit. He extended his call by travelling all over England and Scotland, proclaiming from pulpits made available to him. He encouraged ministers of various churches to unite in prayer, including laymen to pray at home. Stewart's call met with a measure of success, as people prayed for the outpouring of the Holy Spirit, leaving the outcome and mode of fulfillment entirely in the hands of God.[24]

Before assembling with his brethren in the ministry at the Albury Park Prophetic Conference, Edward Irving had already sensed the poor state of religious faith, expressed in his first book, *Babylon and Infidelity Foredoomed of God*, published in 1826. Having also recognized that the Coming of the Lord was near, Irving believed it was encumbent upon the ordained ministry to arrest the situation, by conveying to the people the: "Holy Spirit by the preaching of the Word." Irving continued: "by the sending of Elias who is promised before the dreadful and terrible day of the Lord, and by other mighty and miraculous signs. This outpouring of the Spirit, is known in Scripture by 'the latter rain,' of which I deem the religious revivals of the last thirty years to be as the first droppings of the shower."[25]

The above words of Irving were written in his "Preliminary Discourse" to the translation of Lacunza's *Coming of the Messiah*, in order to reach as many as possible. Irving believed that the Spiritual Gifts of the Apostolic Age, in partial fulfillment of the prophecy of Joel, Chapter 2, really belonged to the church of all ages. Spiritual Gifts had largely disappeared because of a lack of faith. He believed they would be *restored* in a great outpouring of the Holy Spirit prior to the Second Advent, "before the great and notable day of the Lord come" (Acts 2:20). He had such a burden for this message that he committed it to writing, and came out with his book entitled, *On the Restoration of Spiritual Gifts* (1828). Having such an interest and commitment to this message, it is no wonder that he welcomed Stewart's call and joined hands in fostering it.

By 1830 news spread like lightning that the spirit of prophecy, constituting a charismatic revival, had arisen in western Scotland. The students of prophecy, convened at Albury in July, got wind of the phenomenon. At the conclusion of the Conference a clergyman of the Church of England expressed the concensus of the gathering: "That it is our duty to pray for the revival of the gifts manifested in the primitive church; which are wisdom, knowledge, faith, healing, miracles, prophecy, discerning of spirits, kinds of tongues; and that a responsibility lies on us to enquire into the state of those gifts said to be now present in the west of Scotland."[26]

Such was the course of events initiated by Stewart's call to pray for the outpouring of the Holy Spirit, coupled with the writings of Irving, and fostered by the members of the Albury Prophetic Conference. And in the concluding words of the Conference, *we* will now "enquire into the state of those gifts."

Margaret MacDonald's Prophecy of a Secret Coming

In western Scotland during the early part of 1830, centered in the small town of Port Glasgow, about fifteen miles from Fernicarry, lived a young teen-age lassie—Miss Margaret MacDonald, who had been bed-ridden for eighteen months. She was not alone, but was living with her twin brothers, James and George MacDonald, who were eking out an honest living as ship-builders. The MacDonalds were deeply moved by a sermon preached by Alexander J. Scott, then Irving's assistant, concerning the permanence of the miraculous power of the Holy Spirit in the Christian Church, and the probable manifestation of it any time soon. Such sentiments were reinforced by Irving's powerful message along similar lines, since his works, including his translation of Lacunza, had been out for a few years; and since his intensive preaching tour of Scotland from 1828. In response to the call of Stewart and others the MacDonalds held special prayer-meetings in their home for the salvation of souls and for the outpouring of the Holy Spirit.[27]

One morning in April, 1830, Margaret MacDonald arose and declared before her sister: "there will be a mighty baptism of the Spirit this day." When her brother James came home from work that evening, she prayed that he might instantly be endowed with the power of the Holy Spirit. James immediately responded:"I have got it." He then stepped out, walking directly to Margaret's bedside, and addressed her in the words of the twentieth Psalm: "Arise, and stand upright." He took her by the hand and she arose—apparently healed. James then wrote a letter to Mary Campbell who was also ill. In the letter he commanded her "in the name of the Lord to arise." She too was healed. A few days later, during an evening prayer-meeting, James and George MacDonald began suddenly to speak in unknown tongues. Thus commenced the charismatic revival, with the manifestation of the gifts of healing and tongues, which was to spread like wildfire. And these reports are not merely hearsay. They were compiled ten years later from original sources, such as letters and hand-written descriptions, by the eminent physician and clergyman Rev. Robert Norton, M.D., under the title, *Memoirs of James and George MacDonald, of Port Glasgow* (1840). Besides, Norton had also visited western Scotland as an observer, soon after the news came out in 1830.[28]

Besides the story of Margaret MacDonald's healing, and her brothers speaking in tongues, Margaret was the first prominent recipient of the spirit of prophecy during the year 1830. Norton records a transcript of her prophetic revelation excerpted as follows:

> I saw it was just the Lord himself descending from Heaven with a shout, just the glorified man, even Jesus; but that all must, as Stephen was, be *filled with the Holy Ghost*, that they might look up, and see the brightness of the Father's glory. I saw the *error* to be, that men think that it will be *something seen by the natural eye, but 'tis spiritual discernment that is needed, the eye of God in his people....*That we may discern that which cometh *not with observation to the natural eye.* Only those who have the light of God *within them will see the sign of his appearance....*I felt that those who were *filled with the Spirit could see spiritual things*, and feel walking in the midst of them, while those who *had not the Spirit could see nothing—so that two shall be in one bed, the one taken and the other left, because the one has the light of God within* while the other *cannot see the kingdom of Heaven....*I saw that night, and often since, that there will be an outpouring of the Spirit on the body, such as has not been, *a baptism of fire*, that all the dross may be put away. Oh there must and will be such an *indwelling of the Living God* as has not been—the servants of God sealed in their foreheads—great *conformity to Jesus —his holy image seen in his people....This is what we are at present made to pray much for, that speedily we may all be made ready to meet our Lord in the air—and it will be.*[29]

(Italics supplied)

Written within the context of 1 Thessalonians 4, verses 16 and 17, Margaret MacDonald gives quite a cogent account of the *translation* of the righteous living saints, commencing with the *descent* of Christ from Heaven, and concluding with the saints having been caught up to meet the Lord in the air. **First**, notice the translation of the righteous saints is a Partial Translation, the rest of the living saints "had not the Spirit—so that two shall be in one bed, the one taken and the other left, because the one has the light of God within while the other cannot see the Kingdom of Heaven." While there may not be any connection with Lacunza; it is interesting that this Partial Translation view of Margaret MacDonald bears a resemblance to the Partial Resurrection view of Lacunza.

Second, the Partial Translation view of Margaret MacDonald is made up of a spiritual elite. It comprises only those who have received a full outpouring of the Spirit—"a baptism of fire; an indwelling of the living God; and great conformity to Jesus." Again, while there may not be any known connection with Lacunza these spiritual elite of the Partial Translation bear resemblance to the "great saints, saints of extraordinary sanctity," who qualify for the Partial Resurrection view of Lacunza.

Third, and most important to our study is Margaret MacDonald's emphatic *denial* that the Second Coming, as Jesus descends from Heaven, is "something seen by the natural eye." With reference to Matthew 24, verse 30 she said: "only those who have the light of God within them will see the sign of his appearance," rather than by observation through the "natural eye." This view constitutes the introduction of the SECRET COMING or SECRET RAPTURE, that runs counter to the VISIBLE COMING, as portrayed in Scripture.

While Margaret MacDonald related her secret rapture within the context of 1 Thessalonians 4, verses 16 and 17, Dr. Harold Ockenga, a former believer in such a view, declared: "No amount of explaining can make 1 Thessalonians 4:16, 17 a secret rapture. It is the visible accompaniment of the glorious advent of the Lord" (Quoted in *The Gospel of the Kingdom* by P. Mauro, pp. 6, 7).

But there is still more to Margaret MacDonald's revelation. I'll let Norton elaborate on this point:

> Marvelous light was shed upon the Scripture, and especially on the doctrine of the second Advent, by the revived spirit of prophecy. In the following account by Miss M.M.,— of an evening during which the power of the Holy Ghost rested upon her for several successive hours, in mingled prophecy and vision, we have an instance; for we *first* see the distinction between the *final stage of the Lord's coming, when every eye shall see Him, and his prior appearing in glory to them that look for Him.*[30]

(Italics supplied)

Norton was convinced, and believed that Margaret MacDonald's revelation drew a distinction between the *final stage* of the Lord's Coming and His *prior appearing*. That meant Margaret MacDonald was the *first* to DIVIDE the Second Coming into TWO STAGES, or to SPLIT the Second Coming into TWO PHASES. Thus, the long-held doctrine of the Second Advent as a SINGLE UNIFIED EVENT (Hebrews 9:28) was transformed into a TWO-PHASE EVENT, based upon the revelation of a fifteen year old youth.

But Norton believed that the revelation of the two-phase Second Coming was based upon Scripture—that "marvelous light was shed upon the Scripture by the revived Spirit of prophecy."

About the same time that Norton made his comments, Dr. Samuel P. Tregelles, an eminent early Brethren Greek scholar, commented on the origin of the secret rapture revelation and wrote: "It was from that supposed revelation....It came not from Holy Scripture, but from that which falsely pretended to be the Spirit of God.[31]

If Margaret MacDonald's doctrine of a secret rapture and a two-phase Second Coming has no basis in Scripture, it also raises a question of the veracity of the "revived Spirit of prophecy"—to use Norton's term. We therefore apply, in this case, the Scriptural test of a prophet: "To the law and to the testimony: if they speak not according to this word, it is because there is no light in them" (Isaiah 8:20). Since the "revived Spirit of prophecy" did not speak according to the Word of God, there is no light in the prophet—the prophetic revelation is false, and so is the prophet false.

It has to be recognized, that when Stewart and Irving appealed to the church in the British Isles, to pray for the outpouring of the Holy Spirit and for the restoration of Apostolic Gifts, that they expected a genuine outcome. They did not realize how powerful the devil is; that he goes about as a roaring lion seeking whom he may devour (1 Peter 5:8). They did not realize how crafty the devil is; that he can be transformed into an angel of light, and his ministers also into ministers of righteousness (2 Corinthians 11:14, 15). They did not realize, that in spite of their call for the outpouring of the Spirit, that the spirit of the devil would "snatch away" their precious expectation (Matthew 13:4, 19), and pour out false gifts of prophecy, tongues, and healing.

Furthermore, human nature is prone to accept all that is supernatural and miraculous, as proceeding from God. Little does human nature realize that supernatural phenomena may also proceed from the great adversary—the devil. A classic example, is that when Moses' rod was turned into a serpent, the Egyptians duplicated the supernatural, by converting their rods into serpents (Exodus 7:10–12). Then how can one discern the true from the false, the *bona fide* from the bogus? One has to apply the Scriptural tests. Said Jesus: "By their fruits ye shall know them" (Matthew 7:20). John said: "Try the spirits whether they are of God: because many false prophets are gone out into the world" (1 John 4:1). Jeremiah said: "When the word of the prophet shall *come to pass*, then shall the prophet be known, that the Lord hath sent him"

(Jeremiah 28:9; Italics supplied). Add to this small list Isaiah 8, verse 20, which we have already applied to Margaret MacDonald.

Going back to Margaret MacDonald's revelation, there is no doubt that her revelation attracted wide attention. Her views were immediately circulated at the many prayer-meetings, that were held in different towns in the west of Scotland. In Port Glasgow and neighborhood, meetings were held every evening, and bristled with the spread of supernatural phenomena. A delegation arrived there, late August, 1830, comprising a medical doctor, Dr. Thompson, a lawyer, John B. Cardale, Mr. Henderson, and three ladies, all of whom were members of the Church of England, and one was also a member of Irving's congregation. The delegation spent over three weeks conducting an investigation of the spreading supernatural phenomena of prophecy and tongues, including Margaret MacDonald's experiences, and came away favorably impressed. Cardale submitted a glowing report to *The Morning Watch*. Members of the delegation returned to London in October, and reported to a gathering of Church of England ministers, including Edward Irving. This meeting produced conviction of the reality of Spiritual Gifts in the minds of most present. Apparently no Scriptural tests were applied, and at this time no dissenting voice was heard.[32]

Were Christians at that time so gullible to accept these supernatural phenomena as genuine, or was the initial impact of them so overwhelming, that Christians were overtaken by surprise and awe-struck? Nevertheless, after the initial flurry of the phenomena in 1830, tests were applied with great scrutiny, which will be addressed subsequently in this chapter.

Margaret MacDonald's Revelation followed by Morning Watch Article

In the meantime, while the atmosphere in 1830 was so conducive to acceptance of supernatural phenomena, Margaret MacDonald's revelation really took off. The air was fully charged with religious enthusiasm and excitement. Therefore, no sooner had Margaret MacDonald had her revelation, than an article appeared in *The Morning Watch*, dated September, 1830, as an immediate follow-up of Margaret MacDonald's two-phase Second Coming. It was based upon her revelation statement: "Only those who have the light of God *within them will see the sign of his appearance*" (referring to Matthew 24:30).

The author of *The Morning Watch* article, obviously conversant with New Testament Greek, tried to make a distinction between *two words* used in the Greek to describe the Coming of Jesus:

(1) *epiphaneia*, Epiphany, meaning in English—appearance;
(2) *parousia*, meaning in English—presence, or a coming. It was used as a technical term for the visit of a king, hence the Parousia of King Jesus.

First of all the author applied the term *epiphany* to a first phase of the Second Coming in Secret, quoting the first phrase of Matthew 24, verse 30: "And then shall appear (the epiphany) the sign of the Son of Man in Heaven." As stated above, Margaret MacDonald had already portrayed a Secret Coming with this first phrase of the text in mind.

Second, the author of *The Morning Watch* article, says the first phase epiphany, involving the resurrection and translation of the saints, is followed "by a certain period of time, during which all the tribes of the earth shall mourn" (referring to the second phrase of Matthew 24:30). The length of the period of time in which the tribes mourn is not specified.

Third, the author says the second phase *parousia* of the Lord then takes place, which is "his advent to the earth, or *presence thereon.*" This is linked with the third phrase of Matthew 24, verse 30: "And they shall see the Son of Man coming in the clouds of heaven, with power and great glory." The author then quotes Revelation 1, verse 7: "Behold, he cometh with clouds; and every eye shall see him, and they also which pierced him; and all kindreds of the earth shall wail because of him."

To summarize, the author presents:
(1) a first phase (Epiphany) of the Second Coming for the saints—a secret "rapture" (from the Latin Vulgate *rapio* —to snatch away, or be caught up);
(2) an indefinite period of time as an interim in which the wicked mourn;
(3) a second phase (Parousia) of the Second Coming, that is visible to the wicked, who are destroyed.[33]

While the author of *The Morning Watch* article tried to make a case for the Epiphany, as the first phase of the Second Advent, followed by Parousia as the second phase, later the so-called Plymouth Brethren *reversed* these terms. They applied Parousia to the first phase and Epiphany to the second phase.[34] If these terms can be so juggled and switched, it demonstrates they are interchangeable, and therefore the two-phase Second Coming falls away—the terms obviously apply to a single unified event. Modern Dispensationalists must have some difficulty in explaining why Paul uses the Parousia Coming (2 Thessalonians 2:1) in connection with the slaying of the Antichrist, and actually combines the two words *epiphaneia* and *parousia* in a single unified Second Coming: "And then shall that Wicked be revealed, whom the Lord shall consume with the spirit of his mouth, and shall destroy with the brightness *(epiphaneia)* of his coming" *(parousia)* (2 Thessalonians 2:8).

1827: John N. Darby, Father of Dispensationalism

After his ordination as a priest in the Established Church of England, John N. Darby went amongst the poor Irish mountaineers where he remained for the next two years. It was during this time that an accident in 1827 forced him into a period of convalescence, that gave him the opportunity for his initial study and contemplation of his dispensational view of: "The coming of the Lord for the saints."[35] It also brought him to the decision to leave the Established Church the next year, and break away from formalism and clericalism. Then for the next couple of years he went about raising informal congregations, "gathered to Jesus by the Holy Ghost," meeting together as "The Brethren," in fulfillment of the promise: "Where two or three meet together in My Name, there I am in the midst of them." By 1830 congregations of this nature had sprung up in Dublin, Plymouth, and Bristol. Near Bristol was George Muller's famous orphanage, himself a member of the Brethren.[36]

From 1827 to 1830 John Darby was exposed to the writings of Edward Irving, including his English translation of Lacunza's book, and the futuristic teachings of Samuel Maitland and his cohorts. Yet Darby still clung to the day for a year interpretation of the "prophetic numbers," as evidenced by his article in the prophetic periodical from Dublin—*The Christian Herald*, December, 1830. What brought about the change to his futuristic two-phase Second Advent, with a *fixed* period of tribulation between the phases? Was it precipitated by his visit to the home of the MacDonalds, soon after Margaret MacDonald's revelation?[37]

It is difficult to pinpoint Darby's linkage with Margaret MacDonald. But in one of his letters, Darby writes about his new beliefs precipitated by an unidentified young lady: "It is a remarkable circumstance, that a dear young lady, who was instrumental in setting them afloat for me."[38]

On the other hand, since Margaret MacDonald taught a Partial Secret Rapture of the saints at the Second Advent, Darby's statement in refining the Rapture to include *all the saints*, may, or may not have some bearing on a linkage. Here is the statement: "All the saints will be with Christ at His coming... all who are really members of His body must be with Him. You cannot divide the body."[39]

By the year 1831 the Brethren church in Plymouth taught a two-phase Second Advent.[40] From Margaret MacDonald's written revelation, somewhat vague and rather subject to interpretation, Irvingites extracted a secret rapture, and a two-phase Second Advent. But, it is to the credit of Darby, if any credit is due, that these views were cleared of any vagueness, since he gathered all he could to bear on the subject, and clarified, defined, refined, and systematized these views into what we now call Dispensationalism. He drew upon the Futurism of Ribera, Lacunza, and Maitland, and denied the day for a year principle, that he once upheld. He projected an individual Antichrist way into the future, across a vast silent **gap** of time, set in the midst of a "7 year period" of Great Tribulation—a tribulation made up of the events of Matthew 24 and *all* the events of Revelation 6 through 19. On either side of the "7 year period" he placed the phases of the Second Coming—the Secret Rapture *for* the saints at the beginning of the 7 years, and the Revelation *with* the saints at the end of the 7 years.[41] Now this scheme has no support in Scripture, so Darby bent and twisted the Scriptures to fit. This was achieved on the occasion of the third Prophetic Conference at Powerscourt, Dublin, 1833, when Darby made a dogmatic, if not dynamic presentation. He severed the last "7 year period" of Daniel's 70 weeks prophecy, and placed it way into the indefinite future, across a vast chasm, or **gap** of time, to fit his scheme.[42] Coincident with this event, as if to give credence to Futurism, a cheap abridged English edition of Lacunza's book went into circulation in Ireland.

John Darby Opens a Pandora's Box of Prophetic Paraphernalia

Darby's presentation at Powerscourt in 1833, regarding his interpretation of the seventieth week of Daniel 9, drew this comment from his colleague Newton, who was present at the Conference: "The secret rapture was bad enough, but this was worse."[43]

Daniel presented a prophecy known as the "seventy weeks of years" (RSV Daniel 9:24) apportioned to the ancient nation of Israel, and to them alone—all of which is fully discussed in the previous chapter of this book. But Darby molested this prophecy. He severed the seventieth week, comprising seven years, from the sixty-ninth week, creating a vast **gap** of time extending from the Crucifixion to the Consummation. Here is how he expressed it:

> We are properly nowhere, save in the extraordinary SUSPENSION of prophetic testimony, or period, which comes IN BETWEEN THE SIXTY-NINTH AND SEVENTIETH WEEK of Daniel.[44]
>
> (Capitalization supplied)

Dr. Harry A. Ironside, a well known former Pastor of Moody Memorial Church, Chicago, who had experienced association with the Plymouth Brethren, elaborated on Darby's "suspension of prophetic testimony" in glowing terms in his book, *The Great Parenthesis*:

> "Between the sixty-ninth and the seventieth weeks we have a great PARENTHESIS which has now lasted over nineteen hundred years....The moment Messiah died on the cross, the prophetic clock stopped. There has not been a tick upon that clock for nineteen centuries."[45]
>
> (Capitalization supplied)

Ironside's pious words may sound convincing, and similar words have been repeated as a sacred refrain ever since, with the added thought that the "prophetic clock" will not start ticking again until the Rapture.[46] Dilating on the postponement of Daniel's seventieth week of years until after the Rapture, Ironside unequivocally stated: "We have here the BACKBONE of the entire prophetic system of the Bible"[47] (Capitalization supplied).

This "backbone" comprises the severance of the seventieth week from Daniel's "seventy weeks of years," and places it after the first phase Rapture of the Second Coming, adorned with strange embellishments of prophetic paraphernalia. Can this backbone stand up to scrutiny? Let's apply the two-edged sword of Scriptural exegesis (Hebrews 4:12) and pierce this backbone—shattering it.

The accompanying diagram illustrates the severance of the seventieth week from the sixty-ninth week, comprising a unit of a week of years—namely a seven year period. Notice the seven year period is placed 1900 + years after the Messiah—Christ; after the Great Parenthesis, or **Gap**, and ends up at the point of the Rapture of the Second Coming. (See Illustration 8).

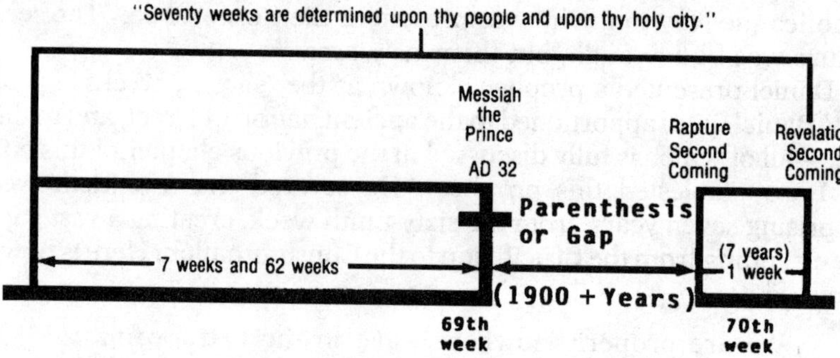

Illustration 8
Futurism's Severance of Daniel's 70th Week from the 69th Week
This severance created a vast Gap of indeterminate time - a Great Parenthesis of 1900+ years.

First of all we look at the *severance of the seventieth week from the sixty-ninth week*, and ask by what permission, by whose authority, can this arbitrary severance be done? Looking at the context of Daniel 9, verses 24 to 27, there is absolutely no word, or intimation, for this severance, or amputation. Neither is there any word or intimation elsewhere in Scripture.

Furthermore, with all due respects to Darby or his supporters, there is *no* suggestion of the "suspension of prophetic testimony," neither did the "prophetic clock" stop, to make way for a great parenthesis of time, before the fulfillment of the seventieth week, comprising a period of seven years. No such suggestion is forthcoming from the context of Daniel 9, verses 24 to 27. Neither is there any suggestion elsewhere in Scripture.

Grammatico-historical exegesis demands contextual interpretation. To amputate the seventieth week from the sixty-ninth week, and place it way into an indefinite future, is absolutely out of context. It calls for extra-biblical sources of authority to do this.

Second, we look at the prophecy of the *"seventy weeks of years"* apportioned to the nation of Israel as a *whole*, comprising 7 weeks + 62 weeks + 1 week. This is a continuous unit of time, without interruption (Daniel 9:24–27). Having already scrutinized this passage of Scripture, we extend our contextual study to include the previous verses to this passage within Daniel, chapter 9. Lo, and behold, we come across this enlightening statement at Daniel 9, verse 2:

In the first year of his reign [ca.538 B.C.] I Daniel understood by books the number of the years, whereof the word of the Lord came to Jeremiah the prophet, that he would accomplish SEVENTY YEARS in the DESOLATIONS OF JERUSALEM.

(Capitalization supplied)

With reference to the seventy years captivity of Israel in the land of Babylon (605 B.C. to 536 B.C.) foretold by the prophet Jeremiah (Jeremiah 25:12; 29:10), Daniel expected in a little while, the "accomplishment" of the prophecy, and the "return to this place"—Jerusalem. Daniel *understood the number of years* to be *seventy years*, plain and simple—a continuous unit of time, without interruption. "Have not we exactly the same reason to *understand* that the *seventy weeks of years* mean what they appear to mean, that Daniel had for understanding that the words *seventy years* were to be taken in accordance with their plain and obvious meaning? Surely the two instances are exactly alike"[48] (Italics supplied).

Out of all consistency, if "seventy years" at Daniel 9, verse 2 is taken at face value (*prima facie*), so must also "seventy weeks of years" at Daniel 9, verse 24, be taken at face value. A primary rule of Grammatico-historical exegesis is to accept the normal, grammatical meaning and usage of the words at the time of writing, ascertaining the common sense meaning. This lexical rule was violated by John Darby's interpretation, when he interrupted the continuity of the seventy weeks, and separated the seventieth week from the adjoining sixty-ninth week.

Besides the "seventy years" and "seventy weeks of years" found in Daniel 9, every other case in Scripture where God foretold a measure of time within which a specified thing was to happen, that time-measure was to be understood in its plain and simple language. For example, the 430 year sojourn of Abraham's posterity in Egypt was accomplished *to a day*—"even the selfsame day it came to pass" (Exodus 12:41; Galatians 3:17). Even the wilderness wandering of the Israelites were 40 consecutive years (Numbers 14:33, 34). Philip Mauro, one time lawyer for the Supreme Court, and at one time a Dispensationalist at heart, penned these words to close this case:"Never has a specified number of time-units, making up a described stretch of time, been taken to mean anything but *continuous* or *consecutive* time-units."[49]

Our **third** consideration is the detached *seventieth week* —a period of seven years adorned with strange embellishments of prophetic paraphernalia. The seven year period, is placed 1900 + years after the Messiah—Christ, after the Great Parenthesis, or Gap of what is called the

Church Age. *This seven year period is commenced* with the Rapture of the
Saved—a first phase of Jesus' Coming *for* the saints in secret. It is
concluded with the Return of Christ in Glory, which is the *visible* Revelation *with the saints*—a second phase of Jesus' Coming to destroy the
Antichrist and establish the kingdom. *During* the seven year period of
Tribulation the 7 Seals, 7 Trumpets, and 7 Bowls or Plagues of Revelation
are unleashed in succession. Please consult the accompanying diagram
showing these points. (See Illustration 9).

In the previous chapter, advocates of the Great Advent Awakening
advanced the *truth* of Daniel 9, verse 27, that portrayed the Messiah
who confirmed the covenant with literal Israel, "thy people," for the
final seven year period. But in the middle of the prophetic seven year
period the Messiah brought an end to the sacrificial system, by "He"
himself becoming the sacrifice in 31 A.D. This is the most glorious
prophetic truth of the Bible. To overturn this truth is tantamount to
blasphemy. Go back to the previous chapter, dear reader, and review
this precious clear-cut truth that Darby was about to overturn,
mutilate, and snatch away.

Darby overturned this truth and systematically taught that
"He"—an individual antagonistic prince, or Antichrist, would make a
seven year covenant—a pact of peace with the Jewish people (For the
misapplication of "He," please consult Appendix B). During this time
the Jewish temple would be rebuilt with the restoration of the sacrificial
system. In the middle of the seven year period the Antichrist would
move into the temple, and according to Darby: "the sacrifice is made to
cease."[50] Similar sentiments were propounded by Jesuit scholar
Ribera, before Darby, and also by Darby's contemporary propo-
nent—the Protestant Maitland. But Darby systematized these fictitious
novelties, and adorned them with the two-stage Second Advent.

The Christian writer Philip Mauro applied the two-edged sword of
Scripture and rent asunder these Antichrist embellishments and novelties stating: "There is not one word of proof in support of any one of the
following propositions, each and all of which must be proved ere the
view in dispute can be considered established:

(1) that a future Roman prince will make a covenant with many
    Jews;
(2) that the *supposed* covenant will be for the term of one week;
(3) that it will have for its purpose to permit the Jews to resume their
    ancient and long abolished temple sacrifices;
(4) that the *supposed* prince will break the *supposed* covenant in the
    midst of the week, and thus 'cause the sacrifice and oblation to
    cease.' We repeat that we are bound to reject the interpretation
    referred to unless *each* and *all* these four propositions (which
    are involved in it) are established by evidence from the Word of
    God; and the fact is that there is *not one word* of proof for *any one*
    of them."[51]

(Italics supplied)

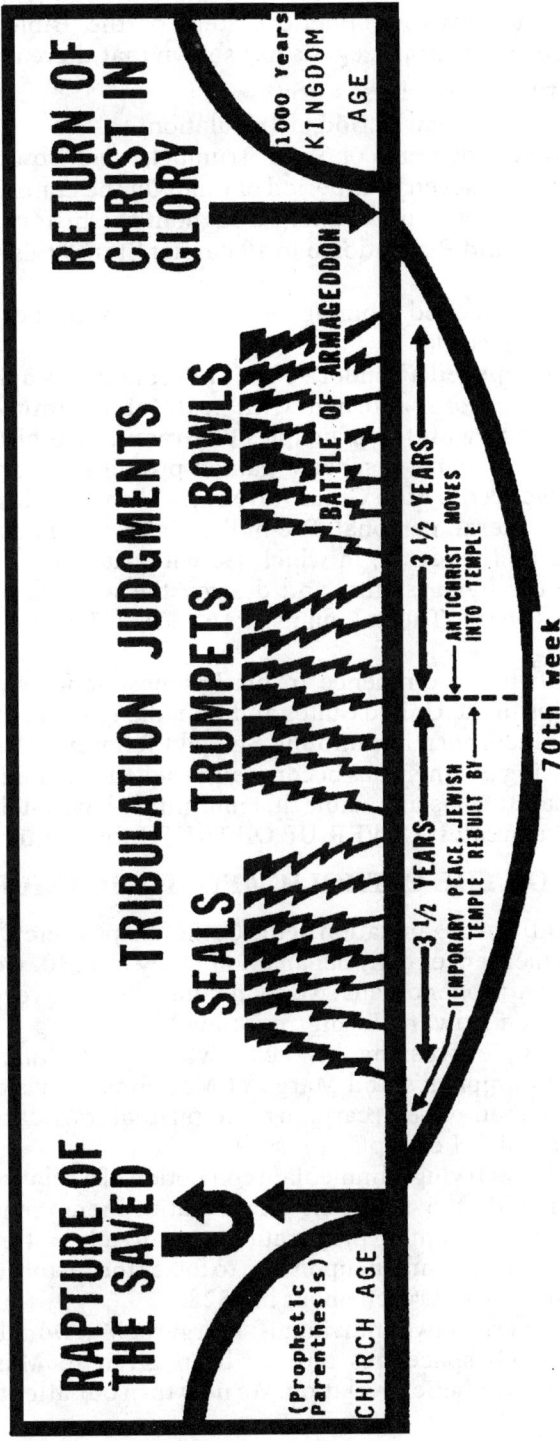

Illustration 9

Futurism's Detached 70th Week of Daniel 9, verse 27

Courtesy L.I. Bates

That does it—the testimony of Scripture has shattered Ironside's "BACKBONE of the entire prophetic system of the Bible." The two-edged sword of Scriptural exegesis has shown that there is:

(1) No such fictitious Antichrist story;

(2) No detached seven year period of Tribulation;

(3) No Tribulation Judgments of Seals, Trumpets, and Bowls to fit into a diminutive seven year period of time. On the contrary, the Seals and Trumpets run parallel throughout the history of the Christian Era, and Revelation 6 to 19 cannot fit into this period of time either;

(4) No two-phase Second Coming with a seven year period in between the phases.

Certainly Darby opened a Pandora's box of Prophetic Paraphernalia, based on *assumptions* adorned with texts of Scripture, but absolutely out of touch with the principles of Grammatico-historical exegesis. Nevertheless, Darby's scheme gained prominence over the Apostolic truth advanced by the Great Advent Awakening. This truth envisaged a visible, literal, personal, Pre-millennial Second Advent of Christ, as a single unified event, in which He will raise the "dead in Christ," translate the living saints, and destroy the wicked and the Antichrist power (See 1 Thessalonians 4:16, 17; 2 Thessalonians 1:7–10; 2:1–8).

Darby gave further prominence to his Dispensational view, by making several trips to the United States and Canada. His scheme was popularized by its incorporation into the Scofield Reference Bible in 1909. With the passing of time it has become entrenched in the minds of Protestant America. But, it is incredible that multitudes have latched on to this scheme—the greatest COVER-UP OF TRUTH this century.

EMERGENCE OF THE CATHOLIC APOSTOLIC CHURCH

Although the official organization of the Catholic Apostolic Church is dated 1833, its emergence really began unofficially in 1830, with the outbreak of charismatic phenomena. No sooner had the news reverberated in the land, than Edward Irving responded by writing a letter, dated June 2, 1830, expressing his acknowledgment thus: "The substance of Mary Campbell's and Margaret MacDonald's visions or revelations, given in their papers, carry to me a spiritual conviction and a spiritual reproof which I cannot express."[52]

Such a letter shows Irving's immediate conviction of a relationship and identification with the resultant charismatic phenomena, for which he directed a program of preparation—as already outlined in this chapter. It was now incumbent upon him to foster the restoration of Spiritual Gifts that he had written about in 1828.

Irving's letter refers to two individuals: Margaret MacDonald and Mary Campbell. Much space has already been given to Margaret MacDonald and her prophetic revelation. We now turn our attention to

Mary Campbell, whose experience took place in the same year as Margaret MacDonald.

Mary Campbell's Healing

In order to preserve continuity in this chapter, I shall pick up from the story of Margaret MacDonald's healing by her brother James—as related earlier in this chapter. After healing Margaret, James wrote a letter to Mary Campbell commanding her in the name of the Lord to arise.

Mary Campbell lived at Fernicarry, about fifteen miles away from Margaret MacDonald. Mary suffered from a form of consumption, that brought about the death of her sister Isabella. She complained of pain in the chest and breathlessness. Presently she received James MacDonald's letter and began to read. In her own words she said:

> I received dear brother James MacDonald's letter, giving an account of his sister's being raised up, and commanding me to 'rise and walk'. I had scarcely read the first page when I was overpowered, and laid it aside for a few minutes; but I had to rest in my mind until I took it up again, and began to read. As I read every word came home with power, and when I came to the command to rise, it came home with a power which no words can describe; it was felt to be indeed the Voice of Christ; it was such a Voice as could not be resisted; a mighty power was instantaneously exerted upon me; I felt as if I had been lifted from off the earth, and all my diseases taken off me at the voice of Christ. I was verily made in a moment to stand upon my feet, leap and walk, sing and rejoice.[53]

Before her healing, Mary Campbell had talked about the subject of healing, lately broached by Irving, that bodily disease was inflicted by Satan, but it could be healed by faith and prayer. On the whole the cases of healing at this time were by the prayer of faith, in some cases accompanied by anointing with olive oil. Apparently there were no faith healers conducting healing crusades. The genuineness of the healings can only be attested by the personal testimonies of the few individuals mentioned herein. For lack of evidence, it is impossible to assess the permanence of the healing, by following up the healing incidents after a number of years. Be that as it may, the number of reported instances in one year among the Irvingites reached a total of forty six in England alone.[54]

Soon after the healing of Mary Campbell and Margaret MacDonald by James MacDonald, Britain was engulfed in a serious epidemic of cholera towards the end of 1831. The MacDonald family survived the epidemic, even though they were exposed day and night while visiting in the neighborhood in their mission of mercy, caring for the sick. However, the MacDonald twin brothers did not survive the illness of "consumption," that took a number of lives. They both died in 1835; and James, who had been instrumental in healing Mary and Margaret, was only 34 years old when he died of consumption. By 1840 both Mary and Margaret had died; and Margaret had not reached the age of 25 years. Such untimely deaths pose a question about the permanence of the healing of these two young women—just a few years before, in 1830. On the other hand, their deaths may have been the will of God, or perhaps the low life expectancy.[55]

Mary Campbell's Gift of Tongues

There could not be a finer religious climate, than that which prevailed in Great Britain, for the endowment of the gift of tongues—an Apostolic gift par excellence. This was the age of the great Advent Awakening. This was the Philadelphian age of brotherly love, and the extension of the Gospel to the heathen—the age of Missions. If ever, there was a need for the gift of tongues, or foreign language—it was now.

William Carey could have benefited with the Spiritual Gift of tongues at his first mission in India. So could Joseph Wolff have benefited as the missionary to the world. So could all those missionaries have benefited, who were grappling with vernacular tongues, preparing translations of the Bible, and sending them on to the British and Foreign Bible Society for publication. Even Edward Irving could have benefited, while translating Lacunza's book from Spanish into English. But, strangely enough, none of these benefited with the Spiritual Gift of tongues. They all applied themselves to the tedious task of the learning and study of language.

It was in such a religious climate as described, that a humble, honest young dressmaker, Mary Campbell talked and prayed for the restoration of Spiritual Gifts bearing upon mission work—something mentioned already by Irving. In fact she was studying language with a view to mission work, and was looking out "every day for the gift of tongues, etc., being poured out upon the church."[56]

Mary Campbell was well aware of Acts of the Apostles, Chapter 2, describing the Pentecostal experience, whereby the apostles were miraculously endowed with the gift of tongues. She, like so many others, recognized that every person from fifteen areas heard the apostles "speak in his own language," or dialect (Acts 2:6). The hearers were amazed to hear the apostles speak their own languages with the same native-born inflection and intonation (Acts 2:8).

All of a sudden, without any previous notice, and in response to her expectation, Mary Campbell one evening in March, 1830, before a few friends, "began to utter sounds to them incomprehensible."[57] She tried to figure out the language, in order to go to the country where it was intelligible, and fulfill her grandest aspirations of mission service. Eventually she announced the gift was the language of the Pellew islands in the southern Pacific Ocean.[58]

Soon after her initial experience, Mary Campbell won the reputation of a gifted prophetess. "She expounded, prophesied, and spoke before crowded meetings."[59] She gave utterances in what she deemed to be Turkish and the language of the Pellew islands. She married W.R. Caird in 1831, with the intention that they go together as missionaries, and was impelled by a Voice that declared to her, that unless she "rose and proceeded without delay to declare the gospel to the heathen, she and her father's house would perish."[60]

The fact of the matter is, that Mary (Campbell) Caird *never* did go to the mission field, and neither was the threat of the Voice carried out. In spite of her disappointment and failure to exercise her so-called gift of tongues as a missionary, Mary clung to her belief and advanced to prominence in the Catholic Apostolic Church. She joined the band of prophetesses called "gifted handmaids"[61]—in fulfillment of Joel's prophecy: "your daughters shall prophesy... and upon the handmaids in those days will I pour out my spirit." Strange, that one can be so deceived, and yet still adhere to a supernatural experience.

But an observer of Mary Caird's supernatural experience was not going to be deceived. The Rev. Robert Story's earliest contact and knowledge of Mary Caird goes back a few years before her first tongues experience. When Mary's sister Isabella died in 1828, Story came out with a Memoir of her most saintly life—6000 copies of which sold in a few weeks. The close observation and scrutiny of Isabella's life was now applied to Mary Caird. One can imagine the publicity that surrounded Mary Caird's experience in the wake of her sister Isabella. And so Story put her tongues experience to the test. Mary submitted some of her utterances in tongues from Scotland, reduced to writing. A distinguished panel of three examined the writing, comprising Sir George Staunton, and Doctors Pusey and Lee, the Professors of Hebrew in the Universities of Oxford and Cambridge. Their tabulated consensus was that the submitted writing, supposedly of the Pellew islands, "contains neither character nor language known in any region under the sun."[62]

Indeed, Story was not deceived, and his observation and writing about Mary's tongues experience in his Memoir—*Life of Robert Story*, left him disappointed at the failure of Mary carrying out what she considered to be a Divine enterprise. The result was that both he, and Rev. John M. Campbell (who also had intimate acquaintance with Mary), together with Irving's assistant, Alexander Scott, all refused to join with the Catholic Apostolic Church at its inauguration, even after earnest solicitations.[63]

Spurious Gifts of Tongues and Prophecy

The purported gift of tongues experienced by Mary (Campbell) Caird was not like the phenomenon of Scripture. The Greek word *glossa*, translated tongue, meaning language—the medium of intelligent communication between individuals is used in Acts, chapter 2, verses 4 and 11. It is equated with the Greek word *dialektos*, meaning literally dialect, used in the same chapter at verses 6 and 8. Clear and consistent interpretation demands, that wherever else in the New Testament *glossa* appears in connection with the gift of tongues, its going to mean exactly what it implies—foreign language. Therefore, *glossa* in the manifestation of the gift of tongues at Caesarea, Acts 10 and 11; at Ephesus, Acts 19; and at Corinth, 1 Corinthians 12 to 14, is none other than foreign language. Mary Caird's gift was not a foreign language—it was unintelligible jargon, inarticulate vocalizing. It was what we call in modern terms: *glossolalia*. It was a fallacious gift of tongues, devoid of Scriptural support.

It has been described, how readily Mary Caird submitted for examination her utterances in tongues, reduced to writing. But that practise was soon forbidden by the power of the spirit, both in England and Scotland—as reported by Robert Baxter in his book, *Narrative of Facts, Characterizing the Supernatural Manifestations in Members of Mr. Irvings Congregation, and Other Individuals, in England and Scotland, and Formerly in the Writer Himself* (1833). Baxter reported that the power of the spirit warned even against the repetition of utterances verbatim. Veiled in such secrecy, errors and contradictions are not easily detected.[64] Supernatural phenomena of this nature casts all the more suspicion on the authenticity of the gifts of tongues and prophecy.

Baxter described the nature of the power that possessed him, before his renunciation of the gift of prophecy: "a power coming upon me which was altogether new, an unnatural, and in many cases an appalling utterance given to me.... It was manifest to me that the power was supernatural; it was therefore, a spirit."[65]

John Cardale, a favorable observer, in contrast, said: "They declare that their organs of speech are made use of by the Spirit of God, and that they utter that which is given to them, and not the expressions of their own conceptions, or their own intention."[66] While that may be true to some extent, there is also an intermingling of their own expressions resulting in subjective utterances. Case in point—Dr. Hugh McNeile, Dean of Ripon, and chairman of the Albury Park Prophetic Conferences, observed a Mr. Taplin's prophetic utterance stating: "It was neither more nor less than is commonly called jargon, uttered—*ore rotundo*, and mingled with Latin words, among which I heard more than once, *amamini, amaminor.* "[67] These words reminded Dr. McNeile of Mr. Taplin's scholastic duties in his "academy"—thus suggesting the subjectivity of the phenomenon, colored by Taplin's own life experience and versatility in Latin, Greek, and Hebrew.[68]

As the number of prophets grew and as the number of prophecies accumulated, so did contradiction, confusion, and charismatic chaos grow. Taplin himself, "chief of the prophets," had been time and again convicted of false prophecy, and time and again received as a true prophet. At one time Taplin, through the voice of prophecy, rebuked Edward Irving. Whereupon Taplin was rebuked by the prophetic utterance of Miss E. Cardale. Such charismatic chaos led the more discerning individuals to question the veracity of the gift of prophecy, while others blithely explained things away, and continued in the delusion.[69]

Baxter was one of those discerning individuals. Having been a "prolific deliverer of prophecies," and well accepted by his assembly, he virtually applied the Biblical test of a prophet (Jeremiah 28:9)—that the word of the prophet must come to pass. He had prophesied, as recorded in his *Narrative*: "that in 1,260 days from January 14th, 1832, the Lord Jesus would come in glory;...that the man of sin should be Louis Napoleon."[70] The non-fulfillment of this prophecy, and over forty other documented prophecies which were signally unfulfilled, led Baxter to publish to the world his reasons for his defection from Irving's following, as expressed in his expose, *Narrative of Facts*. The announcement of Baxter's defection was made in person to Edward Irving on the very morning of Irving's Christological heresy trial (March 13, 1833) before his superiors, the Scottish Presbytery. These developments certainly dealt a heavy blow of disappointment and discouragement upon Irving, and did not augur well for the establishment of the Catholic Apostolic Church, soon thereafter.[71]

In a book printed for private distribution entitled, *My Reasons for retiring from the Catholic Apostolic Church* (1873), H.M. Prior wrote:

> I have heard some thousand so-called prophetic utterances, but (with two exceptions) they have contained nothing beyond the ability of any ordinary man to speak. They were largely composed of quotations from Scripture, and all else they contained has been better expressed from the pulpit. The two exceptions were poetical utterances, and although it is beyond the ability of ordinary men to extemporize poetry, the gift is not so rare as to require us to suppose that any other than human agency was concerned in it. The only thing remarkable about these utterances is the unnatural way in which they are spoken.[72]

In the exhaustive two-volume work, *The History and Doctrines of Irvingism* (1878), the author, Edward Miller, Vicar of Butler's Marston, points out the failure of the prophetic utterances for Christ's Second Coming set for the following dates: 1835 (as predicted by Baxter), 1838, 1845, 1850, and 1866. In concluding statements Miller observes that in the late 1870's the "Prophets are but a small power in the Community," and that the "Unknown Tongues are now things of the past, and are no longer heard in Catholic Apostolic Churches."[73]

The Entrance of Tongues and Prophecy in Irving's Church

The early outbreak of charismatic phenomena in 1830, from the homes of the MacDonald's and Mary Campbell, made no impact upon Irving's large Presbyterian congregation, meeting in the famous Regent Square Church, London, until 1831. Fearing the introduction of charismatic phenomena in this congregation, Irving reluctantly permitted meetings of this nature in the early mornings. But this was not to be. On Sunday morning, October 16th, 1831, a Miss Hall (who later defected) disrupted the service conducted for about 1500 to 2000 people, as they listened to her "sudden, doleful, and unintelligible sounds." Whereupon Irving restored order, and abandoned his sermon for an explanation of 1 Corinthians, chapter fourteen, pertinent to the charismatic interruption. This was the beginning of the end, since the charismatics had gotten a foothold in the church, but it aroused the indignation of the regular Presbyterian congregation. It split the church. And further disruption of Sunday services forced the regular Presbyterian members to file a complaint with the Presbytery of London. The outcome of the matter was that Irving was charged for violating Presbyterian order, by allowing the unauthorized utterances of tongues and prophecy. Irving was deposed, and his charismatic followers of about 800 were debarred from entering the Regent Square Church.[74]

Irving's charismatic followers were now forced to band together as a body, meeting in the house and premises on Newman Street. They needed organization, so the Catholic Apostolic Church was officially born, 1833, ostensibly a restoration of the Apostolic Church. They needed some leadership, but not until Irving was re-ordained an "angel," or bishop of the church. Nevertheless, his ministry in the Catholic Apostolic Church was short-lived. He died of consumption at the age of 42 years, December 8th, 1834.

Since 1825 Irving rose like a meteor and shone brightly, then rapidly paled. He was a pre-eminent Christian—kind-hearted, humble, and consecrated. Although Irving himself, never spoke in tongues or prophesied, he fostered the charismatic movement in Great Britain, and therefore became the veritable "father of modern Pentecostalism."[75]

The Gift of Apostles and Development of the Catholic Apostolic Church

The organization and structure of the Catholic Apostolic Church did not follow the traditional leadership of a church congregation by a Pastor. Instead of Edward Irving, the *virtual founder*, directing the arrangements and destinies of the church, Baxter explained:

> All the changes which took place in Mr. Irving's views and church arrangements, were in *subservience* and *strict obedience to these utterances*, and that from the period of their *introduction* into his church, they were *worshiped as the voice of God in the gift of prophecy*.[76]
>
> (Italics supplied).

The title and name Catholic and Apostolic Church is said to have come about "in obedience to a word of prophecy forbidding any other." But it may also be a take off from the Roman Catholic Church, which is designated the one Holy Catholic and Apostolic Church throughout the world, claiming unbroken existence from the time of Christ. The date of the establishment of the Catholic Apostolic Church almost coincided with the strong promotion of the Oxford Church movement making overtures to Rome by means of tracts. When a distinctive name was unavoidable the Church preferred to be called, 'The Church gathered under apostles." To affix the term Catholic to the Apostolic Church was not to imitate, or relate to the Roman Catholic Church, but to epitomize their ambition and objective to become *universal* and restore the Apostolic Church of the first century in all its aspects.[77]

Taking its cue from the "Seven Churches" of Revelation, Chapters 2 and 3, the Catholic Apostolic Church soon organized seven separate congregations in London naming them "The Seven Churches." The Church borrowed the term "angel," or messenger, from Revelation's "Seven Churches" (Revelation 2 and 3) and appointed an angel, or bishop, for each of the seven churches in London.[78]

No sooner had the gifts of tongues, prophecy, and healing been manifested in 1830, when prayer meetings were held at Port Glasgow and neighborhood pleading for the accompanying gift of apostles. Such craving was based upon Ephesians, Chapter 4, verse 11: "And he gave some, apostles; and some prophets; and some evangelists; and some pastors and teachers." From this verse, coupled with 1 Corinthians, Chapter 12, verse 28, was derived the tenet of a Fourfold Ministry of *apostles, prophets, evangelists, and pastor*s. With the establishment of the Catholic Apostolic Church at Newman Street this concept came to fruition, and became the touchstone of the Church.

The officers of the Church were likened to the furnishings and composition of the ancient Hebrew tabernacle. The *pastor* and elder was compared to the Golden Candlestick. A slew of *evangelists* was appointed, represented by the Pillars of the tabernacle—sixty in number. The *prophets* apparently were not symbolized by anything in the tabernacle, but in the auditorium for worship, they were prominently seated in a row of seven seats—all arrangements ordered, of course, by prophetic utterance. Last, but not least *twelve apostles* were appointed with no relationship to the tabernacle—they constituted the foundation of the temple.[79]

Since the gift of apostles was listed first by Paul's inspired writings to the churches at Ephesus and Corinth, the Catholic Apostolic Church held the gift in high repute. In fact, as we trace its development, a strange doctrine resulted from fanciful interpretation of the book of Revelation by prophetic utterance. The first intimation of the gift came from the initial meetings of the Church assembled in Newman Street, when John Cardale the solicitor already possessing the gift of prophecy, was selected as the first apostle by prophetic utterance. Almost a year later Henry Drummond, the banker, became an apostle by the same approach. By 1835 the perfect quota of twelve apostles was realized. The completion of the number was declared by prophetic utterance to be the birth of the "man child" mentioned in the vision of Revelation,

Chapter 12. The mass withdrawal of the apostles to Albury on the eighth day from their call, represented the circumcision of this "child."[80]

While awaiting their mission in Albury for a year, a prophetic utterance given by Drummond, directed that the world should be divided into twelve "tribes," each of which was assigned to a particular apostle. Cardale was assigned England, as the tribe of Judah, and Drummond was assigned Scotland and Switzerland, as the tribe of Benjamin. After all assignments were made the twelve apostles were to be imbued with the baptism of fire, and that signs, wonders and miracles would follow them. Their commission was to carry out the Sealing of 144,000 of all the "tribes" apportioned to them (Revelation 7:1–8). Each apostle was to save and seal 12,000 for his tribe. This great commission was exact and definite. It had to be accomplished within the life-time of each individual apostle, and before the Second Coming of Christ.[81]

Added to the power of Sealing, the twelve apostles constituted the ultimate court of appeal to settle disputes about Doctrine. All prophecies were to be submitted to the Apostle of the Tribe for the stamp of approval. A complaint had been lodged, that Baxter interpreted his own prophecies, instead of submitting them for interpretation by the apostles. There may have been some tension between the apostles and prophets in this matter. But, apparently there was no question raised about the prophetic utterances, directing the appointment of the apostles and their commission, or the fanciful interpretation of Revelation, Chapters 7, 12, and 14, applied to the apostles.[82]

It is adduced that the outcome of the College of twelve Apostles was a failure. The situation, after sixteen years into the enterprise, was such that Drummond had resumed duties in the English Parliament, two apostles had refused to participate, and two others had either withdrawn, or retired. By the year 1875 more than half of the apostles had died, and not one had attained his quota of 12,000 sealed souls within his life-time—as required by prophetic utterance. The situation was lamented by one of the last stalwart apostles, John Cardale, among other members. The entire membership of the Catholic Apostolic Church at this time had only reached a total of 10,500, half of which were in the British Isles. This figure was a far cry from what was projected—namely 12 multiplied by 12,000 giving a grand total of 144,000. Thus, the twelve-fold Apostolate collapsed, together with the prophetic utterances by which it was launched.[83] The grandiose attempt to restore the fundamentals of the Apostolic Church of the first century, complete with Spiritual Gifts, was a total failure.

Conclusion

In the mid 1870's the Catholic Apostolic Church had 1,500 members in America and the Colonies.[84] Whether there is any connection between the Catholic Apostolic Church and the rise of Pentecostalism in America, in 1901, is unknown. What is known, is that a Methodist minister, Charles Parham, laid his hands upon the head of Agnes Osman, a student at a Bible school in Topeka, Kansas, in 1901, and she received an ecstatic utterance. The emerging movement gained national attention in 1906 through healings at the Azusa Street Mission in Los Angeles.[85] Pentecostalism, or the charismatic movement continued to grow and separate into denominational lines: the Assemblies of God, the Four Square Gospel Church, the United Pentecostal Church, the Apostolic Churches, and so on.[86]

But in 1960 Pentecostalism began to penetrate the mainline denominations when Dennis J. Bennett, rector of St. Mark's Episcopal church in Van Nuys, California, announced to his parishioners that he had experienced the baptism of the Holy Spirit, and received the gift of tongues. Since 1960 Neo-Pentecostalism has penetrated over 100 denominations including Episcopalian, Methodist, Presbyterian, Baptist, and Lutheran churches; and from 1967 it made its way into the Roman Catholic churches.[87] And there is no let up, the Pentecostal—charismatic movement continues to grow in leaps and bounds, uniting denominations across the whole spectrum of Protestantism with unprecedented ecumenical force.

The present-day Pentecostal—charismatic movement shares the same false gifts of healing, prophecy, and tongues, as did the Catholic Apostolic Church as exposed in this chapter. But another sad thing, is that as Pentecostalism arose, it absorbed the false doctrine of a Secret Rapture and a two-phase Second Coming with Futuristic overtones, all wrapped up in a Dispensational scheme found in the Scofield Reference Bible. The union of the false Pentecostal-charismatic movement *in combination with* the Dispensational scheme constitutes: the greatest DUAL COVER-UP OF TRUTH this century.

Chapter 5

SECOND ADVENT AWAKENING IN AMERICA

As we enter the portals of the nineteenth century in America, we are about to behold the grand finale of fulfilling prophecy that will strengthen our faith and belief. At once we are reminded of the principle of prophetic interpretation so clearly enunciated by Jesus: "And now I have told you before it come to pass, that, when it is come to pass, ye might believe" (John 14:29).

The ultimate purpose of prophecy, is for that which is prefigured, or prophesied, to "come to pass"—to take place in an identifiable historical event; and when that happens, our faith is strengthened, that we "might believe." Therefore the passing of time in events is the interpreter of prophecy—simply history unveils or interprets prophecy. Jesus' principle of prophetic interpretation became the Protestant continuous Historicist principle of prophetic interpretation. This exciting principle was followed in America, as one prophecy after another was fulfilled to draw nearer, and nearer: "Looking for that blessed hope, and the glorious appearing of the great God and our Saviour Jesus Christ" (Titus 2:13).

Providential Convergence of Prophetic Interpretation An Ocean Apart

The initial groundwork for the great Second Advent Awakening in America was laid by the introduction of prophetic periodicals: the *Connecticut Evangelical Magazine* (1800); the *Christian Observer* (Anglican) of Boston (1802); and the *Herald of Gospel Liberty* (Christian) launched in 1808 at Portsmouth, New Hampshire, by Elias Smith, one of the founders of the Christian Connection. These three religious periodicals were unusually popular.[1]

The Boston *Christian Observer*, widely read throughout New England, was the American edition of the London *Christian Observer* from the start, without any changes to suit the American mind. Hence the pioneer expositors of the great Advent Awakening in Great Britain appeared in America through articles by such men as William Cuninghame. He taught the Supremacy of the Papal Little Horn of Daniel, Chapter 7, for 1,260 years from the Code of Justinian, 533 A.D., to the French Revolution, 1792, followed by the Pre-Advent Judgment (Daniel 7:9–14, 22, 26) and the "blessed state." He also dated the 2,300 years (Daniel 8:14) from the time of the vision of Daniel.[2] Thus Cuninghame's writings and other British expositors, began to mold American thought from 1807, and again from 1840, when his lengthy treatises, among those of a host of prominent British expositors, was published by Orrin Rogers of Philadelphia. These complete reprints appeared in five volumes as a semimonthly periodical, entitled *The*

Literalist—advocating the literal interpretation of prophecy in opposition to a spiritualizing trend.[3]

In addition the *American Millenarian and Prophetic Review,* another Protestant journal, launched in New York City, in 1842, pressed home the pre-millennial Second Advent and leaned heavily on British expositors. Such was the accumulation of prophetic writings that fostered a phenomenal interest and circulation—binding together the British and American Advent Awakening.[4]

Apart from Cuninghame's article in the 1807 issue of the Boston *Christian Observer,* outlined above, another ground-floor introduction was made by the November, 1810, issue. **John A. Brown's** ground-breaking article taught the *synchronous* or *simultaneous* beginning of the prophecy of the "seventy weeks of years" (490 years) *together with* the 2,300 year prophecy (Daniel 8:14). He dated the commencement from 457 B.C., according to the decree of Artaxerxes to restore and rebuild Jerusalem (Ezra 7:7, 8, 12, 13). Brown traced the 490 years to the cross, and the 2,300 years to end in 1843. Apparently this was the *first* time such an epochal truth was presented with precise dating in Great Britain, and now in America.

But, a Providential aspect about Brown's truth presented in November, 1810, before a British and American readership, was that barely two months later **William C. Davis**, a prominent Presbyterian minister and teacher of South Carolina, quite independently, published his truth of a *synchronous* beginning of the "seventy weeks" with the 2,300 years from 453 B.C., terminating the longer period in 1847, followed by the millennium. The *convergence* of Brown and Davis' prophetic interpretation of Daniel 8 and 9 at a point in time *so close,* and yet in distance, separated by the Atlantic Ocean, has to be more than a coincidence—*it had to be Providential.*[5]

Davis was the *first* American expositor, as far as is known, to expound his truth on Daniel that was published in a pamphlet entitled, *The Millennium, or A Short Sketch on the Rise and Fall of Antichrist.* Several reprints followed consecutively in South Carolina and Kentucky. His pamphlet influenced Presbyterian ministers: Archibald Mason of Scotland, and Joshua Wilson, sometime moderator of Ohio, who preached on prophecy in 1828.[6]

In summation, certain fundamental interpretations of prophecy in America and Great Britain came to be regarded as axiomatic, namely: the day for a year principle; the collapse of the Papacy during the French Revolution terminating the 1,260 year prophecy (Daniel 7:25); the consecutive historical outline prophecies of Daniel; the Papal Antichrist of Daniel 7, of Revelation 13 and 17, and of 2 Thessalonians 2; and the 391 years applied to the Turk (Revelation 9:15).

Another fundamental interpretation of prophecy that came to be regarded as axiomatic during the Advent Awakening in Europe and America must be included in the list. And that is the 2,300 year prophecy terminating in 1843, 1844, or 1847, based upon the simultaneous commencement of the "seventy weeks" and the 2,300 days. Johann

Petri, Reformed pastor of Germany, was the first (in 1768) to outline this prophecy accordingly; thereafter, over seventy international and inter-denominational distinguished expositors followed until 1836, at which time William Miller's first book on prophecy appeared.[7] The event to mark the "cleansing of the sanctuary" (Daniel 8:14) at the termination of the 2,300 year prophecy was still to be ascertained. The next chapter will reveal the event.

Indeed, it has to be recognized that the 2,300 year prophecy is the longest time prophecy in the Bible, and its fulfillment pointed to the last possible date of any prophecy as the great climactic hour. It is no wonder then, that when John Brown (November 1810) and William Davis (January 1811) came upon this prophecy almost simultaneously, merely a couple of months apart, that this sparked a tremendous interest and investigation, that gave rise to a simultaneous Providential Advent Awakening in both Great Britain and America.

FULFILLING PROPHECIES AS SIGNS OF APPROACHING SECOND ADVENT

The glorious Second Advent of Christ has been the transcendent hope of the ages. And the Gospels and Revelation have furnished mankind with spectacular signs of the approaching Advent. As each sign finds fulfillment in some identifying event to which it points, so the climactic Second Advent is drawn nearer, and still nearer. The big thing, however, is to identify the event with the sign; to recognize its fulfillment; to believe it has "come to pass"; to rejoice about its fulfillment, and to tabulate it for future generations—lest with the passing of time it might be lost sight of, or forgotten. Furthermore, it would appear that as mankind entered the "time of the end," namely from about 1750, that there would be a multiplicity of signs in rather rapid succession, to alert mankind of the consummation of the ages in the Second Advent. Now trace four fulfilling signs impacting the Advent Awakening.

(1) Lisbon Earthquake, November 1, 1755

> And *great earthquakes* shall be in divers places, and famines, and pestilences; and fearful sights and great signs shall there be from heaven. Luke 21, verse 11.

> And I beheld when he had opened the sixth seal, and lo there was a *great earthquake*; and the sun became black as sackcloth of hair, and the moon became as blood.
>
> Revelation 6, verse 12.
> *Authorized King James Version*

The city of Lisbon, Portugal, was struck by one of the "greatest earthquakes" ever recorded, on November 1, 1755. Two shock waves occurred, forty minutes apart, causing the waters to recede and surge back through the city, rising fifty feet above its ordinary level. Then the city was engulfed in a conflagration that lasted a whole week. The new quay built entirely of marble, at an immense expense subsided. Over

9000 buildings were destroyed, among them the infamous Palace of the Inquisition—never to be rebuilt. The terror of the people was beyond description, heightened by the fact that the churches were crowded to honor the dead on All Saints Day. Consternation seized them as they ran hither and thither crying out, '*Misericordia! the world's at an end!*' No! It was not the end of the world, but a portent of the end! Nevertheless, the loss of life was immense. "In the course of about six minutes, sixty thousand persons perished."[8]

There is no doubt that the Lisbon earthquake was a "great earthquake," to match the description given in Luke 21:11 and Revelation 6:12, quoted above. The earthquake was so great that it "extended over a tract of at least four millions of square miles."[9] Its shock effects were felt as far as Africa, Britain, Europe, and the West Indies. A tidal wave swept over the coast of Spain, and reached a height over fifty feet at Cadiz. The northern coast of Africa met with great severity: a major section of Algiers was destroyed, and a village of eight thousand inhabitants near Morocco was swallowed up.[10]

In **Great Britain** several issues of *The London Magazine* related the Lisbon earthquake to the "signs" of the Scriptures, pointing out that Lisbon, once the richest city in the world, became the "particular mark of divine displeasure."[11] One of the aspects of God's displeasure was that on the very day of the earthquake, it was planned to burn convicts of the Inquisition, to celebrate the *Auto-da-fe*.[12] Thanks be to God this never happened, and instead the Palace of the Inquisition was destroyed in the earthquake.

Writing in another London journal, *The Gentleman's Magazine*, the author in similar vein to the above writer, noted it was in Lisbon, where "the most dreadful tribunal of the Inquisition emitted the infernal flames with the greatest fury and hottest violence." He then tied the catastrophe of the Lisbon earthquake to Luke 21, verses 25 and 26, declaring it to be "one of the infallible omens," set forth as a herald of the "glorious kingdom of the millennium." This earthquake, he said, should "awaken the world to serious and devout contemplations," and to "compare it with the prophecies relating to, and now fulfilling in this its last days."[13]

Besides the published reports, the clergy of the Anglican Church were not remiss in recognizing the Lisbon earthquake as one of Christ's "signs" of the approaching Second Advent. They saw in the event a clarion call to repentance and humility before God. Therefore, in order to make an indelible impression upon the minds of the people, a day of fasting and prayer was summoned for Friday, February 6, 1756. Church dignitaries rallied the people, and delivered twenty one sermons for the occasion. Bishop Lavington of Exeter referred to the General Fast-Day as "the greatest Call in its kind which has been known in the Memory of any Person living, or (I think) recorded in History." And, as if acknowledging the Countdown to the Second Advent had begun, the bishop concluded none can put "any stop to the Forerunner of the Lord's Coming."[14]

In **America** the news of the Lisbon earthquake was received with prophetic significance. The *Boston Weekly News-Letter* came out with an extra "Postscript" page in folio size, of an eye-witness account of the Lisbon earthquake. On the back of the page appeared advertisements of four Biblical discourses on the earthquake by American ministers of religion.[15]

One of the ministers, Thomas Prentice of the Congregational Church, published a sermon relative to the Lisbon earthquake in fulfillment of "terrible earthquakes mentioned by our Lord Himself." He also related the Lisbon earthquake to the events of the Sixth Seal as a harbinger of the end, quoting Revelation 6, verse 12 through 17: "And I beheld when he had opened the sixth seal, and lo, there was a great earthquake;.... For the great day of his wrath is come; and who shall be able to stand."[16]

(2) The Dark Day, May 19, 1780

> The sun shall be turned into darkness, and the moon into blood, before the great and terrible day of the Lord come. Joel 2, verse 31.

> The sun and the moon shall be darkened, and the stars shall withdraw their shining. Joel 3, verse 15.

> Immediately after the tribulation of those days shall the sun be darkened, and the moon shall not give her light, and the stars shall fall from heaven, and the powers of the heavens shall be shaken. Matthew 24, verse 29.
> *Authorized King James Version*

"The dark day of New England, so familiar to old and young, came May 19, 1780.... Near eleven o'clock it began to grow dark as if night were coming. Men ceased their work; the lowing cattle came to the barns, the bleating sheep huddled by fences, the wild birds screamed and flew to their nests, the fowls went to their roosts.... At night it was so inky dark that a person could not see his hand when held up, nor even a white sheet of paper."[17]

A professor of Harvard University, Samuel Williams, professor of mathematics and philosophy, who observed the mysterious phenomenon of the Dark Day, May19, 1780, wrote an elaborate account for the *Memoirs of the American Academy of Arts and Sciences* (1785); excerpts of which follow in his own words:

> The time of this extraordinary darkness was May 19, 1780. It came on between the hours of ten and eleven a.m., and continued until the middle of the next night....

> The *extent* of this darkness was very remarkable.... It was observed as far east as Falmouth [Portland, Maine]. To the westward we hear of its reaching to the furthest parts of Connecticut, and Albany. To the southward it

was observed all along the seacoasts, and to the north
as far as our settlements extend....

With regard to its *duration*, it continued in this place at
least fourteen hours; but it is probable this was not
exactly the same in different parts of the country.[18]

Of great interest were the comments regarding the cause of the
Dark Day. Under the heading Dark Day, Noah Webster's Dictionary
said: "The true cause of this remarkable phenomenon is not known."[19]
President Timothy Dwight of Yale College, a contemporary, stated: "A
very general opinion prevailed that the day of judgment was at hand."[20]
Sir William Herschel, who discovered the planet Uranus in the year
after the Dark Day, was not able to uncover the cause of the Dark Day.
Nevertheless, Herschel, who transformed astronomy with his forty
eight inch telescope, a veritable marvel of eighteenth century technol-
ogy, explained the Dark Day, a marvel of eighteenth century prophecy,
in these words: "The dark day in Northern America was one of those
wonderful phenomena of nature which will always be read of with
interest, but which philosophy is at a loss to explain."[21]

Dr. Samuel Stearns made this contemporary observation concerning the cause of the Dark Day: "That the darkness was not caused by an
eclipse is manifest by the various positions of the planets of our system
at that time; for the moon was more than one hundred fifty degrees
from the sun all that day." Scientist Stearns went on to say: "The
primary cause must be imputed to Him that walketh through the circuit
of heaven."[22]

Now for a smidgen of an anecdotal nature from the Connecticut
State Legislature—of all places, in session on that notable Dark Day.
One member moved to adjourn, when the inky darkness fell. Then the
opinion of Colonel Abraham Davenport was asked, whereupon he rose
and said:

I am against an adjournment. The day of judgment is
either approaching or it is not. If it is not, there is no
cause for adjournment; if it is, I choose to be found
doing my duty. I wish therefore that candles may be
brought.[23]

This is the scene that John G. Whittier immortalized with his poetic pen:

'Twas on a May day of the far old year
Seventeen hundred eighty, that there fell
Over the bloom and sweet life of the spring,
Over the fresh earth and the heaven of noon,
A horror of great darkness, like the night....

Meanwhile in the old Statehouse, dim as ghosts,
Sat the lawgivers of Connecticut,
Trembling beneath their legislative robes.
'It is the Lord's great day! Let us adjourn',

Some said: and then, as if with one accord,
All eyes were turned to Abraham Davenport.

He rose, slow cleaving with his steady voice
The intolerable hush. 'This well may be
The day of judgment which the world awaits;
But be it so or not, I only know
My present duty, and my Lord's command
To occupy till He come. So at the post
Where He hath set me in His providence,
I choose, for one, to meet Him face to face,

No faithless servant frightened from my task,
But ready when the Lord of the harvest calls;
And therefore, with all reverence, I would say,
Let God do His work, we will see to ours.
Bring in the candles.'[24]

Having noted the observations and descriptions from the secular world, we now cite the significance of the Dark Day from the perspective of the religious world. There were some, who, after studying about the "signs in the sun, and in the moon, and in the stars" (Luke 21:25), *anticipated* their fulfillment. One such individual was Edmund March, M.A., a Congregational minister of Massachusetts, who in 1762 wrote in his book, originally sent to an association of ministers, that he was longing for the Second Coming, and the fulfillment of the darkening of the sun and the falling of the stars (Matthew 24:29).[25]

The *History and Traditions of Marblehead* describes the Dark Day, and the need for artificial lights, noting that birds and beasts went to roost. Samuel Gatchel, deacon of the Second Congregational Church in Marblehead, published a tract contending that the Dark Day was in fulfillment of Joel 3, verse 15. This contemporary commentary appears to be the first of its kind.[26]

To be styled the "day-star" of the pre-millennial Second Advent, more than forty years later, was a great honor conferred on Joshua Spalding. He had studied theology under Jonathan Edwards, and became Pastor of the Tabernacle Church at Salem, Massachusetts,—a continuation of the famous First Church founded in 1629. But his outstanding contribution, that earned his title "day-star," was his widely read book *Sentiments, Concerning the Coming and Kingdom of Christ* published in 1796. In his book of nine lectures he outlined the parallel events of Joel and Matthew 24, verse 29 (quoted above), specifically relating to the period of "tribulation," followed by the fulfillment of the Dark Day, in expectation of the other celestial signs—all of which were stated as a prelude to the Second Advent. Joshua V. Himes, of the Second Advent movement, was so impressed by Spalding's book, that he had it reprinted in 1841, more than forty years after the first publication.[27] He designated it "the day-star of returning light to the American

churches on the subject of the near coming and kingdom of our Lord
Jesus Christ."[28]

Elias Smith, one of the founders of the Christian Connection,
deserves double honors for expressing his prophetic outlook on the
visible signs of the Second Advent in his book *The Day of Judgment*
(1805), and his popular pioneer prophetic periodical *Herald of Gospel
Liberty* (1808). The periodical helped lay the foundation of the American Advent Awakening, together with the *Christian
Observer*—discussed in the introduction to this chapter.[29]

Smith wrote extensively on the Signs (Luke 21:25, 26), drawing
attention to fulfillment in his day and the near future. He wrote: "In the
year 1780, there was something remarkable seen in the sun by day, and
in the moon by night. All who believed in the Bible, thought this a sign of
the coming of the Son of Man." Of the fulfillment of future signs he
wrote: "Christ mentions signs in the stars—whether there has been any
particular signs in the stars, I am not able to determine; but while there
are so many other signs, we may expect them soon." Those words were
penned in 1808, and true to his expectation as coming "soon," and his
faith in fulfillment of future signs—a most spectacular display of falling
stars did take place in 1833.[30]

(3) "The Falling Stars," November 12/13, 1833

Matthew 24:

v.29 Immediately after the tribulation of those days shall
the sun be darkened, and the moon shall not give her
light, and *the stars shall fall from heaven*, and the powers
of the heavens shall be shaken:

v.30 And then shall appear the sign of the Son of Man in
heaven: and then shall all the tribes of the earth mourn,
and they shall see the Son of Man coming in the clouds of
heaven with power and great glory.

(Italics supplied)

Revelation 6:

v.12 And behold when he had opened the sixth seal, and
lo, there was a great earthquake; and the sun became
black as sackcloth of hair, and the moon became as blood;

v.13 And the *stars of heaven fell* unto the earth, even as a
fig tree casteth her untimely figs, when she is shaken of a
mighty wind.

v.14 And the heaven departed as a scroll when it is rolled
together; and every mountain and island were moved out
of their places.

v.17 For the great day of His wrath is come;
and who shall be able to stand?

(Italics supplied)
Authorized King James Version

The greatest display of fireworks celebrating Independence Day on the Fourth of July pales into insignificance, when compared with the display of the celestial "fireworks of the most imposing grandeur, covering the entire vault of heaven with myriads of fireballs, resembling skyrockets,"[31] that took place on the morning of November 13, 1833. This Leonid meteoric shower, the most "extensive and magnificent" exhibition of "shooting stars" ever recorded, was the Divine celebration, commemorating the *nearness* of the Second Coming. (See Picture 7).

The eyewitness account of Denison Olmstead, Professor of Astronomy at Yale, who wrote in the *American Journal of Science and Arts* had this to say about the Falling Stars: "After collecting and collating the accounts in all the periodicals of the country, and also in numerous letters addressed either to my scientific friends or to myself, the following appeared to be the *leading facts* attending the phenomenon. The shower pervaded nearly the whole of North America, having appeared in equal splendor from the British possessions on the north, to the West India Islands and Mexico on the south, and from sixty-one degrees of longitude east of the American coast, quite to the Pacific Ocean on the west. Throughout this immense region, the duration was nearly the same. The meteors began to attract attention by their unusual frequency and brilliancy, from nine to twelve o'clock in the evening, were most striking in their appearance from two to five [o'clock]."[32]

Here is further elaboration on the frequency and brilliancy of the Falling Stars. "There was scarcely a space in the firmament which was not filled at every instant with these falling stars—they fell like flakes of snow."[33] The frequency of shooting stars "at some stations was estimated as high as 200,000 an hour for five or six hours."[34] In Missouri the brilliance of these countless meteors was so great, that common-sized print could be read without much difficulty.[35]

The Caucasians of North America were not the only ones to record the visible sign of the Falling Stars, in the west the American Indians recorded it as "a milestone" in their annual calendars. Among the **Dakota** tribe it was designated the year when "it rained stars," depicted as a cluster of stars, by means of picture writing painted on calendars made of buffalo hide.[36]

From the remoteness of the Dakotas of North America to the remote corners of Central America, the spectacular display of Falling Stars was recorded. It is more than a coincidence, that the lone voice of a devout Roman Catholic magistrate, **Dr. Jose de Rozas**, of Mexico, should swell the chorus of prophetic voices in the world-wide Advent Awakening. Having served as a fiscal lawyer, and then as defense counsel for prisoners of the Inquisition in Mexico, Rozas became acquainted with so-called heretical writings, which led him to a study of the Scriptures and Lacunza's masterpiece, which he ultimately defended in a treatise. But his unique contribution, without equal in

"The stars of heaven fell unto the earth, even as a fig tree casteth her untimely figs, when she is shaken of a mighty wind." Rev. 6:13.

Picture 7
Great Leonid Meteoric Shower, November 13, 1833
This event of "Falling Stars" was the most extensive and magnificent exhibition of "shooting stars" ever recorded. The phenomenal event exactly matched the description of falling stars foretold at Revelation 6:13.

Spanish America, or even in Catholic Europe, was his *Consultation with the Wise Men About the Nearness of the Second Coming of Our Lord Jesus Christ* (1835), in which he followed Lacunza's proposition of literal interpretation of Scripture. By independent scholarship, and with great delight, Rozas announced 1847 as the termination of the 2,300 day-years (Daniel 8:14), clearly linking Daniel 8 and 9, commencing the prophecy with the command of Artaxerxes, to restore and build Jerusalem, which he placed in 454 B.C. The climax, however, of Rozas' unique treatise, was his discourse on the signs of the times, with emphasis on the Meteoric Shower of November 13, 1833, in fulfillment of prophecy. His precise description from personal observation, from sundry letters and the press, demonstrated the extent of the Falling Stars in Mexico.[37]

The impact of the Falling Stars found its way into many journals of the day. Here is a choice one by Dr. Henry D. Ward, a well-known Episcopalian minister of New York:

> We felt in our hearts, that it was a sign of the last days. For, truly, 'the stars of heaven fell *unto the earth*, even as a fig tree casteth her untimely figs, when she is shaken of a mighty wind.'—Revelation 6:13. This language of the prophet has always been received as metaphorical. Yesterday it was literally fulfilled....
>
> The stars fell 'Even as a fig tree casteth her untimely figs, when she is shaken of a mighty wind.' Here is the exactness of the prophet. The falling stars did not come, as if from several trees shaken, but from one....They fell, not as *ripe* fruit falls. Far from it. But they *flew*, they WERE CAST, like the *unripe* fruit, which at first refuses to leave the branch; and, when it does break its hold, flies swiftly, *strait off*, descending; and in the multitude falling some cross the track of others, as they are thrown with more or less force....
>
> No philosopher or scholar has told or recorded an event, like that of yesterday morning. A prophet of 1800 years ago foretold it exactly, if we will be at the trouble of understanding stars falling, to mean falling-stars.[38]

The exact description by the prophet John on the Falling Stars, illustrated by the fig tree casting its untimely figs, was not only recorded in writing. Henry J. Pickering, editor of *The Old Countryman*, a New York weekly, actually supervised the drawing of a *woodcut*, according to the specifications of his observation. Reproductions of the woodcut appeared in various journals and newspapers. The specifications of the woodcut turned out to be a replica of the prophet John's description, exhibiting the meteoric shower *emanating* from a common center or radiant, just like the ribs of a gigantic umbrella radiating from a single point of divergence. (See Illustration 10).

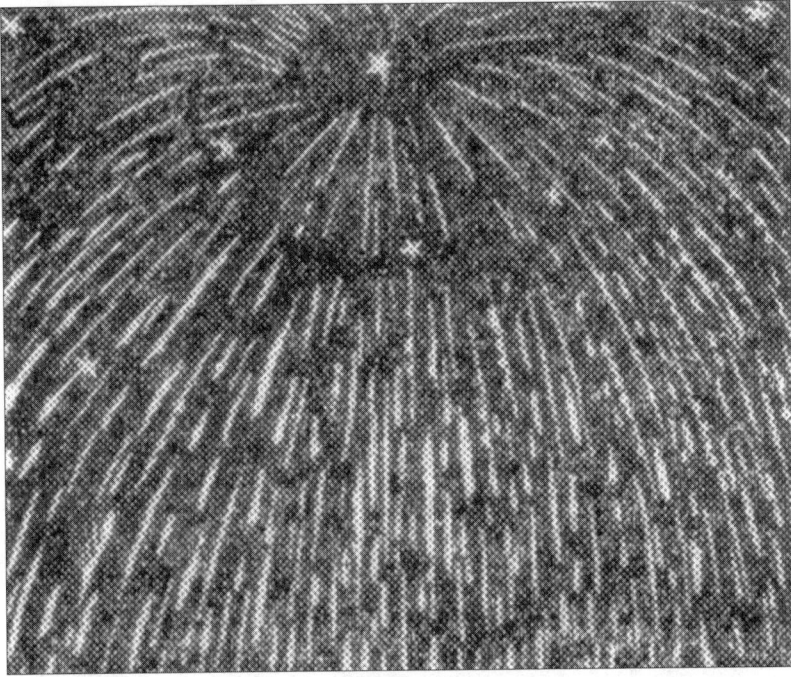

Illustration 10
Editor Pickering's Woodcut Captures Personal Observation of Falling Stars
The only surviving contemporary drawing of the Falling Stars, November 13, 1833. As seen by the naked eye, this amazing depiction shows a point of divergence, resembling the prophet's description of a fig tree casting its untimely figs, when shaken of a mighty wind (Revelation 6:13). The depiction was reprinted in *Mechanic's Magazine*, November, 1833.

It may be possible to obtain a glimpse of the magnitude of the Falling Stars from the perspective of astronomy. It is known as a Leonid Meteoric Shower, because it appears to come from within the "sickle" of the constellation of Leo. It comprises a swarm, or stream of small cosmic particles traveling through space in a vast elliptical path—a continual orbit touching the earth's orbit at one end, and reaching a little beyond the orbit of the planet Uranus at the other end. The stream of meteors completes its orbit every thirty three years, and precisely on November 12/13, 1833, the *denser* central core of the stream, about 120,000 miles in diameter, came into view over North America, creating an extensive meteoric *shower*. This direct hit was afforded by the alignment of the planets and their three-dimensional, delicately balanced, gravitational pull in 1833, which on other occasions, either thirty three years before, or after, has not been that precise, or predictable.

The magnificence of the 1833 meteoric shower was further enhanced by the fact that the orbits of the earth and the Leonids were opposite to each other; and when the earth, hurtling through space at eighteen miles a second, *crossed* obliquely the orbital path of the Leonids, rushing at twenty six miles a second, there was a celestial head-on collision. The 1833 Leonid meteors (not meteorites) flashed into incandescence and burned up on striking the atmosphere around our earth. This resulted in a spectacular shower of the swiftest and hottest meteors, radiating from a common center, and appearing head-on, over the heads of Americans with such power, that a Kentuckian wrote, "In every direction I could hear men, women, and children screaming, 'the judgment day is come!'"[39] (See Illustration 11).

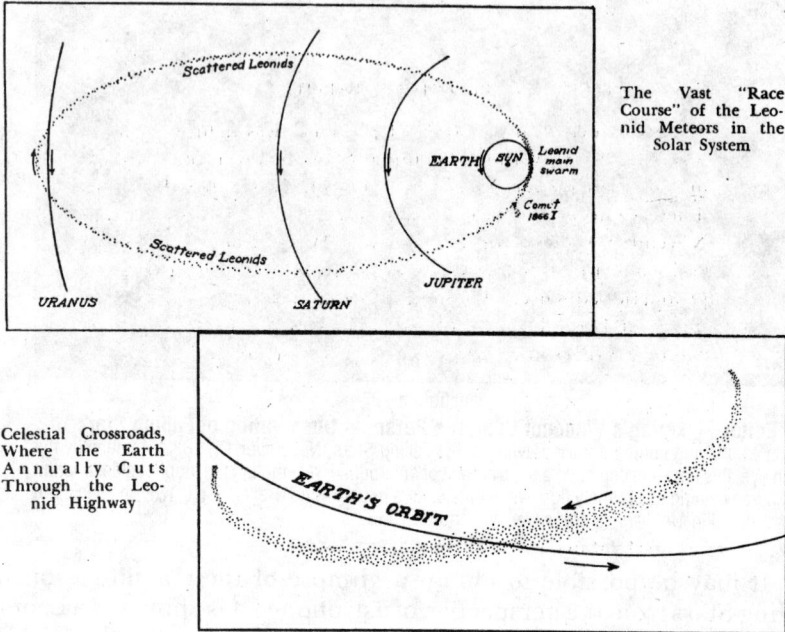

The Vast "Race Course" of the Leonid Meteors in the Solar System

Celestial Crossroads, Where the Earth Annually Cuts Through the Leonid Highway

Courtesy *The Telescope*, Oct., 1934   Illustration 11

Phenomenal Orbit of Leonid Meteors - Falling Stars

(Upper) Note vast elliptical orbit of Leonid Meteors extending from the Earth's orbit at one end, and passing just beyond the orbit of Uranus at the other end. The Leonids complete their circuit in 33 years, the elongated denser "main swarm" of cosmic particles may take 3 years to pass a certain area of the Earth. (Lower) Note the Earth's orbit and the orbit of the Leonids are opposite to each other. Since they clash obliquely at cosmic speed, the celestial head-on collision affords a spectacular, on-coming, overhead, display of directly shooting celestial fireworks - that peaked November 12/13, 1833, to fulfill Revelation 6:13.

Since the dense core of the Leonid meteoric stream of 1833 was greatly *elongated*, it took three years to pass the crossroads, where it met the earth's atmosphere. Hence, on November 13, 1831, a shower of falling stars was seen on the coast of Spain. Again on November 12/13, 1832, a small shower of Leonid meteors was reported from England (48 meteors in five minutes), Switzerland, the Tyrol, Russia, the Red Sea, India, and off Pernambuco, Brazil.[40] Obviously these sightings over two years in Europe and Asia, bear no comparison with North America, during the third year in 1833. But they do provide a world-wide composite fulfillment over three years, of the prophecy of Matthew 24:29 and Revelation 6:13.

It has to be borne in mind that the Leonid meteors appear like clock-work in our sky *annually*, about mid-November, brought about by the widely scattered, or separated stragglers of the meteoric stream, continually in orbit. Every thirty three years, such as in 1766, 1799, 1833, and 1866 a Leonid meteoric shower took place, when the dense central core of the meteoric stream struck our atmosphere. The Leonid Meteoric shower of November 12/13, 1833, reached an unprecedented peak in frequency, brilliance, and extent to fulfill the specifications of the prophecy of Jesus and John. But the *timing* of this 1833 shower to take place *after* the Dark Day of 1780, instead of *before* the Dark Day, has to be Providential, sticking to the sequence of Matthew 24:29 and Revelation 6:12, 13.

The Leonid meteoric shower of 1833 made an impact on the astronomers of the day, generating a keen interest in future repetitions every thirty three years. After a diminished shower in 1866 expectations for 1899 were high, despite the warning of two English astronomers, whose calculations showed that "planetary perturbations" might have shifted the broad Leonid stream enough to miss the earth.[41] The expectation was so great that *Chamber's Astronomy* of 1899 even went ahead and published the meteoric shower: "may be expected to reappear with *great brilliancy* in 1899."[42] The disappointment, however, was intense, when the meteors failed to appear in any numbers, and a historian of astronomy penned these disappointing words in 1902: "We can no longer count upon the Leonids. Their glory for scenic purposes, is departed."[43] And nearly fifty years later, Sir Harold S. Jones, director of the Royal Observatory at Greenwich, England, added his doleful comment doubting "whether these spectacular displays will occur again."[44]

Since 1833 there has been a proportional diminution in the number of meteors in each successive repetition of Leonid showers. Only 80 meteors per hour were tabulated for 1931, compared with anywhere from 60,000 to 200,000 per hour in 1833.[45] Thus, He who guides the stars in their courses (Job 38:32), selected November 12/13, 1833, for the Leonid meteoric shower of the Ages—a landmark sign in the skies, never to be superseded. This sign, that drew world-wide attention, and gripped the imagination for years to come, was expressed by the clergyman-scientist Dr. Thomas Milner, while addressing the British public in 1852: "In many districts, the mass of the population were terror-struck, and the more enlightened were awed at contemplating so vivid a picture of the apocalyptic image—that of the stars of heaven falling to the earth, even as a fig tree casting her untimely figs, when she is shaken of a mighty wind."[46]

Needless to say, the religiously enlightened were certainly awe-struck, when they realized that the verses *after* Matthew 24:29 and Revelation 6:13 ushered in the Second Coming of Christ. Hence the "Falling Stars" of 1833 was recognized as the LAST VISIBLE SIGN before the Second Advent, and this gave great impetus to the Advent Awakening.

(4) Collapse of Ottoman Turkish Empire, August 11, 1840

Considering the **Fifth Trumpet** of Revelation, Chapter 9, it was generally held that the "fallen Star" (verse 1) was Mohammed, who "opened the bottomless pit" (verse 2) of the Arabian desert wastes, to release the Saracen hordes like locusts (verse 3), to ravage the Eastern Roman empire of Byzantium. But it was Othman, a "king" from the bottomless pit (verse 11), who, after consolidating the principal Mohammedan tribes into one grand monarchy, attacked the Greek Byzantine empire, by invading Nicomedia on July 27, 1299. For five prophetic months (verses 5, 10), that is 5 multiplied by 30 equals 150 days, or 150 years, on the *day for a year principle*, these Moslem hordes made incursions upon Byzantium. They continued until Greek independence was voluntarily surrendered into the hands of the Ottoman Turks, when the last Greek emperor died, and his brother Deacozes ascended the throne by permission of the Turkish sultan in 1449. Thus the 150 year prophecy (1299 to 1449) was "exactly fulfilled," according to the Advent preacher Josiah Litch, who by the way, also recognized the sign of the "Falling Stars" in 1833.[47]

Under the **Sixth Trumpet** the power of the Ottoman Turks was unleashed by the "four angels" of the Euphrates region (Revelation 9, verses 14, 15), namely the four leading *sultanies* of the Ottoman empire: Aleppo, Iconium, Damascus, and Baghdad. They were destined to carry out their exploits for a period of time measured in symbolic prophetic language, that is a prophetic day standing for a literal year. The text spells it out as follows: "prepared for an hour, and a day, and a month, and a year, for to slay the third part of men" (verse 15). The conversion to literal time is: a day is *one year*, a month of 30 days is *30 years*, a year of 360 days is *360 years*. Since a symbolic hour is a twenty-fourth of a day, and a day stands for a year, a twenty-fourth of a year of 360 days, would be 360 divided by 24, which is *15 days*. Adding the conversion to literal time: 15 days + 1 year + 30 years + 360 years gives a total of 391 years and 15 days.

By adding 391 years and 15 days to July 27, 1449, would bring us to August 11, 1840, when the second period would end with the collapse of the Ottoman Turkish power. A Providential coincidence ruled, that just as Greek independence was voluntarily surrendered into the hands of the Ottoman Turks on July 27, 1449, so likewise, the Ottoman Turks in turn, voluntarily surrendered their power into the hands of the European nations on August 11, 1840.

Here are the circumstances and the setting that brought about the collapse of the Ottoman Turkish empire on August 11, 1840. The Ottoman empire was shrinking as it lost possessions slice by slice, until, in 1838 trouble broke out between the sultan and his vassal Mehemet Ali, pasha of Egypt. A patched-up peace followed for a little while, but hostilities broke out again the next year. The sultan's army was defeated, his naval fleet was captured and taken to Egypt, and

Constantinople quivered in a tenuous situation. Whereupon the sultan appealed to the four European powers to intervene. Britain, Russia, Austria, and Prussia quickly convened a conference in London, and drew up an *ultimatum* to be presented to Egypt. The ultimatum reached the pasha of Egypt in Alexandria on the very day, August 11, 1840, and fulfilled the prophecy of 391 years and 15 days exactly (Revelation 9:15). At the same time the European powers pledged to take any steps necessary in the event of further hostilities. Consequently the sultan of the Ottoman Turkish empire had voluntarily surrendered his independence and power to the European nations—and has existed ever since, only by the sufferance of these Christian nations. Having virtually collapsed into the friendly arms of the great European nations, the Ottoman Turks, from that day on, were called "The Sick Man of the East."

The study of the prophecy of the Fifth and Sixth Trumpets of Revelation, chapter nine, excited wide-spread interest. More so, because **Dr. Josiah Litch** of Philadelphia, a prominent Advent preacher of the Methodist church, *predicted* the fall of the Ottoman empire TWO YEARS BEFORE THE EVENT. His 200 page book, published in June of 1838, predicted the outcome "in A.D. 1840, sometime in the month of August."[48] Then in the year 1840, a number of days before the event, Litch made a PRECISE PREDICTION that appeared in the August 1st issue of the popular periodical *Signs of the Times* as follows:

> Allowing the first period, 150 years, to have been exactly fulfilled before Deacozes ascended the throne by permission of the Turks, and that the 391 years, fifteen days, commenced at the close of the first period, it will end on the 11th OF AUGUST, 1840, when the Ottoman power in Constantinople may be expected to be broken. And this, I believe, will be found to be the case.[49]
>
> (Capitalization supplied)

From the first publication of Litch's book in 1838, on the predicted fall of the Ottoman power, until the time set for the fulfillment of the prophecy in 1840, thousands watched with bated breath for the outcome. Without reserve, Litch fanned the fervor by two editions of his book *An Address to the Clergy*, supplemented by articles in various public journals. When the news of the loss of Ottoman supremacy right on time, hit the headlines, and was flashed to the unbelieving world, the effect was startling. Within a few months, it is reported, Litch "received letters from more than one thousand prominent infidels, some of them leaders of infidel clubs, in which they stated they had given up the battle against the Bible and had accepted it as God's revelation to man." Some expressed themselves in such words as these: "We have said that expositors of prophecy quote from the musty pages of history to substantiate their claims of prophetic fulfillments, but in this case we have the living facts before our eyes."[50]

Of all the fulfillments of prophecy, the eclipse of Ottoman Turkish power on August 11, 1840, gave a wonderful impetus to the great Advent Awakening, that was by this time, transformed into a Second Advent Movement.

Summary
OUTLINE OF FULFILLED PROPHECIES

Matthew 24:29, 30—The Signs of Jesus

The Prophecy	The Fulfillment
Tribulation	Persecution under Pagan & Papal Rome
Sun Darkened	Dark Day, May 19, 1780
Stars Fall	Falling Stars, November 12/13, 1833

"The powers of the heavens shall be shaken":

v.30 "Then shall all the tribes of the earth mourn, and they shall see the Son of Man Coming in the clouds of heaven with power and great glory."

Revelation 6:9, 12–14, 16, 17—Fifth and Sixth Seals

The Prophecy	The Fulfillment
v.9 Those Slain for the Word of God	Persecution under Papal Rome
v.12 Great Earthquake	Lisbon Earthquake, November 1, 1755
Sun Darkened	Dark Day, May 19, 1780
v.13 Stars Fall	Falling Stars, November 12/13, 1833

v.14 "And the heaven departed as a scroll when it is rolled together."

vs.16, 17 "And said to the mountains and rocks, Fall on us, and hide us from the face of Him that sitteth on the throne... For the great day of His wrath is come; and who shall be able to stand?

Revelation 9:5, 10, 14, 15—Fifth and Sixth Trumpets

The Prophecy	The Fulfillment
vs.5,10 A power to hurt men 5 months =150 years.	Ottoman Turks ravage Byzantine empire July 27, 1299 to July 27, 1449.
vs.14,15 Powers loosed from Euphrates for hour, day, month, year = 391 years, 15 days.	Ottoman Turk Supremacy from July 27, 1449 to August 11, 1840.

The 1,260 year period of Papal Supremacy, terminating at the time of the French Revolution in 1798 (Daniel 7:25; Revelation 13:5), that was considered as axiomatic, may be added to the above Outline of Fulfilled Prophecies. Jesus' famous Mount Olivet discourse on the prophetic Signs pointing to His Second Coming, drew attention to a period of Tribulation prior to the Dark Day. Jesus said that except those days of Tribulation be shortened, there should no flesh be saved (Matthew 24:21). Persecution, or Tribulation, under Papal Rome was so rife, that if the time period of 1,260 years was not shortened, few lives would be saved. Therefore, instead of Papal Roman persecution continuing unabated until 1798, it was cut short, and the Dark Day sign appeared 1780 "immediately after the tribulation of those days" (Matthew 24:29).

Furthermore, the Lisbon earthquake sign of the Sixth Seal occurred 1755, and also shortened the Papal persecution under the Fifth Seal, whose martyrs cried out asking how much longer should they suffer persecution (Revelation 6:9–11). Remember, as already stated, the Lisbon earthquake of 1755, prevented the scheduled mass burning of heretics, known as the Auto-da-fe, and destroyed the Palace of the Inquisition—never to be rebuilt. Obviously the Providential timing of the Lisbon earthquake cut short the power of Papal tyranny, and physically knocked out one of its strongholds in Portugal. Moreover, the cry of the saints was heard by God, who prevented the mass burning scheduled for All Saints Day, the very day of the earthquake.

Close scrutiny of the afore-mentioned Outline of Fulfilled Prophecies shows the parallel sequence of the Signs of Jesus and the Fifth and Sixth Seals. The parallel is so close, it almost looks like John copied the sequence of the Signs of Jesus. Furthermore, the historical fulfillment of the sequence followed exactly the prophetic order—all to the glory of God and Divine inspiration.

An important conclusion that can be drawn from the parallel sequence of the Signs of Jesus and the Fifth and Sixth Seals, is that it placed mankind squarely between the last sign of the Falling Stars of 1833, and the Sign of the Second Coming of Jesus. Likewise, the fulfillment of the Fifth and Sixth Trumpets, placed mankind in 1840, on the eve of the Seventh Trumpet, when "the mystery of God should be finished" (Revelation 10:7). And if that was the case of mankind in the 1840's, how much greater must be the expectation of the Second Coming for us who are living on borrowed time, more than a hundred and fifty years later. Even so, Come Lord Jesus!

As one considers the Signs of Jesus and the Signs of John, the Revelator, one is led to question why were they given? Answer—they were given to arrest the attention of mankind that God is speaking, and that mankind needs to recognize the Almighty God and repent. Consequently the sign of the Lisbon "earthquake had made all men thoughtful," wrote Tallentyre, on the *Life of Voltaire*. Even the French philosopher, Voltaire, "was profoundly moved" by the earthquake, and plans for the opening of a theater at Lausanne, for the special performance of some of Voltaire's rationalistic dramas was postponed, because "they mistrusted their love of the drama, and filled the churches instead."[51] Likewise, the fulfillment of the Sixth Trumpet in the collapse of the Ottoman Turkish empire, August 11, 1840, elicited a startled recognition of the Almighty God and Divine inspiration from a thousand infidels.

By far the greatest reason why the Signs of Jesus were given, is best stated by Jesus, himself: "When ye shall see all these things, know that it [the Second Advent] is near, even at the doors" (Matthew 24:33). Luke's record adds this statement: "When these things begin *to come to pass*, then look up, and lift up your heads; for your redemption draweth nigh" (Luke 21:28; Italics supplied). How wonderful! How natural, and plausible to watch for the fulfillment of the signs, *to come to pass* in the events of history, pointing nearer, and still nearer to the climactic event of the Second Advent.

On the other hand, how futile it is to accept an alternative view, to pin one's hopes on the fulfillment of the Signs of Jesus—all bunched up, in a diminutive period of time *after* a so-called Secret Rapture, as taught by Lacunza and Darby, whose view is permeating modern Protestantism. The futility of this view is further aggravated by the fact, that Christ's given reason of *nearness* for the Second Advent, by means of fulfilling signs, would have no relevance for mankind today. Furthermore, to place the signs of Matthew, chapter twenty four, together with the Seals and Trumpets of Revelation into this contrived diminutive period of seven years—all labeled Tribulation Judgments, simply adds more coals to the fire of erroneous doctrine, and robs mankind of these relevant prophetic truths of Jesus and John *prior* to the Second Advent.

Allowing the fire of erroneous doctrine to burn out, let's applaud the historic literal fulfillment of the Signs of Jesus and the Seals and Trumpets of John, the Revelator, *before* the Second Coming—not *after*. Let us then proceed and pick up the momentum, as the Advent Awakening grows into a Second Advent Movement. The dynamics of the movement will center around the 2,300 days of Daniel, to be discussed in the next chapter.

Chapter 6

THE SECOND ADVENT MOVEMENT IN AMERICA

The Second Advent Awakening in America might well have remained just an Awakening, as it did in England, if it were not for an American Reformer, William Miller, who transformed it into a Second Advent Movement. Like a modern Jonah, the tenor of Miller's preaching was prophetic: Jonah preached, "Yet forty days, and Nineveh shall be overthrown" (Jonah 3:4); Miller recorded, "I was thus brought, in 1818, at the close of my two year's study of the Scriptures, to the solemn conclusion, that in about twenty-five years from that time [1818] all the affairs of our present state would be wound up."[1]

But the prophetic preaching of both Jonah and Miller, after much reticence and hesitation, had an underlying message that resulted in conversion and reformation, and the inhabitants of Nineveh and North America "turned from their evil way" (Jonah 3:10). The following biographical sketch of the conversion and call of William Miller illustrates what he sincerely lived out in his prophetic preaching: to prepare a people to meet their God.[2]

Intellectual Development of William Miller

William Miller (1782–1849), the eldest of sixteen children, grew up on a frontier farm of a hundred acres at Low Hampton, near Lake Champlain, New York. His mother first taught him to read, and from an early age he cultivated a thirst for knowledge, and a love of reading to such an extent, that his companions at the district school considered him as a "prodigy for learning"; and "it was generally admitted that his attainments exceeded those of the teachers usually employed." Miller's omnivorous reading knew no bounds. He read books from the private libraries of a judge and a congressman, and from the first large public library in Vermont at Poultney, where he settled after marrying at the age of twenty one in 1803. Endowed with a retentive memory, Miller's strong mind was packed with historical facts from ancient and modern history, which served him well later on, in the illustration of the prophecies.

Deistical Development of Miller

But, in Poultney, he also ran into grave spiritual and intellectual difficulties when he associated with Deists for the next *twelve years*, imbibing deistical sentiments from the works of Voltaire, Volney, Hume, Paine, Ethan Allen, and others. Like a Deist, Miller advanced deistical arguments on the supposed inconsistencies, contradictions, and the mysticisms of the Bible, and could not regard the Bible as inspired, and dismissed it as the work of designing men. He did, however, believe in a "Supreme Being, as brought to view by the works of Nature and Providence," but not yet in Revelation. Before the close of his deistic experience he concluded: "I began to suspect that deism tended to a belief in *annihilation*, which was always very abhorrent to my feelings" (Italics supplied). Yet in this deistical morass, he desired something better, such as a *hereafter*, or future existence.

It may have been in the Providence of God that Miller spent twelve years with deistic philosophy, and became more or less, a Deist of the Deists, in order that in later years, he would know how to demolish all deistic arguments with a plain thus saith the Lord. No doubt Miller's experience paralleled that of Paul, who before his conversion, was a strict Pharisee (Acts 26:5), in order to refute their arguments in later years and present Jesus.

Conversion of Miller

God permitted Miller to plumb the depths of deistic philosophy to recognize its futility, so that when Christian conversion occurred, the change would be so marked and dramatic. The place for the beginning of his conversion was not on the Damascus Road, but back in Low Hampton, New York, to which he retired in 1816 at the age of thirty four. He secured a two hundred acre farm, where he built a comfortable double story farm house, alongside a beautiful maple grove. Having retired from public life he resumed farming, and this afforded an ideal setting for him to engage in extensive reading and reflection.

Out on the farm, one day, he caught himself in the very act of taking the name of God in vain, in contravention of the third commandment, a habit he had acquired while serving in the military for a short time. The Holy Spirit instantly convicted him of its sinfulness, so he retired to his beautiful grove where he meditated on the matter. He was then led to question how a just Being could consistently save those who violated the laws of justice. The works of Nature or of Providence did not answer his question. He tried to penetrate the mystery of the connection between the present and a future state of existence. He found that his former views gave him no assurance of happiness beyond the present life. All was dark beyond the grave. Years later he described his quandary at this time as follows:

"Annihilation was a cold and chilling thought, and accountability was sure destruction to all. The heavens were as brass over my head, and the earth as iron under my feet. *Eternity! —what was it? And death—why was it?* The more I reasoned, the further I was from demonstration.... I knew that there was a wrong, but knew not how or where to find the right. I mourned, but without hope."[3]

Little did Miller realize at the time when he took the name of God in vain, and was convicted with a knowledge of his condition as a sinner, that according to the great church historian M. D'Aubigne, this is the first step in the process of a sound Christian experience of conversion, or salvation. The next step is the knowledge of the grace of God manifested in deliverance from our fallen condition, or salvation from our fallen sinful condition. But the Savior has to be sought. The occasion presented itself, when in the absence of the pastor, Miller, who was not a church member, was asked to read a selected sermon on Isaiah 53 in the nearby brick church, one Sunday. Soon after he commenced reading, he was overcome with emotion and took to his seat weeping, while the congregation deeply sympathized. Soon after he said:

> Suddenly, the character of a Saviour was vividly impressed upon my mind. It seemed that there might be a Being so good and compassionate as to himself atone for our transgressions, and thereby save us from suffering the penalty of sin. I immediately felt how lovely such a Being must be; and imagined that I could cast myself into the arms of, and trust in the mercy of, such an One. But the question arose, How can it be proved that such a Being does exist? Aside from the Bible, I found that I could get no evidence of the existence of such a Saviour, or even of a *future state*. I felt that to believe in such a Saviour without evidence would be visionary in the extreme. I saw that the Bible did bring to view just such a Saviour as I needed; and I was perplexed to find how an uninspired book should develop principles so perfectly adapted to the wants of a fallen world. I was constrained to admit that the Scriptures must be a *revelation* from God. They became my delight, and in Jesus I found a friend. The Saviour became to me the chiefest among ten thousand; and the Scriptures, which before were dark and *contradictory*, now became the lamp to my feet and light to my path.[4]

(Italics supplied)

The year 1816 marked a new era in the life of the 34 year old William Miller. His deistic friends regarded his yielding deism to the truth of God's Word, and his departure from them, as the loss of a standard-bearer. The die was cast, and he had taken his stand for life as a soldier of the cross. Nevertheless, he felt the taunts of deism, and met the challenge of a friend with this reply, "Give me time, and I will harmonize all those apparent contradictions to my own satisfaction, or I will be a Deist still."

So thorough was Miller's conversion that he immediately erected the family altar, opened his home for prayer meetings, became a stanch pillar of the little Hampton Baptist Church, and for the next two years studied his Bible intensely. He often spent whole nights and days in methodical study.

Miller's Principles of Biblical and Prophetic Interpretation

Laying aside all preconceived opinions as best he could, and dispensing with commentaries, William Miller compared Scripture with Scripture, with the aid of marginal references in his Bible, and Crudens Concordance. Without realizing it, he read the Bible applying the very Protestant principles of Grammatico-historical exegesis. He read the Scriptures naturally, recognizing their natural, obvious meaning, and sense, within their context. He went so far in methodical study that he formulated fourteen "Rules of Interpretation" incorporating: the literal common sense meaning (Rule 7); the synthesis principle of bringing Scripture together with Scripture to arrive at a clear, consistent meaning (Rule 4); "Scripture must be its own expositor" (Rule 5); "God has revealed things to come by visions, in figures and parables" (Rule 6); "Figures always have a figurative meaning, and are used much in prophecy to represent future things, times and events,—such as beasts, meaning kingdoms, Daniel 7:8, 17; waters, meaning people, Revelation 17:1, 15; day, meaning year, Ezekiel 4:6" (Rule 8).

Miller's Rule 13 on prophetic interpretation is remarkable and comprehensive stating:

> To know whether we have the true historical event for the fulfillment of a prophecy: If you find every word of the prophecy (after the figures are understood) is *literally fulfilled*, then you may know that your history is the true event; but if one word lacks a fulfillment, then you must look for another event, or wait its future development; for God takes care that *history* and *prophecy shall agree*, so that the true believing children of God may never be ashamed. Psalm 22:5. Isaiah 45:17–19. 1 Peter 2:6. Revelation 17:17. Acts 3:18.[5]
>
> (Italics supplied)

Miller's Intensive Two Year Study of Scripture

Having come out of a deistic background, it can be expected that Miller's *first* approach to his intensive two year study of the Scriptures, would be to harmonize all the apparent inconsistencies, and contradictions of Scripture. This was achieved to his satisfaction, and he could declare unequivocally that "the Bible is a *system of revealed truths*, so clearly and simply given, that the wayfaring man, though a fool, need not err therein."[6] (Italics supplied).

Of paramount importance was the fact that Miller did not commence his intensive study of the Scriptures in 1816, with the expectation of finding the *time* of the end of the world, and the Second Advent of Christ.[7] This was his subsequent finding; but there were previous discoveries that led to this alarming finding. His *first* major conclusion reached was that "the popular views of the spiritual reign of Christ—a temporal millennium *before the end of the world*, and the Jews return—are not sustained by the Word of God."[8] He believed in a literal, personal, PRE-MILLENNIAL SECOND ADVENT that was near at hand. Next, evidence that vitally affected his mind, was the chronological prophecies of fixed periods of time that had been fulfilled literally. He felt the prophetic periods were as much a portion of the Word of God, entitled to serious consideration, and ought not to be passed over.[9] He discovered that in every case where time had been revealed, every event was accomplished as predicted (except the case of Nineveh, in Jonah).[10]

Then Miller was confronted with the 2,300 prophetic days (Daniel 8:14), and regarded the time as symbolical, each day standing for a year according to all the "standard Protestant commentators." Miller consulted the "best chronologers," such as Ussher, and the "best historians" of his day, and commenced the 2,300 years synchronously with the seventy weeks (Daniel 9:24–27), from 457 B.C., terminating about 1843 A.D.

Thus Miller was brought, in 1818, at the close of his two years study, to the startling conclusion that the end of the world, and the Second Advent, would take place in about 1843. At this juncture he exclaimed, "I could at first hardly believe the result to which I had arrived; but the evidence struck me with such force that I could not resist my convictions."[11] (Please see Reference Note 11).

Miller's intensive two year study of the Scriptures brought him great joy and satisfaction personally. He also answered the objections of the Deists by harmonizing the apparent contradictions, and was delighted to find that the Bible was inspired, meeting the Deist charge that it was *not* inspired. It was his attraction to the prophetic element of the Bible that convinced him of the Divine Inspiration of the Bible. But now he was confronted with the 2,300 day-year prophecy that pointed to the end of the world in 1843, and what was he going to do about it. He thought that he was the only one that had made such a discovery. Little did he realize at the time, that other great students of prophecy in England and America had come to similar conclusions before he did (as already outlined in this book). Gradually in time, he found out that others had arrived at such conclusions.

Miller's Sincerity and Four Year Review

The sincerity of Miller is evidenced by his reaction to his great discovery, expressed in these words, "I therefore feared to present it, lest by some possibility I should be in error, and be the means of misleading any."[12] So Miller assiduously reviewed and restudied his position for the *next four years* —something few men have ever done. He mustered many objections that might militate against his conclusions—to test their validity. He looked into the text, among others, that pointed out: "Of that day and hour knoweth no man" (Matthew 24:36). But on scrutiny of the context, he was assured "we may know when it is nigh, even at the doors." Nevertheless, Miller painstakingly avoided setting a specific day for the termination of the 2,300 year prophecy. His later published lectures carried the words, "about the year 1843"; his oral lectures invariably declared 1843, stating *if* there was no mistake in his calculations. But his colleagues censured him for inserting the word IF. He then published in December of 1842, that the Lord would come some time between March 21, 1843, and March 21, 1844. When his published time passed without any event, he frankly acknowledged his disappointment in reference to the *exact* time. Then it was articulated, that the terminal date was related to the 10th day of the seventh month of the typical day of Atonement, which coincided with October 22, (Leviticus 23:27). Miller did not go along with this date set by the "seventh month movement," as it was called. It was not until about two or three weeks prior to October 22, 1844, that Miller finally acquiesced, feeling it must be the work of God.[13] Such caution demonstrated clearly that Miller was not an enthusiast, or a charlatan, in his approach to the awesome revelations of Scripture.

Miller's Twenty Articles of Faith

By the year 1822, having completed his four year review, Miller wrote out his creed that he simply called "my faith," comprising twenty articles (after which the writing of the document breaks off). His articles of faith begin with belief in the inspiration of the Bible as a revelation of God to man, the only rule for our practise, and a guide to our faith. He expressed his belief in the Trinity, the Creation and Fall of Man, Salvation through the death of Christ, and the agency of the Holy Spirit in accomplishing salvation. He believed that Christ is an offering of God for redemption from sin, a sacrifice for sin which justice demanded, and "that all those who confess their sins on the head of this victim, may expect forgiveness of sin through the blood of the atonement, which is in Christ Jesus, the great High Priest in the Holy of Holies" (Article VIII). Article IX read: "I believe the atonement to be made by the intercession of Jesus Christ, and the sprinkling of His blood in the Holy of Holies, and upon the mercy seat and people; by which means the offended is reconciled to the offender, the offender is brought into subjection to the will of God; and the effect is forgiveness of sin, union to the Divine person, and to the household of faith."[14]

Such was the force and thrust of Gospel prerogatives foremost in Miller's thinking, followed by the keeping power of Christ, the necessity of the new birth, and the cleansing of the earth by fire, to become the renewed eternal abode of the glorified believers. Article XIV introduced the Second Advent and the destruction of the wicked. Only at Article XV does Miller refer to the nearness of the Second Coming, "even at the door, on or before 1843." The subsequent Articles of Faith refer to a literal resurrection of the just at the Second Advent, followed by a literal resurrection of the unjust at the close of the millennium. The document of faith ends on election, baptism by immersion, and the Lord's Supper.[15]

Miller's Providential Call

Having reached this climactic point of his Christian experience and faith in 1822, Miller still did not enter any public ministry, resisting any impressions of duty to go out as a public teacher until 1831. His strongest impressions during this time centered around the text in

Ezekiel 33, verses 8 and 9 with the words: "Go and tell it to the world." Just as Jonah resisted the commission of God to "Go unto Nineveh, that great city, and preach" (Jonah 3:2), so Miller resisted the call of God for *nine long years*, hoping and praying that God would raise up some minister for this mission. But one Saturday morning in 1831 the impression to "Go and tell it to the world," came through suddenly, and with more force, that he entered into a colloquy, covenanting with God that if God would open the way by arranging an *invitation* for Miller to speak publicly in any place, he would respond.

Lo and behold, in about a half hour from the time of Miller's covenant with God, his nephew arrived with an *invitation* to return with him, to fulfill a preaching appointment on the Second Coming, in the absence of the minister. Miller's immediate response to the invitation was one of anger that he had covenanted with God, and so he left his nephew waiting, while he spent an hour in his maple grove, wrestling with God for release from his covenant. Miller then returned to meet his waiting nephew with peace in his heart, to stand by his covenant, and after dinner they both traveled together sixteen miles to Dresden. His first public lecture on prophecy was so well received, that he was asked to continue preaching throughout the week, resulting in a revival among those who attended from the community and nearby towns. From that first public lecture, he was to go on and deliver lecture after lecture, which numbered about 4,000 from 1840 to 1844 alone—in something like 500 different towns.[16]

As soon as Miller returned home from his lecture series in Dresden, he found a letter from the Baptist minister of Poultney, Vermont, *inviting* him to lecture there, even though he had not heard of the Dresden visit. Miller promptly responded, and from then onward he was inundated with invitations from Congregational, Baptist, and Methodist churches. And in fulfillment of his covenant with God he declared, "I have never labored in any place to which I was not previously *invited*" [17] (Italics supplied).

Miller's Credentials

To Miller's own inner conviction of his Providential call, was added, to his surprise, the issuance of a license to preach from the church of his conversion in Low Hampton, New York, in 1833. Then, precisely two years later, as a result of his initial preaching, Miller received a Ministerial Recommendation commending him to the public as a "lecturer on the prophecies." The Certificate was signed by more than twenty Baptist ministers, and seventeen ministers of various denominations in New York, Vermont, Massachusetts, and Canada. Such developments gave Miller more confidence, and endeared him to the people.

Miller's Entry Into the Large Cities

From 1834 Miller went into full-time preaching as a solitary worker until 1839. While he delivered 800 lectures, and spread his book of sixteen lectures everywhere, he was confined during this period to small towns and rural areas. But Miller's entrance into Massachusetts for the first time in 1839, led to his meeting Dr. Josiah Litch in the Lowell lectures, and Joshua V. Himes in the Exeter lectures. Then Himes invited him to preach the first of several sessions of lectures in the large city of Boston—ushering in a new phase in the expanding Second Advent movement. Entrance into the large cities had begun, and Miller's solitary labor ended, as ministers like Presbyterian Charles Fitch, Methodist Josiah Litch, and Joshua Himes of the Christian Connection became his right-hand men, embracing his views and preaching his message in cities far and wide.

Power of the Printed Page

Prior to Miller's several courses of oral lectures in Boston (population 93,000), his book of lectures paved the way for the deep interest that eventually sprang up in Boston and environs. In 1838 a copy of his lectures fell into the hands of the editor of the Boston *Daily Times*, who promptly gave wide publicity, by publishing a series of reprints of the lectures in that paper.

About the same time another copy of lectures was placed in the hands of Josiah Litch, who after accepting Miller's views, published a 48 page *Review of Mr. Miller's Lectures*. This was followed up by his own convictions in a 204 page book, *The Probability of the Second Coming of Christ about A.D. 1843*. Litch had observed the prophecy of Falling Stars in 1833, but in this work the calculation on the predicted fall of the Ottoman Turkish power in August, 1840, was first given to the world. This work circulated throughout New England and excited some interest. But when the predicted event was fulfilled on August 11, 1840, it elicited great interest, and gave impetus to Miller's movement.

Miller's meeting with Joshua Himes, not only resulted in inviting Miller to preach in the large city of Boston, as a prelude to entering metropolitan America, but Himes arranged for a wider circulation of Miller's lectures, with the publication of a new revised edition of 5,000 copies. In addition Himes published the first number of the Boston weekly periodical *Signs of the Times* in 1840, that grew to a circulation of 50,000 in two years time. He then launched a daily of 10,000 copies an issue called the *Midnight Cry*, during the weeks of an evangelistic drive in New York City, in 1842. All told, 600,000 pieces of literature were distributed in that city by 1843. A similar pattern was followed in conjunction with major series of lectures in important cities, frequently circulating periodicals along with the lecture series, for a period of thirteen weeks. Under the dynamic leadership of Himes, about thirty capable editors were active with their periodicals in the movement. By the end of 1843 the circulation of Second Advent periodicals had reached a million, and by mid-1844 five million copies. This was a marvelous accomplishment, since the population of America at that time was about seventeen million. Such was the unrivaled battery of periodicals that swept over the United States, from Maine to the

Mississippi, from Quebec to Washington, D.C., as an angel of mercy and love to thousands.

The Spearhead of General Conferences

It would appear that whatever happened in Boston would set the pace and the course of the Second Advent movement. A committee headed by William Miller called for "The First General Conference of Second Advent Believers" to convene in Boston, in Himes' church, scheduled for October, 1840. About twenty ministers of different denominations mingled among the group of about two hundred in attendance, to give expression to their beliefs, to harmonize variant viewpoints, and to present a united front to the world. Dr. Henry Ward, Episcopalian Rector of New York City, who contributed a remarkable article at the time of the Falling Stars of 1833, was appointed chairman of the conference. The conference was a success, and it was voted to publish 10,000 copies of the report of the deliberations, including the addresses given, to be sent to all ministers, missionaries, and theological seminaries. The high caliber of this first conference became the paradigm of fifteen successive conferences, all of which had the marked effect of solidifying the Second Advent movement, and giving it direction.

Camp Meetings Shake the Nation

Boston was again the venue for the twelfth General Conference in 1842, with retired sea captain Joseph Bates as chairman, Joshua Himes as secretary, and Baptist minister Thomas M. Preble, among others serving on the large committee. An important decision was made to have far reaching results. It was decided to hold great Camp Meetings to reach the masses, as the Methodists had successfully done. The decision was implemented the same year, under the direction of Litch in East Canada, and Himes in East Kingston, New Hampshire. Seven to ten thousand people daily attended the latter camp meeting, and contributed a thousand dollars worth in gold, silver, and jewelry, for the furtherance of the cause—certainly a tidy sum for those days. This was the forerunner of over 120 camp meetings for the next two years, drawing a half million souls.

At the close of each camp meeting the parting scene was unforgettable. The believers formed a giant circle encompassing the entire camp. Then it would be broken to form an outer circle and an inner circle, the believers facing each other. Those in the outer circle stood still, while those in the inner circle filed past them, until each one had shaken hands, or embraced every one else. Voices choked with emotion as they bade each other farewell, and exhorted one another to be faithful until Jesus' Coming in Glory. The camp meetings were so spirited and successful, that Josiah Litch felt "it was a movement which shook the nation."

A Streamlined Proclamation

Another far-reaching decision at the Boston Conference in 1842 was to lithograph 300 copies of a large prophetic chart, fondly known as the "1843 Chart." This composite chart, meticulously designed by Charles Fitch and Apollos Hale, beautifully illustrated the prophecies of Daniel and the Revelation. Its use superseded all previously used charts, and identified the public presentations of the movement. The chart was a powerful visual aid in simplifying the prophetic presentations. By far the greatest effect in the use of the chart, however, was that it *unified* the presentation of a distinct message—every lecturer and preacher giving the message a certain sound, clear and simple. The lithographing of 300 copies of the "1843 Chart" demonstrated the large number of lecturers making full use of them, and riding the crest of the wave, in a movement destined to terminate in 1843, or thereabouts.

The Movement Intensifies

From 1840 onwards the proclamation of the Second Advent message intensified, through the increasing volume and distribution of the printed page; through the direction and unified onslaught of the general conferences; through the multiplication of giant camp meetings; through the innovative use of America's largest canvas "Big Tent" seating 6,000, used in combination with camp meetings, or where prophetic lectures were debarred; and through streamlined presentations in churches, tabernacles, auditoriums, halls, and the groves. All of these avenues of approach were used to the full by a coordinated team, eventually reaching a total of about five hundred preachers, and fifteen hundred public lecturers. Without question, the Second Advent movement made the greatest impact on the minds of the American people, within the short space of thirteen years (1831–1844), more than any other religious movement in the history of the nation. (See Picture 8).

After Miller met Josiah Litch, the first prominent minister to come to his side, and after gaining the support of Joshua Himes and Charles Fitch, a strong bond of friendship and cooperation was forged between them. As the pace of the movement gained momentum they never tramped on one another's toes, or tripped over each other's feet. Miller and Himes teamed up on lecture tours in the great city of New York (population nearly 400,000), Philadelphia (93,000), and Washington, D.C. (23,000), and fostered interest there. However, Litch first awakened an interest in Philadelphia, and later launched the 16 page periodical, the *Philadelphia Alarm*, before pioneering in Baltimore (102,000). Himes took the Big Tent to Rochester and Buffalo, and then on to Cincinnati (46,000) Ohio's largest city. But Fitch proclaimed the Second Advent message to the faculty and students of Oberlin Institute and established himself in Cleveland (6,000), Ohio. Such was the hand in glove ministry of these men.

While Miller's right-hand men looked to him for leadership, Himes, in many ways, was the leading figure in the movement. He was a

© Review & Herald Pub. association   Picture 8   Harry Anderson, Artist

William Miller - Leader of the Great Second Advent Movement

William Miller held thousands spell-bound with his powerful prophetic expositions. Behind him is a copy of Charles Fitch's Prophetic Chart, used by all heralds of the Second Advent.

great publicist, promoter and organizer—managing conferences and giant camp meetings, as well as holding about five thousand meetings, and running a great publishing and distribution project smoothly. Himes was a human dynamo, accomplishing a feat perhaps unequaled in ecclesiastical history. And Miller was quite at ease, to delegate much authority to Himes. Needless to say, that except for Fitch who served well until his death in 1844, Litch and Himes held up Miller's hands throughout the movement, and after the Great Disappointment of 1844—when the expected Second Advent did not occur, they still stood at his side.

The Movement Reaches a Climax

As the Second Advent movement came closer to the climactic date for the expected Second Advent, so did the opposition rise with increased friction. On top of this, Fitch in the summer of 1843 began to preach, that since much of Christendom had rejected the truth of the Second Advent, they were to be constituted as the Daughters of Mother Babylon (Revelation 17:5). He contended that Babylon was no longer limited to Papal Rome, but now also included the daughters—an apostate Protestantism. Fitch therefore preached the call for Advent believers to separate from the churches, and heed the call to "Come out of her, my people" (Revelation 18:4). Fitch's call to "Come Out" was rather timely, since clergy and laity sympathetic to the Advent movement were already being evicted from the churches, and others were quietly separating and forming associations for prayer and fellow-ship, anyway. But Fitch's call caught fire, as it were, in the Second Advent movement, and precipitated a mass separation. Fifty to one hundred thousand abandoned their former church affiliations, and formed distinctive groups of their own to prepare for the expected Second Advent.[18]

The personal, literal, Pre-millennial Second Advent was indeed the faith of the primitive church, or the Apostolic Church. Another mark of the Apostolic Church arose in Miller's Second Advent movement: "the doctrine of annihilation and the soul's unconsciousness in death." It was first presented by former Methodist minister George Storrs, while preaching on the Second Advent in New York City, in 1842. While Storrs' truth, that he had studied for five years, did not spread through-out the Advent movement, Charles Fitch was his first ministerial convert in January, 1844, including several prominent ministers in England. Storrs' work entitled *An Enquiry: Are the Souls of the Wicked Immortal? In Six Sermons* must have had some influence, since about 200,000 copies were published.[19]

As the climactic day October 22, 1844, equivalent to the "tenth day of the seventh month" (Leviticus 23:27) approached, Advent believers earnestly prepared for the Second Coming, just like a person on his deathbed, who faces the end, makes all possible preparations to meet his God. The Advent steam presses in Boston and elsewhere continued to admonish their believers to avoid everything foolish and fanatical, and to search their own hearts.[20] Advent believers, sold their properties, and turned in the proceeds to foster the publication of literature, as a last ditch effort to sound the warning message. They also settled all debts.

During the last week before the expected great event of Christ's return, merchants closed their stores, mechanics forsook their workshops, farmers left their crops of potatoes and apples unharvested, clerks, magistrates, and teachers resigned their posts. They assembled in buildings and houses for prayer and exhortation, while in Boston, New York, and Philadelphia, evening meetings were suspended, because of hostile disturbances. In some places the disturbances were so rife, that stones were cast, mobs threatened and hissed, and gather-ings were broken up. Nevertheless, facing much provocation, Advent believers remained steadfast, patient, and avoided retaliation. The prospect of meeting their Lord and Savior superseded all else, and in joyful anticipation their conduct was exemplary, heeding the admoni-tion of their sober-minded leaders. Finally the fateful day arrived, the solemn hours slipped by, night fell, and the sun arose as usual the next morning, October 23, and the Lord Jesus had not returned. The sweet expectation had turned to bitter disappointment.[21] (Please see this Reference Note 21).

Was the Second Advent Movement a Heresy?

If we consider the Providential call of Miller, and the Providential openings and *invitations* for Miller to preach his views, we have to conclude that the movement led by him, was ordained by God. Miller's remarkable conversion and sweet acceptance of Jesus, and his setting forth of the priorities of the Gospel—in every sermon stressing regeneration, justification, sanctification, and glorification, yet always in the setting of Christ's imminent return, must have the sanction of God. Said Miller, "My whole object was a desire to convert souls, to notify the world of a coming judgment, and to induce my fellow-men to make that preparation of heart which will enable them to meet their God in peace."[22] Any movement that has, as its objective, the saving of souls has the authorization of God, for it is God's paramount purpose "not willing that any should perish, but that all should come to repentance" (2 Peter 3:9).

Applying the test of authenticity to Miller, found in the words: "By their fruits ye shall know them" (Matthew 7:20) we continue. Miller sacrificed the comfortable life of a farmer, and expended his energies and means as an itinerant evangelist, penetrating all the New England and Middle States, Ohio, Michigan, Maryland, and Canada East and West. His lectures were heard by at least 500,000,[23] his tally of conversions about 6,000, of whom 700 were infidels, and about 200 ministers embraced his views. None of these fruits of his labors were for self-aggrandizement, or for the establishment of a following, or church, after him. Wrote Miller, "I always told them to go where they would feel at home; and I never favored any one denomination in my advice to such."[24]

If Miller's message of the end of the world in 1844 was a heresy, so also was Jonah's message: "Yet forty days, and Nineveh shall be overthrown" (Jonah 3:4). It has been noted elsewhere that Miller scrutinized the prophecies and found fulfillment in every case where time had been revealed, except in Jonah's message of Nineveh's destruction. How ironic, that as Jonah's message failed of fulfillment, so did Miller's message fail. But that did not make Jonah or Miller false prophets, it was the design of God that they led such movements of revival. Nevertheless, Jonah was "displeased exceedingly" and disappointed when the destruction of Nineveh was not fulfilled, feeling that he was a false prophet. On the other hand, Miller was terribly disappointed that Jesus did not return in 1844, but was pleased that Providence over-ruled in the preaching of the *definite* time, October 22, 1844 and wrote to Himes:

> It is to me almost a demonstration, that God's hand is seen in this thing. Many thousands, to all human appearance, have been made to study the Scriptures by the preaching of the *time*; and by that means, through

faith and the sprinkling of the blood of Christ, have
been reconciled to God.[25]

(Italics supplied)

It is to be recognized that there is ever the human, as well as the divine
element, present in the best of religious movements. The failure of Miller's
movement was to interpret the meaning of the "cleansing of the sanctuary" in the 2,300 day-year prophecy (Daniel 8:14). Even Christ's disciples
could not be accused of heresy, when they suffered great disappointment
at the Crucifixion—because they had not rightly interpreted one of the key
statements of the prophets concerning Christ, that He had not come to set
up a material kingdom and deliver the Jews, but that He must suffer
humiliation and death, before He could be glorified.

One grave mistake in the interpretation of prophecy is that one cannot
be dogmatic and punctilious in pinpointing the meaning of *unfulfilled
prophecy*. The interpreters were so sure that the future event of the
"cleansing of the sanctuary" meant in the words of Miller, the cleansing of
the "Earth and the Church" at the Second Advent, at which time the saints
are cleansed, or "justified (as it reads in the margin)"[26] according to Daniel
8:14. Such precise interpretation did in fact run counter to Miller's own
rule of prophetic interpretation: "but if *one word* lacks a *fulfillment*, then
you must look for another event, or *wait its future development*" (Italics
supplied).[27]

Nevertheless, the Second Advent movement was on the right track,
and came very close to the meaning of the "cleansing of the sanctuary"
from August 1844, in what was called the "seventh month movement."
Fifteen months prior to this time Miller noted in a letter to Himes, that the
three Levitical *spring* festivals of Passover, Unleavened Bread, and Pentecost "had their fulfillment in Christ's First Advent." He next deduced that
the three *autumn* festivals in the seventh month, namely the Feast of
Trumpets, the Day of Atonement, and the Feast of Tabernacles (Leviticus
23:24–37) "can only have their fulfillment at His Second Advent."[28]
Needless to say, that a century earlier, Sir Isaac Newton, who formulated
the law of gravitation, wrote a book on Apocalyptic Prophecy, and drew
the same conclusions about the Hebrew Feasts as did Miller.

Miller set forth a series of reasons for the position he took, such as this:
"The atonement was made on the tenth day of the seventh month [in the
typical service], and this is certainly typical of the atonement Christ is *now*
making for us.... When the high priest came out of the holy of holies [in the
typical service], after making the atonement, he blessed the people... so
will our great High Priest. Heb. 9:28. This was on the seventh month tenth
day."[29]

Miller's view that the three Levitical autumn festivals in the seventh
month pointed forward to the Second Advent for their fulfillment, lay
dormant until August 1844, when newly ordained Samuel S. Snow electrified the camp meeting at Exeter, New Hampshire. He clinched Miller's
view, believing that the autumnal festivals would be fulfilled in connection
with the Second Advent, even with regard to the specific "tenth day of the

seventh month" (Leviticus 23:27) for the typical Day of Atonement, which coincided with October 22, 1844, according to the Karaite calendar. Snow's new light took hold and spread like a bush fire through the movement, strongly supported by George Storrs, Joseph Bates, James White, T.M. Preble, and eventually by the prominent leaders. Miller himself came on board about two weeks before October 22.[30]

Miller's view that Christ's high priestly intercession in the Holy of Holies of the heavenly sanctuary, applying the benefits of His atoning sacrifice, and terminating on the tenth day of the seventh month, with his *emergence* from the sanctuary to bless the people in the Second Advent (Hebrews 9:28), really came to the forefront of the movement from August, 1844. But, while the leaders continually made such applications of the proceedings of the typical Levitical Day of Atonement to the Second Advent, they missed some *key points*. They missed the point that the earthly sanctuary had two apartments: the first apartment, the Holy Place, for the daily ministration of the high priest (Hebrews 9:1, 2, 6); the second apartment, the Most Holy Place, or Holy of Holies, into which the high priest *entered* only "once every year" (Hebrews 9:7). He entered on the specific tenth day of the seventh month, the Day of Atonement, to *cleanse* the sanctuary, and then to *emerge* from it to bless the people (Leviticus 16:23, 24). Therefore, to follow through with an application, it meant the "cleansing of the sanctuary" was an interim event, an event *prior to*, and *before* the emergence of the high priest from the sanctuary to bless the people.

Acknowledging the fact that the earthly sanctuary with two apartments was a replica, a pattern, a shadow, or figure (Hebrews 8:2, 5; 9:9) of the heavenly sanctuary with two apartments; it would mean that Christ's *emergence from* the heavenly sanctuary, to cleanse the Earth and Church at the Second Advent on October 22, 1844, was a mistaken interpretation.

If we apply the analogy of the Day of Atonement festival squarely to the last days relative to the Second Advent, then the truth of the matter is that Christ left his daily ministration in the Holy Place of the heavenly sanctuary where He had been since His Ascension; and made His *entrance into* the Most Holy Place of the heavenly sanctuary, to *begin* the cleansing of the sanctuary from October 22, 1844. Therefore—Christ's *emergence* from the heavenly sanctuary takes place *after* the cleansing is completed, at the Second Advent. Chapter nine of Hebrews drives home the purification, or cleansing of "heavenly things" (verse 23) *prior to*, and *before* Christ's *emergence* from heaven at the Second Advent (verse 28). Please see the accompanying diagrams, Illustration 12.

The accompanying diagrams show the different views of Miller and Edson. The *key points* missed by Miller and associates were eventually taught by Hiram Edson—to be discussed fully in the next chapter.

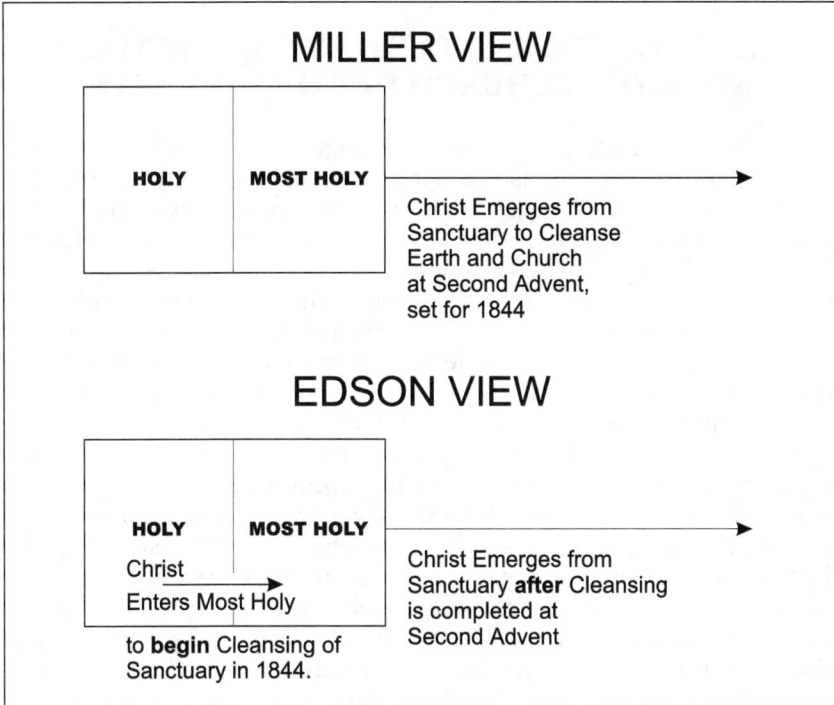

MILLER VIEW

HOLY MOST HOLY

Christ Emerges from
Sanctuary to Cleanse
Earth and Church
at Second Advent,
set for 1844

EDSON VIEW

HOLY MOST HOLY

Christ
Enters Most Holy

to **begin** Cleansing of
Sanctuary in 1844.

Christ Emerges from
Sanctuary **after** Cleansing
is completed at
Second Advent

Illustration 12

**Christ's Ministry in the Heavenly Sanctuary comprising two apartments - the Holy,
and the Most Holy**

Note that the Earthly Sanctuary, or Tabernacle, had two apartments (Hebrews 9:6,7) being an "example and shadow of heavenly things": where Christ our High Priest ministers "in the true tabernacle, which the Lord pitched and not man" (Hebrews 8:5, 1, 2).

Chapter 7

EMERGENCE AND RESTORATION OF THE APOSTOLIC CHURCH OF THE LAST DAYS

At this juncture, let us turn back the pages of Redemptive History to the first century, and behold the inception of the Apostolic Church. The disciples *missed the key points* of the great prophecies: that Christ would be "brought as a lamb to the slaughter, ...cut off out of the land of the living" (Isaiah 53:7, 8; Cited Acts 8:32, 33), and that Messiah would be "cut off...and in the midst of the week he shall cause the sacrifice and oblation to cease" (Daniel 9:26, 27). Strange that the disciples missed the point of Christ's sacrificial death regarding the First Advent, as the followers of Miller missed the meaning of the "cleansing of the sanctuary" pointing to the Second Advent. Christ's Crucifixion pointed to the end of the seventy weeks prophecy of Daniel, chapter nine. The "cleansing of the sanctuary" pointed to the termination of the 2,300 day-year prophecy (Daniel 8:14), of which the seventy weeks forms a part.

But the fact that the disciples were oblivious to the suffering and death of Christ, brought them great disappointment. When the expectation of the setting up of a Messianic material kingdom was dashed to pieces, the disciples were bitterly disappointed, discouraged and dismayed. Is it safe to say that God permitted such overwhelming disappointment, if not even ordained it, so that when they came out of it, the contrast between the disappointment and the prospects of what lay before them, would be all the more amazing. "Weeping may endure for a night, but joy cometh in the morning" (Psalm 30:5).

Little did the disciples realize at the time of their bitter disappointment, that hope was just around the corner, that new light was about to break forth, that the Holy Spirit was itching to imbue them with power at Pentecost. The disappointment was indeed short-lived, the new light—the truth of the Resurrection almost immediately burst forth, and dispelled the darkness of disappointment and despair. Next thing the disciples regrouped, and preached with power at Pentecost, and became witnesses "unto the uttermost part of the earth" (Acts 1:8). Furthermore, above all else, the sheep that were scattered through disappointment, regrouped, into "one fold" (John 10:16)—the united body of the Apostolic Church, and "they continued steadfastly in the apostles' doctrine and fellowship" (Acts 2:42), under "one Lord, one faith" (Ephesians 4:5).

In passing, may we reflect on the preaching of Jonah. Do we realize the disappointment that overtook him, when his God-given message of doom to Nineveh failed. He was so distraught, feeling like a false prophet, that he wanted God to take his life (Jonah 4:3). Little did he realize that hope and truth were near at hand. The practical experience of the plant, the worm, and the wind, was new light to him, that buoyed his spirits and lifted him from the depths of despair.

Now coming to the Great Disappointment of October 22, 1844, when the followers of Miller did not realize their hopes of the Second Advent of Christ. Untold thousands experienced an unprecedented disappointment, on a magnitude perhaps unequaled in history. Yet, was this bitter disappointment itself, in the design of God? Was there light at the end of the dark tunnel? Such questions will be answered presently.

At the time of their disappointment Miller's followers did not expect, at all, that "unto the upright there ariseth light in the darkness" (Psalm 112:4). Their case was not hopeless, God's "people shall never be ashamed" (Joel 2:26). They didn't have the slightest notion that the solution to their understanding of the "cleansing of the sanctuary" was virtually hours away, and that within the year 1844, they would "prophesy again" (Revelation 10:11), and be endowed with the gift of a prophet (Joel 2:28, 29; Ephesians 4:11). Miller's followers, who felt that the great Second Advent movement had collapsed with the Great Disappointment, were in for a surprise, because it was destined to regroup as a movement of destiny, imbued by the Holy Spirit, conquering one land after another, "having the everlasting Gospel to preach unto...every nation, and kindred, and tongue, and people" (Revelation 14:6).

The disappointed followers of Miller, did not realize at the time of the Great Disappointment, that "the path of the just is as the shining light, that shineth more and more unto the perfect day" (Proverbs 4:18). They did not realize that they were on the verge of becoming "restorers of paths to dwell in" (Isaiah 58:12)—restorers of great truths that had either been lost, or fallen into disrepute. This would result in the Restoration of the Apostolic Church, continuing "steadfastly in the apostles' doctrine and fellowship" (Acts 2:42). They did not realize, that monumental truths, were about to break in on their path as new light—shining light, ever growing more brightly.

Providential Breakthrough on the Cleansing of the Sanctuary

We have to go back to the setting of the Great Disappointment and trace the first steps toward the realization of the sentiments expressed above. The followers of Miller had not only missed the essential meaning of the "cleansing of the sanctuary," but they did not follow Miller's own principle of prophetic interpretation: to "wait its future development." Jesus himself enunciated such a principle in these words, "I have told you before it come to pass, that, when it is *come to pass, ye might believe*" (John 14:29; Italics supplied). Almost immediately, or within hours after the *passing* of the fateful hour October 22, 1844, the meaning of the "cleansing of the sanctuary" penetrated the mind of Hiram Edson, like a shaft of light, and he *believed*. (See Picture 9).

Hiram Edson of Port Gibson, New York, on the old Erie Canal, was the leader of the Advent believers, followers of Miller, in that community. A group of believers gathered in Edson's home and keenly awaited the Coming of the Lord, but when night fell, and He had not come, they

Picture 9
Hiram Edson's sudden Illuminating Insight on the Sanctuary Cleansing
While walking across a cornfield on the morning after the Great Disappointment of October 22, 1844, the thought flashed into Edson's mind: that on this fateful date Christ, our High Priest, entered the Most Holy place of the Heavenly Sanctuary, rather than emerging from it in the Second Advent.

"wept, and wept, till the day dawn" of October 23. At this point Edson implored some of his brethren:

> 'Let us go to the barn.' We entered the granary, shut the doors about us and bowed before the Lord. We prayed earnestly, for we felt our necessity. We continued in earnest prayer until the witness of the Spirit was given that our prayer was accepted, and that light should be given—our disappointment be explained, and made clear and satisfactory.
>
> After breakfast I said to one of my brethren 'Let us go and see, and encourage some of our brethren'. We started, and while passing through a large field I was stopped about midway of the field. Heaven seemed open to my view, and I saw distinctly and clearly that instead of our High Priest *coming out of* the Most Holy of the heavenly sanctuary to come to this earth on the tenth day of the seventh month, at the end of the 2,300 days, He for the first time *entered* on that day the second apartment of that sanctuary; and that He had a *work to perform in the Most Holy* before coming to this earth. That He came to the marriage at that time; in other words, to the Ancient of days *to receive a kingdom*, dominion, and glory; and we must wait for His return *from the wedding*....
>
> While I was thus standing in the midst of the field, my comrade passed on almost beyond speaking distance before missing me. He inquired why I was stopping so long. I replied, 'The Lord was answering our morning prayer, by giving light with regard to our disappointment'.[1]

(Italics supplied)

What the leaders had *missed* during the three month period of emphasis on the "seventh month concept" before October 22, 1844, (as previously discussed at the end of the previous chapter), Hiram Edson saw like a bright flash of light illuminating the whole question. (See Illustration 12 again: Edson View). His illuminating insight had resulted, from applying the analogy of the Day of Atonement fully and squarely to an Antitypical Day of Atonement, equated with the cleansing or reconciling (Leviticus 16:19, 20, 30) of the heavenly sanctuary in a Pre-Advent judgment. Edson linked the work of cleansing that Christ had "to perform in the Most Holy before coming to this earth," *with* His interim appearance before the "Ancient of Days to receive a kingdom" (Daniel 7:13, 14). Thus the cleansing of the heavenly sanctuary involved a Pre-Advent Judgment *in favor* of the saints of the Most High, and the time came for the saints to possess the kingdom (Daniel 7:22).

Remember Cuninghame (See Chapter 3), in Great Britain, had dilated on the Pre-Advent Judgment of Daniel 7, and linked it with Revelation 14:7 announcing "the hour of God's judgment was come." But Cuninghame failed to link "the *hour* of God's judgment" with the "cleansing of the sanctuary," beginning at that fateful *hour* —October 22, 1844, according to Daniel 8:14. Therefore Edson's conviction of truth in the large field on the day after the Great Disappointment, *synthesized* the great truth of a Pre-Advent Judgment *with* the cleansing of the sanctuary, that "justified" (Hebrew connotation noted by Edson) the saints, making them up for the possession of the kingdom of glory, soon to be ushered in with the Second Advent (Daniel 7:22, 27).

Edson's conviction of truth was the solution to the mystery of Daniel 8:14, bringing together all the pieces of the prophetic puzzle, that earnest men in Great Britain and America had struggled with for a third of a century. And to think that Edson's conviction of truth came on the morning after the Great Disappointment, corroborated the accuracy of their calculations to the date, October 22, 1844,—what could be more timely than this? But there was more to the Providential breakthrough on the morning after the Great Disappointment—that is, even more new light and incentive. Great thoughts coursed through Edson's mind while he stood motionless in the large field in rapt meditation. His mind was directed to Revelation, chapter 10, stating, "I could see the vision had spoken and did not lie." Edson saw that the "little book open," held in the hand of the angel (Revelation 10:2), was the "little book" of Daniel that was "shut up," or closed to understanding, until the "time of the end" (Daniel 12:4, 8, 9). He recognized that he himself was living in the "time of the end," and that the mysteries of Daniel were indeed "open" to investigation and understanding, and the implications of Daniel 8:14 came sharply into focus. Edson immediately saw that the connection of the eating of the "little book" of Daniel, that was as "sweet as honey" in the mouth (Revelation 10:10), was *related* to the sweet message of the Second Advent that had assumed great proportions as a movement centering around Daniel 8:14. Next he noted, that as soon as John the Revelator had digested the "little book," his "belly was bitter" (Revelation 10:10). Again Edson identified the bitter digestion of the "little book" *with* the bitter Great Disappointment, so fresh in the minds of thousands of believers. There was no mistaking that the experience of the sweet Second Advent Movement, and the bitter Great Disappointment surrounding the opening of the mysteries of the little book of Daniel, was prophesied in Revelation 10, and that God had a hand in all that took place according to His will and Divine Forecast. Edson expressed himself aptly in these words, "WE had eaten the little book; it had been sweet in our mouth, and it had now become bitter in our belly, embittering our whole being."[2]

"Prophesy Again"

As Edson mused longer in the large field, the Trumpet sound of the Seventh angel echoed in his ears, pertaining to the concluding verses of

Revelation, chapters 10 and 11: "Thou must prophesy again" (Revelation 10:11), and "the temple of God was opened in heaven, and there was seen in his temple the ark of his testament" (Revelation 11:19). The former statement, "Thou must prophesy again," was a great incentive for him personally, to publicize his conviction of truth that came to him in the large field. Furthermore, on a far larger scale, it was an incentive to continuity. It meant that the Second Advent movement had not collapsed in the Great Disappointment—it was to continue, to regain momentum, and to accomplish its end—to prepare a people to meet their God in the Second Advent, with no *specific time* set for the event. It was not to die on the vine, but to bear much fruit reaching to the ends of the earth—"to every nation, and kindred, and tongue, and people" declaring: the First Angel's message that "the hour of His judgment is come," followed by the Second and Third Angels' messages (Revelation 14:6–12).

While Edson was to "prophesy again" on the sanctuary question, Joseph Bates, one of Miller's right-hand men, prophesied again on the Third Angel's message. He introduced the new truth of the Sabbath, and placed it in a prophetic setting, explaining the Mark of the Beast and the Seal of God (Revelation 7, 13, 14) in his works, *The Seventh Day Sabbath, A Perpetual Sign* (1846 and 1847), and *A Seal of the Living God* (1849). Besides Edson and Bates, others swelled the ranks to "prophesy again," such as James and Ellen White, to name the more prominent. And all the while, these champions of prophetic interpretation, without exception, maintained the Historicist position.

Impact of the Sanctuary Message

Returning to the narrative, after Edson's conviction of truth in the large field, he gave attention to painstaking review of his cornfield conviction, in a regularly called study group, with Owen R.L. Crosier and Dr. Franklin B. Hahn, a physician of Canandaigua, New York. After several months of study, Crosier, who had a flair for writing, embodied their conclusions in a series of articles appearing first in the *Day-Dawn* of Canandaigua, and then in a lengthy detailed article in the popular *Day-Star*, as an Extra, published in Cincinnati, February 7, 1846. The fact that the article had the endorsing signatures of Edson and Hahn, carried much weight with the reading public far and wide. The articles made an impact in the East and were accepted by Joseph Bates of New Bedford, Massachusetts, and James White of Portland, Maine. However, before Ellen Harmon of Maine married James White, she had a vision relating Jesus' entry into the Holy of Holies of the heavenly sanctuary, published a year later as a brief communication in the *Day-Star*, March 14, 1846. Nevertheless, Ellen Harmon's communication was penned and mailed to the editor before she could have seen Crosier's amplified article in the *Day-Star* Extra. Obviously there was no collusion here, since Miss Harmon was entirely unaware, that the sanctuary truth put forth by Crosier's lengthy article, was the product of Scriptural evidence by concerted group study, conducted by Bible students entirely unknown to her.

Crosier's comprehensive article was so well received, that it became the early standard exposition of the sanctuary message, essential parts of which were republished a number of times, as the best presentation available on the sanctuary question. The exposition shed light on the entire question of the Great Disappointment, and on the justification of the Second Advent movement. Moreover, it made a distinctive contribution to Christian theology.

Mergence of Sanctuary and Sabbath Messages

After Crosier's articles had made their way in New England, it was decided to call for a conference to be held at Edson's home, inviting the scattered Advent believers. James White made the effort to come, but was called back to conduct a funeral. Joseph Bates arrived at the conference and preached the Sabbath truth. Edson listened intently, having already meditated in the cornfield on John's vision of the temple in heaven housing the Ark of the Testament containing the Ten Commandments (Revelation 11:19), together with a few thoughts on the Sabbath commandment penned by Thomas M. Preble. When Bates finished his presentation, Edson was ecstatic and convinced of the Sabbath truth. He shot out of his seat and electrified the audience with the exclamation: "That is light and truth! The seventh day is the Sabbath, and I am with you to keep it!"[3] Thus, the connection was made between the Sabbath message and the Sanctuary message at this historic conference. The merging of these two messages was the first step in forging a body of believers, destined to restore the fundamentals of the Apostolic Church.

Mergence of Sabbath and Second Advent Messages

But how did the Sabbath truth arise among the scattered Advent believers after the Great Disappointment? How did the Sabbath truth merge with the Second Advent truth? It all came about when a Seventh Day Baptist, Rachel Oakes, after taking communion in a small Christian church of Advent believers in the village of Washington, New Hampshire, challenged the preacher Frederick Wheeler, about keeping all the commandments, including the fourth regarding the Sabbath. Wheeler took the outspoken challenge seriously, and began to observe the Sabbath from March, 1844. Next Thomas M. Preble, a strong Second Advent preacher associated with Miller, accepted the Sabbath from Rachel Oakes or Wheeler in August, 1844. He then submitted a revealing article on the Sabbath to the periodical *Hope of Israel*, published February, 1845, in Portland, Maine. The following month this article appeared in tract form and brought the Sabbath to Joseph Bates, who in turn came out with his own 48 page tract *The Seventh Day Sabbath, A Perpetual Sign*, in 1846. Bates' tract led James and Ellen White to accept the Sabbath soon after their marriage in August, 1846. The Whites were convinced by Bates' presentation of clear Scriptural and historical evidence and declared: "In the autumn of 1846 we began to observe the Bible Sabbath, and to teach and defend it." At this time there were about fifty Advent believers observing the Sabbath in New England, the congregation at Washington, New Hampshire, forming the nucleus.[4]

Three-fold Emergence of Truths

It is remarkable, if not amazing, that immediately after the Great Disappointment, *three* great lines of truth suddenly, and almost simultaneously emerged from three isolated and independent places—all in the year 1844. The day after the Great Disappointment, the sanctuary truth dawned upon the mind of Hiram Edson, and after concerted group study, it was proclaimed and published from Western New York. The Sabbath truth, so foreign to the Second Advent movement, took root in Washington, New Hampshire, and was vigorously advocated by Joseph Bates and others in Massachusetts and New Hampshire. By December of that fateful year 1844, the Spiritual Gift of Prophecy, ever so foreign to the Second Advent movement, if not to the Christian world as a whole, began to be felt by a sizable group around Portland, Maine, when young Ellen Harmon had her first vision. This unaccountable three-pronged emergence of monumental truths was soon to merge and unite with other truths. The convergence of these truths into one body of doctrine was initiated in 1848, through a series of Sabbath conferences, to be discussed presently. (Please see Map Illustration 13).

Illustration 13
Providential Mergence of Three Independent Doctrines
The Sanctuary Message of Hiram Edson emerged from Port Gibson, New York. The Sabbath truth came from Washington, New Hampshire, and was soon afterward proclaimed by Joseph Bates. The Prophetic Gift was manifested in Ellen White at Portland, Maine. These three independent doctrines emerged almost simultaneously, in the year 1844, and soon merged into a unified message.

Third Emergence of Truth: The Prophetic Gift

But first, we consider the emergence of the third monumental truth: the gift of prophecy. The true gift of prophecy arose against a background of a false prophetic movement epitomized in the "fruits" (Matthew 7:20) of: the Mormon prophet Joseph Smith, who was assassinated in 1844; the Shaker prophetess, Ann Lee, who claimed she was Christ incarnate in female flesh; the Catholic Apostolic Church in England, as previously discussed in Chapter Four. In view of this background it is no wonder, that even the General Conference held May, 1843, in Boston, during the Second Advent movement under Miller, adopted this sweeping action: "We have no confidence whatever in any visions, dreams, or private revelations."⁵ Judged by human reasoning, with such a background in mind, it would certainly appear to be an inappropriate time to raise a true prophet. Yet one must realize God said, "My thoughts are not your thoughts, neither are your ways My ways" (Isaiah 55:8). So in spite of this unfavorable background God raised Ellen Harmon, and she faced great prejudice.

On the other hand, the gift of prophecy arose against another background, that urgently called for comfort and healing. Remember that thousands of sincere and earnest Christians had their hopes dashed in pieces at the Great Disappointment, many of whom gave up their faith and lost their way. If ever there was a time to fulfill God's promises to these Advent believers, it was now—they desperately needed that "balm in Gilead" (Jeremiah 8:22). So in the hour of their greatest need and worst extremity God fulfilled the promise promptly: "Comfort ye, comfort ye my people" (Isaiah 40;1). God gave a vision of comfort to seventeen year old Ellen Harmon, during the morning worship hour with some other young women of the Advent faith, in the home of Mrs. Elizabeth Haines, in South Portland, Maine, December, 1844.⁶ The content of the vision portrayed the travail and travels of the Advent people on their way to the city of God. The portrayal did not explain the *nature* of the Great Disappointment; that came through personal Bible study by Edson and his colleagues. The portrayal did, however, carry the Advent travelers to the Second Advent, and assured safe entry into the City of God, if they "kept their eyes fixed on Jesus." This first vision of Ellen Harmon was no religious reverie, and did not spring subjectively from her personal beliefs (neither did any other vision, for that matter). Neither did it arise from her acquaintances in Portland, since she and all of them believed that the Millerite movement was an aberration, a tragic mistake. The effect, therefore, of the vision *changed* the belief of Ellen Harmon, and encouraged and comforted her to press on, "looking unto Jesus, the author and finisher of our faith (Hebrews 12:2). Likewise, when she related the vision to others in Portland "about sixty fully believed it to be of God."⁷ They were comforted and convinced, believing that the Millerite movement actually fulfilled a Divine purpose—it was Providential, not aberrational.

Integrity of the Prophetic Gift

From the time of Ellen Harmon's first vision, until the publication of 250 copies of it in broadside form for distribution in April 1846, she came under scrutiny, from none other than Joseph Bates. He observed her in vision a number of times and reported in April, 1847:

> I listened to every word, and watched every move to detect deception, or mesmeric influence. And I thank God for the opportunity I have had with others to witness these things. I can now confidently speak for myself. I believe the work is of God, and is given to comfort and strengthen His 'scattered', 'torn' and 'peeled people'.[8]

The integrity of the prophetic gift was generally ever on the line, and all the Scriptural tests of authenticity were applied to Ellen (Harmon) White, such as the fulfillment of her predictions (Jeremiah 28:9). Certainly the Scriptural test: "by their fruits ye shall know them" (Matthew 7:20) was applied with impunity, especially after seventy years of prophetic ministry (1844–1915). Ellen White's bitterest critic and defector from the faith, Dudley M. Canright, attended her funeral, and with tears running down his cheeks, paid this tribute to her, "There is a noble Christian woman gone."[9] While Ellen White never accepted the role of infallibility, nor claimed the title of prophet, preferring to be called a "messenger"[10] and "servant" of God, the editorial in *The Independent*, a leading New York weekly, laid claim to the title at the time of her death, in these words: "She lived the life and did the work of a worthy prophetess, the most admirable of the American succession."[11] In her book *Great Women of the Christian Faith*, Edith Dean refers to Ellen White as "the pioneer and guide of her church." She wrote further, "Certainly she was a spokesman for God. Like the prophets of old, her life was marked by humility, simplicity, austerity, divine learning, and devotion. And like them, she turned to God for healing and help. So firm did her faith become that she accomplished the miraculous for Adventists."[12]

Physical Phenomena of a Prophet in Vision

Back in the early pioneer days the Scriptural tests of the fulfillment of predictions (Jeremiah 28:9), or the "fruits" of ministry (Matthew 7:20), were still too premature to apply, since they required the passage of time, before application of the tests. However, in those early days, observers were concerned about the physical phenomena regarding the manner in which visions were given. John N. Loughborough, first chronicler of those pioneer days, and author of six books, saw Ellen White in vision about fifty times, sometimes in the presence of physicians who examined her while in vision. Chosen from a file of authentic eye witnesses, Loughborough's testimony is the most concise. Thus he describes the state of Ellen White in vision, a number of years after his first observation in 1852:

> In passing into vision she gives three enrapturing shouts of "Glory!" which echo and re-echo, the second, and especially the third, fainter, but more thrilling than the first, the voice resembling that of one quite a distance from you, and just going out of hearing. For about four or five seconds she seems to drop down like a person in a swoon, or one having *lost his strength*; she then seems to be filled with *superhuman strength*, sometimes rising at once to her feet and walking about the room. There are frequent movements of her hands and arms, pointing to the right or left as her head turns. All these movements are made in a most graceful manner. In whatever position the hand or arm may be placed, it is *impossible for any one to move it*. Her *eyes are always open*, but she does not wink; her head is raised, and she is looking upward, not with a vacant stare, but with a pleasant expression, only differing from the normal in that she appears to be looking intently at some distant object. She *does not breathe*, yet her pulse beats regularly. Her countenance is pleasant, and the colour of her face as florid as in her natural state.[13]

(Italics supplied)

Ellen White's "passing into vision" with the sense of transportation, totally oblivious to her surroundings, resembles that of Paul (2 Corinthians 12:1–4). Her eyes remaining open, without blinking, or even the dilation of the pupils, finds its counterpart in Numbers, chapter 24, verses 3, 4, 16. Her initial momentary loss of strength, followed by "superhuman strength," in which it is "impossible for any one to move" the gestures of the hand or arm, finds a parallel with Daniel in vision, at Daniel, chapter 10, verses 7–10, 16–19. The observable physical phenomena of Ellen White in vision bears resemblance to the Swedish child preachers (Chapter 3), who like Ellen White also experienced absence of breathing, similar to Daniel (Daniel 10:17).

There is no question, but that the Lord chose the weakest of the weak, when He endowed Ellen White with the Gift of Prophecy. James White raised the question regarding the possible effect of the visions upon her constitution and strength stating: "when she had her first vision, she was an emaciated invalid, given up by her friends and physicians to die of consumption. She then weighed about eighty pounds. Her nervous condition was such that she could not write, and was dependent on one sitting near her at the table to even pour her drink from the cup to the saucer. And notwithstanding her anxieties and mental agonies, in consequence of her duty to bring her views before the public... her health and physical and mental strength have improved from the day she had her first vision."[14] She had some 2,000 visions over a seventy year period of fruitful ministry.

Relationship of Ellen White's Visions to the Scriptures

As early as 1847, James White pointed out the relationship of Ellen White's visions to the Scriptures. His initial published declaration appeared in the first small joint work, *A Word to the Little Flock*, as follows: "I conclude that there is not one Second Advent believer who will take the ground, that all of the prophecy of Joel, quoted by Peter, was fulfilled on the day of Pentecost.... A part of this prophecy was fulfilled on the day of Pentecost; and ALL of it is to be fulfilled 'IN THE LAST DAYS, SAITH GOD'. Dreams and visions are among the signs that precede the great and notable day of the Lord [Joel 2:28–32; Acts 2:16–20]. And as the signs of that day have been, and still are fulfilling, it must be clear to every unprejudiced mind, that the time has fully come when the children of God may *expect dreams and visions from the Lord*....The Bible is a perfect and *complete revelation. It is our rule of faith and practise*. But this is no reason, why God may not show the past, present, and future fulfillment of His word, in these *last days*, by dreams and visions; according to Peter's testimony [Acts 2:16–20]. True visions are given to lead us to God, and His written word; but those that are given for a new *rule of faith and practise*, separate from the Bible, cannot be from God, and should be rejected."[15] (Italics and Square Brackets supplied).

Several years later Ellen White followed up on her husband's statement of the relationship of her visions to the Scriptures. She acknowledged that her prophetic gift of visions was in fulfillment of Joel's prophecy, but her visions and writings did not add to, or supersede, surpass, or supplant the Bible. Here is her statement verbatim:

> I recommend to you, dear reader, the Word of God as
> the rule of your faith and practise. By the Word we are
> to be judged. God has in that Word, promised to give
> visions in the 'LAST DAYS': not for a new rule of faith,
> but for the comfort of his people, and to correct those
> who err from Bible truth.[16]

Restoration of Apostolic Church with Spiritual Gifts

Besides James White's explanation of Ellen White's prophetic gift of visions in fulfillment of Joel's prophecy, he also implied unwittingly, that God was forging the restoration of the Apostolic Church in the last days, with the restoration of Spiritual Gifts as related by Paul: "He gave some, apostles; and some, prophets... for the perfecting of the saints... till we all come in the unity of the faith" (Ephesians 4:11–13). Bearing Paul's message in mind James White elaborated, pointing out the necessity of Ellen White's prophetic gift to the scattered, weakened church: "God in much mercy has pitied the weakness of his people, and has set the gifts in the gospel church to correct our errors, and to lead us to his Living Word. Paul says that they are for the 'perfecting of the saints', 'till we all come in the unity of the faith'. The extreme necessity of the church in its imperfect state is God's opportunity to maintain the gifts of the Spirit.... But if a portion of the church err from the truths of the Bible, and become weak, and sickly, and the flock become scattered, so that it seems necessary for God to employ the gifts of the Spirit to correct, revive and heal the erring, we should let him work."[17]

1848 Sabbath Conferences Unify the Faith

"He gave... some, prophets... for the perfecting of the saints... till we all come in the unity of the faith," had to be the marching orders urged by the Holy Spirit to bring his scattered, weak and erring people together to iron out their doctrinal differences in six successive Sabbath Conferences in 1848. The purpose of these conferences, according to James White, was the "uniting [of] the brethren on the great truths connected with the message of the third angel."[18] In the year following the conclusion of the 1848 conferences the goal of perfecting the saints in the unity of the faith had been achieved. James White could confidently write: "The scattering time we have had; it is in the past, and now the time for the saints to be gathered into the unity of the faith, and be sealed by one holy, uniting truth *has come*. Yes, Brother, *it has come*."[19]

The six Sabbath Conferences were held in different homes of Advent believers in various states, the first two had an attendance of fifty and thirty five respectively. The main speakers were, Joseph Bates and James White who addressed the subjects of the ten commandments, the Sabbath, the Second Advent, and the three angels' messages. The third conference was held in Hiram Edson's barn, Port Gibson, New York, reminiscent of his original experience, and therefore he was the chief speaker on the sanctuary message. While the conferences were orderly, "there were hardly two agreed. Each was strenuous for his views, declaring that they were according to the Bible."[20] Nevertheless, the Advent believers many times "remained together until late at night, and sometimes through the entire night, praying for light and studying the Word."[21] The role of Ellen White in these conferences was true to her prophetic call, to perfect the saints, facilitating the "unity of the faith" by playing down differences, and de-emphasizing minor points. Thus she was able "to correct those who err from Bible truth"—to use her own words. After the vigorous conference held in Brother Arnold's barn in Volney, New York, she noted that many yielded their errors, and united "upon the third angels' message. Our meeting ended victoriously. Truth gained the victory."[22]

The immediate result of the six Sabbath Conferences of 1848 was the convergence and consolidation of three great lines of truth into a unified body of doctrine, comprising: (1) the sanctuary message from Port Gibson, Western New York; (2) the Sabbath message from Washington, New Hampshire; (3) the prophetic gift manifested in Ellen

White of Portland, Maine. To the fundamental doctrines of Salvation (Soteriology) and the literal, audible, visible pre-millennial Second Advent (Eschatology), was added the prophetic understanding of the three angels' messages (Revelation 14:6–12), with special emphasis and identity with the third angels' message "unfurling the banner on which was inscribed, 'The commandments of God and the faith of Jesus'"[23] (Revelation 14:12).

These truths were constituted as "landmark" truths with the addition of one more, that surfaced at the 1848 Sabbath Conference quite surprisingly. It was the state of man after death, more specifically the "non-immortality" of the soul, and the total annihilation of the wicked (Revelation 20:12–14). This last named truth was a carry-over from the great Second Advent movement, where it was introduced mainly by George Storrs. Nevertheless, this landmark truth surfaced just on time in 1848, to reject the beginning of modern Spiritualism, the first mysterious "rappings" of which, captured the fancy of the Fox sisters at Hydesville, near Rochester, New York, in 1848. These rappings were interpreted as crude communications from the spirits or souls of the dead, purportedly immortal, thus perpetrating the serpent Satan's original lie, "Ye shall not surely die" (Genesis 3:4). The essence of this lie is engraved on the present-day memorial church Obelisk, at the "International Shrine of Spiritualism," Rochester, that reads: "There is no Death, There are no Dead."

A Vision Warns Against Spiritualism

An interesting footnote to the above story demonstrates the validity of the prophetic gift of Ellen White, who accepted the truth of the "non-immortality" of the soul from the proof texts used in conversation with her Methodist mother back in 1844.[24] She received a revelation in March of 1849 as follows: "I saw that the mysterious knocking in New York and other places was the power of Satan, and that such things would be more and more common, clothed in a religious garb so as to lull the deceived to greater security and to draw the minds of God's people, if possible, to those things and cause them to doubt the teachings and power of the Holy Ghost."[25]

Restoration of the Apostolic Church of the Last Days

Going back to the 1848 Sabbath Conferences, unbeknown to the leaders and contributors, they were forging the restoration of the Apostolic Church of the last days, to continue "steadfastly in the apostles' doctrine" (Acts 2:42). Before them was a model church: Saved by Faith (Acts 2:36–38); Separated by Baptism (Acts 2:38); Spirit Endowed through the Gift of Prophecy (Acts 2:38; Ephesians 4:11–13); Sanctified in Life (Acts 2:43), observing the ten commandments (Romans 7:12; John 14:15), and the Sabbath (Exodus 20:8; 31:13; Mark 2:27, 28; Acts 18:1–4, 11), not in order to be saved, but because they are saved. Furthermore, this model church was steadfast in the Apostles' Doctrine of: the Judgment (Acts 10:42, 17:31, 24:25; Romans 2:16,

14:10, 12; 2 Corinthians 5:10; 1 Peter 4:17); Christ's High Priestly Ministry (Hebrews 7:25, 8:1–6, 9:22–24); Christ's Second Coming (Hebrews 9:28; 1 Thessalonians 4:13–17; Acts 1:9–11); and Christ's teaching on the Sleep of Death (John 11:11–14; Acts 7:55–60), including the annihilation of the wicked (Matthew 10:28). There was still more to come. They were on the eve of another facet of the Apostolic Church model—that is a church that is Successful in Witness.

1848 "Publishing" Vision

During the sixth and last of the 1848 Sabbath Conferences held in Otis Nichol's home, in Dorchester, Massachusetts, Ellen White came out of vision with a message directed to James White:

> I have a message for you. You must begin to print a little paper and send it out to the people. Let it be small at first; but as the people read, they will send you means with which to print, and it will be a success from the first. From this small beginning *it was shown to me to be like streams of light that went clear round the world.*[26] (See Picture 10).
>
> (Italics supplied)

While the 1848 Sabbath Conferences resulted in the consolidation of a unified body of doctrine, the need for publication of a unified message through the power of the printed page immediately presented itself. And this came about through the Spirit of Prophecy. It must have been an overwhelming thought to a group of Christian stragglers, whose followers were not even numbered in several hundreds, to entertain a publishing enterprise that would belt the globe "like streams of light that went clear round the world." World-wide dissemination of their message was the furthest from their minds. It was a bold prediction, demonstrating the dynamism of the prophetic gift through a twenty one year old woman. Nevertheless, undaunted, the young man James White launched the first number of the periodical *Present Truth* in July, 1849, without the necessary financial resources at hand. Still the periodical was mailed on the wings of prayer, and followed up in 1850 with the *Advent Review*. This was the humble beginning of a publishing venture that was "a success from the first," that has indeed gone "clear round the world" in *fulfillment of the prediction*. Today fifty six publishing houses scattered around the world, in about forty countries, are turning out periodicals and books in over 260 languages, including Braille for the blind. And these books are being sold by a world-wide army of over 20,000 colporteurs.[27]

1875 "Publishing" Vision

As a follow-up to Ellen White's vision to commence publishing a periodical in 1848, she had a remarkable publishing vision in 1875. While in vision she made exclamatory remarks such as: "A light! More light! Much light!" This was in reference to the dark world she saw in

© Review & Herald Pub. association   Picture 10   Harry Anderson, Artist

Ellen White's Prophetic Gift in Action

Her vision in 1848 to begin a Publishing Work that would spread "like streams of light that went clear round the world," gave great impetus to a group of Christian stragglers. The bold prediction eventually attained dramatic fulfillment.

vision, being lit up progressively by more lights of truth, until the whole world was lighted. Coming out of vision she reported having observed printing presses running in many foreign lands. She was asked which lands? Ellen White replied that if she ever saw them, she would recognize them. However, she remembered one—Australia. Her hearers were astounded, because there was no work at all in Australia at the time of this vision in 1875. There was only one press, one health institution, and one junior college—all located at Battle Creek, Michigan.[28]

Nevertheless, in 1885 a full ten years after the publishing vision of 1875, Ellen White visited Europe, where she labored for two years. On seeing the presses in both Basel, Switzerland, and Christiania-Oslo, Norway, she remarked, "I have seen these presses before"—recognizing what she had seen in vision ten years before. She was even familiar with the present circumstances of the work in these places, for instance, she asked to meet, what she described as an "older man," who worked in the pressroom at Basel. The bystanders were amazed at her uncanny knowledge of the pressroom and the foreman, an older man, who was absent for that day.[29]

Six years later, in December, 1891, Ellen White arrived in Australia, where she lived and pioneered the cause for nine years. Since initial work only started in Australia in 1885, it is phenomenal that Ellen White saw in vision the Australian press operating at least ten years before. Now, in the first week of 1892 she visited the pressroom in Melbourne, Australia. Immediately upon her entry in the pressroom, she said, "I have seen this place before. I have seen these persons, and I know the conditions existing among the workers in this department. There is a lack of unity here, and a lack of harmony." The workers were taken aback at her supernatural knowledge of the situation. But soon afterwards she wrote words of kind counsel to the workers that brought about important changes.[30]

A Vision Establishes a College

It is clear that Ellen White's publishing vision of 1875 made an impact far and wide—in America, Europe, and Australia, demonstrating to the workers that the Holy Spirit was the dynamic power energizing their endeavors world-wide. While the brethren in Australia, at Ellen White's urging, were looking for land to establish a college, she had a vision of a stretch of land, with a conspicuous freshly plowed furrow, about six feet long and nine inches deep. The brethren and the government fruit expert reported that the land selected was unsuitable for a missionary college, to be supported by agriculture and horticulture. But when Ellen White viewed the tract of land, she came across a freshly plowed furrow matching what appeared to her in vision, and that clinched the decision to secure the property. However, the purchase of the property took a surprising turn. It took the timely visit of a South African, Anna Lindsay, daughter of Mrs. A.E. Wessels, among the first white converts in South Africa, to purchase the property with a gift of $5,000. By 1897 the Australasian Missionary College at Cooranbong, seventy five miles north of Sydney, opened its doors with four teachers and ten students. But before the school term closed there were fifty students enrolled, and contrary to the false reports of poor soil, Ellen White's prediction that "God can furnish a table in the wilderness" (Letter 350, 1907) came to fruition. The college became a showpiece, exhibiting the authenticity of prophetic vision. A prolific vineyard and orchard, not only furnished a table of luscious fruit, but a canning factory on the campus supplied the cities also. In addition a dairy was provided, and a small health food factory was installed. Carpentry, painting, and printing became important industries—there was plenty of work available for students to earn money to pay their way for their courses of study. And from this college went forth a stream of missionaries to the South Pacific and elsewhere in the world.[31]

The Australian Missionary College is typical of a string of about ninety accredited colleges around the world, nine of which are in North America, including three universities. All of these are the result of a Christian education program fostered by Ellen White, when she contributed to the establishment of the first college in Battle Creek, Michigan (1874). The overall result is that the Adventist Church operates the second largest Protestant parochial school system in the United States. Outside the United States, they operate the largest elementary school system of any Protestant Church.

Counsel of a Prophet Establishes a Mission

While living in distant Australia, Ellen White was even instrumental in the establishment of the first mission station in heathen lands. It was a touch and go affair. And if it were not for her intervention, the mission enterprise may not have taken off. As the story goes, the first Dutch converts in South Africa, Pieter and Philip Wessels were delegates to a General Conference session in Battle Creek in 1893, where it was suggested that the time had come to open work among the indigenous African people. The Wessels brothers immediately rose to their feet and pledged $15,000 for the project. Next, they returned to South Africa and obtained a grant of land, as a donation, from Cecil J. Rhodes, Prime Minister of the Cape Colony, and chairman of the Charter Company occupying Rhodesia (later named Zimbabwe). But the Foreign Mission Board in America balked at the idea of accepting the land as a donation, advocating it should be paid for. They were adamant in their decision, and drafted a letter to be sent to Rhodes. Meanwhile the South African brethren saw no reason why the grant of land should not be received as a donation, and were concerned that if the letter reached Rhodes, he might be offended, and even thwart the mission venture. Whereupon S.N. Haskell in South Africa wrote to Ellen White in Australia, requesting her counsel in the matter. Before the Board's letter intended for Rhodes was sent out, Ellen White's letter reached the Board, advising that "what they [Rhodes] would give, we should be privileged to receive." That was final—the land was accepted as a donation as originally planned, and Solusi Mission was established on 12,000 acres, thirty miles from Bulawayo, Zimbabwe, among the Makalanga tribe of Africans in 1895.[32]

"Successful in Witness"

Solusi Mission (recently declared a university) was the forerunner of a string of missions in Zimbabwe, Zambia, Malawi, Tanzania, Kenya, and Uganda, whose total membership now exceeds one million, having just eclipsed the total membership of the home base—the United States. And that is just a segment of the world-wide membership approaching ten million souls. Souls in the world field are presently being baptized at the average rate of 1,400 a day.[33] That brings to mind a partial fulfillment of Ellen White's prediction in 1905: "The time is coming when there will be as many converts in a day as there were on the day of Pentecost, after the disciples had received the Holy Spirit."[34] Thus, the restored Apostolic Church of the last days can claim the qualification of being "Successful in Witness," having penetrated nearly every country of the world, and represented in more countries than any other single Protestant Church.[35]

Chapter 8

UNUSUAL CHARACTERISTIC OF THE RESTORED APOSTOLIC CHURCH OF THE LAST DAYS

1863, Church Organization

The year 1863 was important for two reasons. First, the restored Apostolic Church of the last days, having formulated a unified platform of faith and doctrine, lacked an organizational framework; in fact there was an aversion to it for years. Finally, guided by Ellen White, they formally organized the General Conference of Seventh-day Adventists, naming John Byington, the first president, to direct 3,500 members with his headquarters in Battle Creek, Michigan, in 1863. The second important development that year, was to introduce to the church the unusual characteristic of the Apostolic Church—the apostles' doctrine of the Body Temple: "Do you not know that you are the temple of God and that the Spirit of God dwells in you" (1 Corinthians 3:16, NKJV).

Analogy: Ancient Israel and Spiritual Israel

But before going into the doctrine of the Body Temple, let's strike an interesting analogy. Consider ancient Israel, who came out of Egyptian bondage and were bound for Canaan. They were brought out of Egypt and preserved by a prophet—Moses (Hosea 12:13). God gave them a sanctuary (Exodus 25:8), the Ten Commandments (Exodus 20:1–17), the Sabbath, and manna from heaven daily, excluding the Sabbath day, for a period of forty years (Exodus 16), together with the Levitical Health laws. These Health laws governed the prevention, disinfection, and isolation of disease, including personal hygiene, cleanliness, sanitation, and dietary laws. Private and public health was a prominent feature in the camp of Israel. They were the cleanest people in ancient times, taking a bath once a week, and because they diligently hearkened to the voice of the Lord, and kept all His statutes, they escaped contraction of Egyptian diseases (Exodus 15:26). It is no wonder that "there was not one feeble person among their tribes" (Psalm 105:37), for God declared, "I am the Lord that healeth thee" (Exodus 15:26).

Now consider the parallels of Spiritual Israel with Ancient Israel. The Spiritual Israel of the mid-nineteenth century came out of the Great Disappointment of 1844, still bound for the heavenly Canaan, traveling on life's journey toward the City of God. They were brought out of the Great Disappointment, preserved and comforted by a prophetess—Ellen White. No sooner had they come out, than they were given the sanctuary truth (the meaning of Daniel 8:14), the Ten Commandments (Revelation 11:19, 14:12), and the Sabbath message. Then like manna from heaven, to bless them on their journey to the heavenly Canaan, they were nourished with angels' food (Psalm 78:25)—a dietary regime par excellence, incorporated in a comprehensive forty five minute health vision, revealed to Ellen White in 1863, while visiting in Otsego, thirty miles from Battle Creek, Michigan.

Prevailing Health Outlook in America

The impact of the principles of the health vision are best understood, when we consider the background of the customs and practises of the time. Heavy blood-letting was the panacea of the day, buttressed by "heroic" medication of poisonous drugs, including emetics of antimony tartrate and the like, in addition to fierce purgings with calomel (mercurous chloride). Apart from physicians, apothecaries (as druggists were called) could diagnose illness, and prescribe and sell any medicine or drug—and any one could be an apothecary. The American Medical Association, founded in 1847, had no power to regulate medical education or practise. Polypharmacy was energetically applied, that is: give all the poisonous drugs, such as arsenic, morphine, strychnine, opium, calomel, etc.—keep trying, at least one will work. A cynical saying was repeated in those days, "Saul has slain his thousands, but calomel has slain its ten thousands." Like the voice of one crying in the wilderness, Dr. Holmes in 1860, while hanging on to opium and wine as pain killers, said that the "whole *materia medica*, as now used could be sunk to the bottom of the sea."

As for the general public, they cared little about sanitation, personal health, hygiene, and nutrition. People were afraid of the "deadly night air," and closed their windows to keep the fresh air out of bedrooms. Physicians defended the use of tobacco as a prophylaxis against the night air, and as a stimulant to the lungs. Case in point:preacher J.N. Loughborough formed the habit of smoking cigars as a result of the physician's advice to curb a lung disease, until he realized its ineffectiveness, and the filthiness of the habit.[1] People shunned ventilation and sunlight. They considered bathing in winter to be hazardous. Flesh foods and heavy, greasy, and highly spiced dishes comprised the daily fare. The frontier folk subsisted on salted pork, black coffee, and corn bread, prepared with large amounts of lard.

Health Vision, 1863

Ellen White's health vision of 1863 appealed to the Scriptures as an incentive to healthful living. The vision called for a return to the Edenic Diet: fruits, nuts, grains, and vegetables (Genesis 1:29, 3:18), as the best for man; and an abandonment of the flesh diet, permitted to meet the emergency of Noah's Flood, when all plant life had been destroyed. Moreover, God had blessed ancient Israel with manna, rather than flesh meat, during their forty years wandering in the wilderness, thereby providing the better diet. More specifically in the tabulation of the health vision "God expressly commanded the children of Israel not to eat swine's flesh" (Leviticus 11:7, 8; Deuteronomy 14:7, 8).[2]

The health vision appealed to the concept of the Body Temple to "be preserved in as healthy a condition as possible," as a "sacred duty," thereby glorifying God (1 Corinthians 6:19, 20). Therefore the Body Temple ought not to be defiled with liquor, tobacco, snuff, tea, coffee, and poisonous drugs. Highly spiced and seasoned foods, gluttony and overwork, came under the heading of "intemperance."[3]

The health vision inveighed heavily against heroic drug medication, identifying specific drugs, and advocated that "nature alone possesses curative powers." The health message identified all the customs, practises and life-style of the general public, and advocated rational, natural healing agents: fresh air, pure water (both for internal and external needs—hydrotherapy), sunlight, physical exercise, adequate rest, personal hygiene, fasting for brief periods, a balanced vegetarian diet, and trust in God.[4]

Health Vision Reveals Psychosomatic Approach

Ellen White's health vision proclaimed a sound psychosomatic approach, beyond her day. She wrote: "The power of the will is a mighty soother of the nerves, and can resist much disease, simply by not yielding to ailments, and settling down into a state of inactivity." She went on, "there is a class of individuals who have no real located disease. But as they believe they are dangerously diseased, they are in reality invalids. The mind is diseased, and many die of disease, which exists alone in the imagination."[5] The psychosomatic theme was later expanded in *Ministry of Healing* (1905).

Health Vision Reveals Tobacco—a Malignant Poison

Modern scientific research only caught up with Ellen White's health vision in 1962, when the Royal College of Physicians in London reported the relation between smoking and the malignant cancer of the lung. She reported a hundred years before the Physicians, that "tobacco is a poison of the most deceitful and *malignant* kind, having an exciting, then a paralyzing influence upon the nerves of the body. It is all the more dangerous because its effects upon the system are so slow, and at first scarcely perceivable. Multitudes have fallen victims to its poisonous influence. They have surely murdered themselves by this slow poison" (Italics supplied).[6] In her later great work *Ministry of Healing*, Ellen White characterized tobacco as a "most malignant poison."[7] In the same book, while knowing nothing of the effects of high "cholesterol" she wrote: "The oil, as eaten in the olive, is far preferable to animal oil or fat."[8] Space permits one more health revelation given to Ellen White, who was unacquainted with our household terms of E.K.G.'s and C.A.T. scans. But in 1869 she wrote: "Whatever disturbs the circulation of the electric currents in the nervous system lessens the strength of the vital powers, and the result is a deadening of the sensibilities of the mind."[9] On another occasion she said that the nervous "system is vitalized by the electrical force of the brain to resist disease."[10]

Health Vision Principles Applied

Five years before the health vision of 1863, Ellen White rebuked the preacher Stephen N. Haskell for his making the eating of pork a test of church membership. Now after the vision it did become a test of fellowship, and was clearly revealed to be unfit for human consumption. But the eating of flesh meat of clean animals, namely, "the ox, the sheep, and the goat" (Deuteronomy 14:4), never became a test of church membership, and the vegetarian regime was to be promoted as conducive to good health. Hence in obedience to her health vision, Ellen White revised her eating habits to "two meals a day" on the vegetarian plan. She discarded completely her meat-eating habit, and dispensed with lard, and spices of all kinds. The result after about a year's practise, was that her health had never been better—she was relieved of her childhood affliction of heart trouble and dropsy, and lost twenty five pounds in weight.[11] She was so thrilled with her health vision that she could rightly certify, like Paul, that she neither received it of man, neither was she taught it, but by the revelation of Jesus Christ (Galatians 1:11, 12).

Second Health Vision

Ellen White's Christmas gift, 1865, was a second health vision, in which she was instructed that the church should provide a "home for the afflicted," where care could be given, with instruction in healthful living. The dream came true the next year, with the establishment in Battle Creek (population 5,000) of the Western Health Reform Institute. It was modeled after Dr. James C. Jackson's Hydropathic Institution in Dansville, New York. But the Institute did not make much headway, until Dr. John H. Kellogg became medical superintendent in 1876, having been groomed from his youth for the position by the Whites. Kellogg arrived with a regular M.D. from Bellevue Hospital Medical College in New York City, the recognized nation's leading medical school. Within two years Kellogg built an elegant five story building for $50,000, that began the "grand hotel" era for the institution, named the Medical and Surgical Sanitarium of Battle Creek. Before the end of the century two large wings had been added to make Battle Creek Sanitarium the most prestigious and famous institution in America. And Kellogg had been catapulted to the forefront of the cutting edge, as scientific medicine moved in. (See Picture 11).

The Famous Battle Creek Sanitarium

What was happening at Battle Creek Sanitarium? Answer, just about everything. Dr. John H. Kellogg remained at the Sanitarium for sixty seven years (1876–1943) building a reputation for himself and his prize institution. Within two years of his arrival at the Sanitarium he introduced a School of Hygiene to train prospective medical students. By 1895 he launched the American Medical Missionary College with four years of study, and graduated nearly two hundred physicians during its fifteen year existence. He teamed up with Dr. Kate Lindsay, graduate of the University of Michigan, who founded a School of Nursing, among the first organized anywhere in the United States.

Picture 11
World-famous Battle Creek Sanitarium - A Veritable Health Mecca
This picture of the Sanitarium taken before 1902, does not show the extent of the two large wings added a few years before. The focus of attention is on the elegant central building completed in 1878, that began the "grand hotel" era of the famous institution. In 1927 the Towers Addition was started to accommodate 1,300 sanitarium patients.

Dr. Kellogg spared no pains in effecting grandiose schemes in developing a grand hotel-health resort atmosphere for his Sanitarium, having the advantage of a "salubrious location," with access to four hundred acres of fruit, dairy, and garden farms, and offering guests twenty family-size cottages to stay in. But Kellogg did apply the principles of the 1863 health vision to the full—scientifically streamlining hydrotherapy, and producing the book *Rational Hydrotherapy* that became the accepted text in the field. He strongly urged corrective exercise that aids digestion, helps control obesity, and gives a sense of well being to mind and body. A large gymnasium was provided with exercise machines and aerobic type exercise to the accompaniment of music. A swimming pool encouraged swimming, that Kellogg believed was one of the best forms of exercise. Walking and cycling was also promoted, Kellogg himself rode his bicycle until he was ninety years old. Other health vision principles he promoted were proper rest, sufficient exposure to fresh air and sunshine.

Meatless Diet and Breakfast Cereals

Perhaps the greatest contribution of Kellogg in carrying out the principles of the 1863 health vision, was as a dietitian in the area of wholesome nutrition. While he eliminated meat from the Sanitarium table, he introduced the first vegetable protein dishes designed to resemble meat, with varying combinations of wheat gluten, peanut meal, and flavorings—marketed as Nuttose and Protose. The first peanut butter and flaked cereals came from Kellogg's kitchen at the Sanitarium—the wheat cereal was marketed as Granose Flakes. Dr. Kellogg's brother Will joined hands with him in the kitchen, but eventually left, and formed the Battle Creek Toasted Corn Flake Company. Charles W. Post, a patient at the Sanitarium, also learned the secrets of food processing in the kitchen, and left to patent Postum, a cereal coffee, including the cereal Post Toasties. Thus, the cereal breakfast-food industry had its origin in the church oriented Sanitarium, and reshaped the health and eating habits of the American nation and elsewhere.

Dr. Kellogg's Prodigious Output

Dr. Kellogg was not only an efficient physician and an outstanding abdominal surgeon, but he was a health reformer—a veritable health evangelist, lecturing and writing about health. He gave weekly lectures at the Sanitarium attracting audiences up to two hundred from America and abroad. He edited a health magazine *Good Health*, and was a prodigious writer—some of his books were sold to hundreds of thousands of people. His *Home Hand Book of Domestic Hygiene and Rational Medicine* had just under 1700 pages of encyclopedic material, to reach the man in the street. It is no wonder, then, that the health evangelist, Dr. Kellogg, could attract famous guests, and more than 36,000 patients to his Health Mecca by the year 1900, and still attract another 92,000 patients by the year 1920.[12] After Dr. Kellogg's death, Battle Creek Sanitarium went into decline and settled for mediocrity.

The Sanitarium Concept copied Far and Wide

Owing to the success of the Battle Creek Sanitarium by the year 1895, six sanitariums were spawned in the United States and overseas. But the year 1897 saw the establishment of more prominent sanitariums in Australia, South Africa, and Denmark. The Medical and Surgical Sanitarium near Sydney was established with the arrival from Battle Creek Sanitarium of Dr. E.R. Caro and several trained nurses in 1897. Before long plans were laid for a more representative sanitarium. John Wessels of South Africa came to help locate a suitable site, and Dr. Merritt G. Kellogg, Dr. John Kellogg's brother, who pioneered St. Helena Sanitarium in California, drew up the plans for a 100 bed multi-storied hospital. The Sydney Sanitarium was completed in 1903 for $25,000 with a Sanitarium Health Food Agency. Twelve large factories now produce Sanitarium brand products, including breakfast cereals—Granose, Weet Bix, and flakes, and have captured the market throughout Australasia, furnishing a multi-million dollar business to finance mission operations in the South Pacific.[13] Since the establishment of Sydney Sanitarium about another half-dozen sanitarium-hospitals have developed in the Australasian Division.

Pieter and Henry Wessels in South Africa were ready with $25,000 in hand to establish a sanitarium in Claremont, near Cape Town, South Africa. Architect W.C. Sisley, who had drawn some plans for Battle Creek Sanitarium agreed to draw the plans for the Claremont Sanitarium. A four story building with fifty one rooms, a gymnasium, and facilities for a bakery and a laundry was opened to the public in 1897. It was advertised as the South African Medical and Surgical Sanitarium, the largest health resort in South Africa, to be conducted on rational and scientific principles, patterned after Battle Creek Sanitarium. Dr. R.S. Anthony was installed as superintendent, with Dr. Kate Lindsay and a contingent of seven nurses from Battle Creek Sanitarium. The society of Cape Town welcomed the Claremont Sanitarium as a prestigious institution, having served the South African nation well, until its closure in 1925.[14]

A celebrated sanitarium in Europe was established in 1897, near Copenhagen, Denmark, named the Skodsborg Sanitarium. It was initially nicknamed the Cabbage Hotel because it served vegetarian meals. Nevertheless, Skodsborg Sanitarium became famous through royal patronage, and its medical director Dr. J.C. Ottosen was knighted by the king. Besides Skodsborg Sanitarium, about another twenty sanitarium-hospitals are operating in the European Division.[15]

The phenomenal growth of sanitariums is to be noted at around the turn of the century. In 1901 they numbered 27 large and small hospitals in the United States, Australia, New Zealand, the Pacific Islands, South Africa, Denmark, Switzerland, Germany, England, India, and Mexico.[16] As we approach the twenty first century the globe is girded with 111 hospitals with a patient bed capacity ranging from 50 to 300 beds, and 15 hospitals with a bed capacity ranging from 300 to 1000 beds (1986 figures), besides several hundred smaller hospitals, dispensaries, clinics, and launches.[17]

Results of Obedience to the Health Vision

The Spiritual Israel of the last days have endeavored to obey the laws of God contained in the ten commandments, and have obeyed the "laws of health" contained in the Bible and in the health vision of 1863, pertinent to the Edenic Diet and the concept of the Body Temple. Therefore they can expect to escape contraction of the diseases of the rest of the world, and the Lord will heal them (Exodus 15:26). The results bear out obedience to the health message. A study conducted in the 1960's, concluded that the tens of thousands of Seventh-day Adventists living in Southern California, who did not smoke or drink, who tended to follow a modified vegetarian diet, with strict adherence to a regime of exercise and good hygiene, had a distinct health advantage over their Californian counterparts. "Statistics from the study indicate that compared death for death, with the general population of California, 70 per cent fewer Adventists die from all types of cancer; 68 per cent fewer of respiratory diseases; 88 per cent fewer from tuberculosis; and 85 per cent fewer from pulmonary emphysema."[18] The Adventist Mortality Study in

1978 reflected that "coronary heart disease among California Seventh-day Adventists was 60 per cent that of California non-smokers."[19]

With such statistics in mind it would be expected that the Adventist life-style would contribute to greater life expectancy. It was reported in 1967 that Adventists in California had a "five to six year greater life expectancy than their non-Adventist counterparts."[20] But in 1989 it jumped dramatically, "the average life expectancy of a 35 year old Adventist male is 47.0 additional years, an 8.9 year advantage over the Californian male."[21] Studies based on smaller samples in Europe revealed an 8.9 year life expectancy advantage for Adventist men in Holland, and 9.5 years in southern Poland.[22] On that blessed note we add, "May your tribe multiply."

Prize Institution Established upon a Vision

A prophetic dream coming true *after four years*, was to Ellen White "one of the most wonderful providences that the Lord has opened before us."[23] It was the securing of a functional sanitarium, thoroughly equipped and furnished in Redlands, California, called Loma Linda. It fulfilled the specifications of her vision of: "an occupied building, outside the city, and there are fruit trees on the sanitarium grounds."[24] When Ellen White visited Loma Linda sanitarium in 1905, four years after her vision, she recognized the fulfillment of all specifications, even to the canopylike pepper trees on the grounds.[25] (See Picture 12).

The Providence of the Lord was further demonstrated in the purchase of Loma Linda. The selling price had been reduced by steps from $110,000 to $40,000. But to purchase Loma Linda seemed impossible, since the Southern California Conference was already financially strapped with two sanitariums, Paradise Valley and Glendale, just secured in 1904. The terms of purchase were set at $20,000, before the end of the year, and the balance within another three years. However, from unexpected sources the entire $40,000 was paid within six months.[26]

Loma Linda College of Medical Evangelists was dedicated in 1906 with a School of Nursing in place, followed by a regular School of Medicine in 1910, whereby graduates would be prepared to pass the examinations required by law. Before long Loma Linda became the largest of all the institutions of the church, achieving university status, complete with a hospital providing over 500 beds. And its influence has been felt around the world. Well over 300 physicians, barely a tenth of all the School of Medicine graduates, have served in the church's overseas mission hospitals, as veritable Medical Evangelists.[27] The author himself, has two sons and a daughter-in-law, that have graduated as medical doctors from Loma Linda University.

Picture 12
Loma Linda University Medical Center and Medical School (right)
Loma Linda University has sent more medical workers overseas than all other U.S. health science schools combined. It also has the largest continuing education program in the world - due in part to the Heart Team which has made 837 trips abroad in 30 years since 1963. The team of heart surgeons has visited countries in Asia and offered gratis open-heart surgery. The University, having completed 100 infant heart transplants, is a leader in pediatric heart and lung transplantation, and is a leader in charitable medical practice. The new Children's Hospital has 275 beds, 72 of them are in one of the world's largest newborn intensive care units.

Conclusion

Much of the foregoing material has demonstrated the effects of what happens when a "handmaiden" is endowed by the Holy Spirit in these last days with the gift of prophecy, and "shall see visions," according to Peter's testimony (Acts 2:16–20). The effects of Ellen White's first vision, the vision against spiritualism, the publishing vision, the vision of the presses, the visions to establish the Australian college and Loma Linda, and the health visions—have all been traced, basically as the Acts of the Holy Spirit, much like the Acts of the Apostles written by Luke, are in reality the Acts of the Holy Spirit. And just as the Acts of the Apostles and the Epistles, including Revelation (96 A.D.), were written over nearly seventy years to shape the Apostolic Church (31–96 A.D.), so the Acts of the Holy Spirit were fulfilled in the ministry of Ellen White for seventy years (1844–1915), "for the perfecting of the saints," to shape the Apostolic Church of the Last Days.

Unlike the prophets of the Catholic Apostolic Church, Ellen White's visions were not given for a "new rule of faith and practice"—to use the term quoted by her and James White elsewhere in this chapter. In fact, Ellen White herself learned monumental truths from the Scriptures presented to her. She learned: the prophecies and the Second

Advent truth from William Miller; the sanctuary truth from the Scriptural article of Crosier; the state of man in death from proof texts used in conversation with her mother; the Sabbath from Joseph Bates; sunset Sabbath observance from Scriptural evidence presented by John Andrews (1855);[28] tithe on income to support the ministry from a committee studying the Scriptures (1878);[29] and so the list goes on.

Nevertheless, as time went on, Ellen White learned and grew in her understanding of the Scriptures, matched by a maturation in her writing. The extent of her writing was expressed by the historian, George W. James: "This remarkable woman, though almost entirely self-educated, has written and published more books and in more languages, which circulate to a greater extent, than the written works of any woman of history."[30]

Ellen White's first major work only appeared in 1858, tracing the Conflict of the Ages, a theme revealing the contending forces of good and evil from Eden to Eden restored, based upon Biblical history and the history of the Christian Church. The theme of this work of 200 odd pages was rewritten and greatly amplified from 1888 to 1915, comprising five volumes with from 600 to 800 pages each, under the following titles: *Patriarchs and Prophets, Prophets and Kings, Desire of Ages* on the life of Christ, *Acts of the Apostles, Great Controversy* —dealing with the history of the Christian Church contending for vital Scriptural truths, such as truths comprising the "apostles' doctrine" (Acts 2:42).

Ellen White wrote much more than the above, so well, and with such conviction, that she virtually became the spokesperson for her church. Unlike the Catholic Apostolic Church, whose twelve apostles constituted the ultimate court of appeal to settle doctrinal disputes (See Chapter 4), the writings and teachings of the prophetess Ellen White, do *not* constitute the court of final appeal. In fact neither she, nor her writings are a test of church membership. Ellen White herself cleared the matter when she declared: "The Holy Scriptures are to be accepted as an authoritative, infallible revelation of His will. They are the standard of character, the revealer of doctrines, and the test of experience."[31] Indeed, this church stands squarely on the testimony of Scripture and the Scripture alone—*sola scriptura*, and continues "steadfastly in the apostles' doctrine" (Acts 2:42), thereby constituting the Apostolic Church of the Last Days.

And now to leave a final word ringing in your ears. It is the overall objective of this Restored Apostolic Church in these last days, to evangelize the world and preach the "everlasting gospel" (Revelation 14:6). Second, by means of its global education program, from the parochial school level to the college level, to teach the everlasting gospel. Third, by means of its vast global network of medical missions and hospitals, to bring healing to a suffering world. Thus the Restored Apostolic Church is determined to occupy till Jesus Comes (Luke 19:13), and follow the example of Christ who went about teaching, preaching and healing (Matthew 9:35).

REFERENCE NOTES

CHAPTER 1

1. Modeled after the Outline found in John Phillips, *100 Sermon Outlines from the New Testament* (Chicago: Moody Press, 1979), p. 40.
2. Dr. William Temple, *Nature, Man and God*, p. 460.

CHAPTER 2

1. Charles J. Hefele, *A History of the Christian Councils*, trans. H.N. Oxenham (Edinburgh: T. & T. Clark, 1896), II, 316.
2. Leslie Hardinge, *The Celtic Church in Britain* (Brushton, New York: Teach Services, Inc., 1995), pp. 48–50, 209, 210.
3. *Ibid.*, p. 211.
4. Alphons Bellesheim, *History of the Catholic Church of Scotland* (London: William Blackwood & Sons, 1887), I, 249, 250.
   For further reading on the subject See T. Ratcliffe Barnett, *Margaret of Scotland: Queen and Saint* (London: Oliver & Boyd, 1926).
   The following references corroborate Celtic Sabbath observance:
   A.C. Flick, *The Rise of the Medieval Church*, p. 237;
   A. Lang, *A History of Scotland*, I, 96;
   W.F. Skene, *Celtic Scotland*, III, 349, 350.
5. A.H. Lewis, *Seventh Day Baptists in Europe and America*, I, 29.
6. Leo Sherley-Price, trans., *Bede, A History of the English Church and People* (Edinburgh, Great Britain: R. & R. Clark Ltd., 1965), pp. 100–102.
7. Leslie Hardinge, pp. 11, 12.
8. *Ibid.*, p. 50
9. *Ibid.*, pp. 196, 197, 202.
10. Adamnan, *Life of Columba* trans. W. Huyshe (London: George Routledge & Sons, 1922), p. L1.
11. J.H. Merle D'Aubigne, *History of the Reformation of the Sixteenth Century*, b. 17, chap. 1, par. 21.
12. William Cathcart, *The Ancient British and Irish Churches* (London: Baptist Tract & Bible Society, 1894), p. 185.
13. Alban Butler, *Lives of the Saints* (Edinburgh: 1799, and London: 1815, 1854), VI, 139.
14. Augustus Neander, *General History of the Christian Religion and Church* (London: Geo. Bell & Sons, 1871), III, 17.
15. D'Aubigne, b. 17, chap. 2.
16. Leo Sherley-Price, trans., *Bede*, pp. 101, 102.
17. *Ibid.*, p. 294.
18. *Ibid.*, p. 144.

19. Leslie Hardinge, pp. 64, 65.
20. *Ibid.*, p. 57.
21. *Ibid.*, pp. 101, 102, 108.
22. *Ibid.*, p. 119.
23. *Ibid.*, pp. 60–63.
24. *Ibid.*, pp. 71–73.
25. Benedict Fitzpatrick, *Ireland and the Foundations of Europe* (New York: Funk & Wagnalls Company, 1927), p. 15.
26. Benedict Fitzpatrick, *Ireland and the Making of Britain.* (4th ed. New York: Funk & Wagnalls Company, 1921), p. 12; See also Henry S. Williams, ed. *The Historians' History of the World*, XXI, 342.
27. Benjamin G. Wilkinson, *Truth Triumphant, The Church in the Wilderness* (Brushton, New York: Teach Services, Inc., 1994), pp. 184–196.
28. Albert H. Newman, *A Manual of Church History* (Philadelphia: The American Baptist Publishing Society, 1933), I, 376.
29. *Maxima Bibliotheca Veterum Patrum, apud Anissonios, Lugdunum*, France, 1677, XIV, 201–216.
30. Walter Map, Walter Map's *"De Nugis Curialium ,"* trans. M.R. James (London: The Honourable Society of Cymmrodorian, 1923), pp. 65, 66.
31. A. Monastier, *A History of the Vaudois Church* (rev.; New York: Lane & Scott, 1849), p. 103.
32. References made in this chapter to the Noble Lesson, or the Treatises Concerning Antichrist, Purgatory, Invocation of Saints, and the Sacraments, come from the complete documents found in Samuel Morland, *The History of the Evangelical Churches of the Valleys of Piemont* (London: Printed by H. Hills for A. Byfield, 1658), pp. 99–120, 142–159.
33. Giorgio Tourn, *The Waldensians, The First 800 Years* (1174–1974), trans. C.P. Merlino (Turin: Claudiana Editrice, 1980), pp. 76, 77.
34. William S. Gilly, *Waldensian Researches* (London: C.J.G. & F. Rivington, 1831), p. 61.
35. J.J.I. von Dollinger, *Beitrage zur Sektenge-schichte des Mittelalters* (Munchen: C.H. Beck'she Verlagsbuchhandlung, 1890), II, 327, 662.
36. Robert Cox, *The Literature of the Sabbath Question* (Edinburgh: Maclachlan & Stewart, 1865), II, 201, 202.
37. Monastier, p. 104.
38. Henri Arnoud, *The Glorious Recovery by the Vaudois of their Valleys*, trans. and ed., H.D. Acland, (London: John Murray, 1827), p. xiv.
39. Henry S. Burrage, *A History of the Anabaptists in Switzerland* (New York: Burt Franklin, Published by Lennox Hill Pub., 1973), pp. 19, 20.
40. *Ibid.*, pp. 65–94.

41. *Ibid.*, pp. 95–115, 167, 168.
42. *Ibid.*, pp. 129, 116–120.
43. LeRoy E. Froom, *The Conditionalist Faith of Our Fathers* (Washington, D.C.: Review & Herald Publishing Assn., 1965), II, 149, 136–138.
44. Francis Blackburne, *A Short Historical View of the Controversy concerning an Intermediate State* (London: Printed for F. Field, 1765), pp. 12, 13; See also C.F. Hudson, *Debt and Grace*, p. 346.
45. Quoted in Froom, II, 75.
46. Quoted in Froom, II, 138–142.
47. Quoted in J.N. Andrews, *History of the Sabbath and First Day of the Week* (2nd ed.; Battle Creek, Michigan, 1873), p. 640.
48. Henry C. Vedder, *Balthasar Hubmaier The Leader of the Anabaptists* (New York: G.P. Putman's Sons, The Knickerbocker Press, 1905), pp. 151–153.
49. Quoted in Andrews, p. 641.
50. Vedder, pp. 164–167.
51. *Ibid.*, pp. 163–170, 176, 215, 248–256.
52. *Ibid.*, p. 270.

CHAPTER 3

1. Edward Miller, *The History and Doctrines of Irvingism* (London: C. Kegan Paul & Co., 1878), I, 30–45.
2. *The Christian Herald*, Vol. 1, Preface, pp. [iii], iv; December, 1831 (Vol. 2, No. 24), p. 287.
3. James H. Frere, *The Great Continental Revolution Marking the Expiration of the Times of the Gentiles, A.D. 1847–8* (London: J. Hatchard & Son, 1848), pp. 85–87.
4. Joseph Wolff, *Researches and Missionary Labours Among the Jews, Mohammedans, and Other Sects* (London: James Nisbet & Co., 1835), pp. 263, 264;
The Christian Herald, December 1831 (Vol. 2, No. 24), pp. 275–279;
The Morning Watch, September, 1829 (Vol. 1, No. 3), pp. 294–296.
5. *Dialogues on Prophecy*, Vol. 1, pp. ii, iii, 322, 323;
The Morning Watch, June, 1831 (Vol. 3, No.2), p. 472.
While there were those who counted the 1260 years from 538 to 1798, others computed from Justinian's Code in 533 to 1793, during the French Revolution and the Napoleonic Code (*The Morning Watch*, December, 1829, Vol. 1, No. 4, pp. 547, 550).
6. Leopold Ranke, *The History of the Popes* (London: Henry G. Bohn, 1853), II, 459.
7. Adam Clarke, *Commentary*, notes on Daniel 7:25.
8. *The Christian Observer*, November, 1807 (Vol. 6, No. 71), p. 701;
William Cuninghame, *The Political Destiny of the Earth as*

Revealed in the Bible (Philadelphia: Orrin Rogers, 1840), pp. 29–33.

9. William Cuninghame, *A Dissertation on the Seals and Trumpets of the Apocalypse* (London: J. Hatchard, 1813), pp. 308, 309.

10. William Cuninghame, *The Scheme of Prophetic Arrangement of the Revelation* (London: Thomas Cadell, 1826), p. 111.

11. *The Morning Watch*, September, 1830 (Vol. 2, No.4), pp. 916, 917; *The Christian Herald*, April, 1830 (Vol.1, No.4), p. 56.

12. E.B. Elliott, *Horae Apocalypticae*, or *A Commentary on the Apocalypse*, (5th ed., London: Seeley, Jackson, and Halliday, 1862), IV, 287, 294.

13. William Cuninghame, *A Dissertation on the Seals and Trumpets of the Apocalypse*, pp. 94–104, 144, 145.

14. *The Christian Observer*, June, 1808 (Vol. 7, No. 78), pp. 345–348.

15. *Ibid.*, November, 1810 (Vol. 9, No. 107), pp. 668–669; William Cuninghame, *The Scheme of Prophetic Arrangement of the Revelation*, pp. 76–78; *Dialogues on Prophecy*, Vol. 2, pp. 326, 327.

16. The term days is literally evening-morning from the Hebrew *ereb boqer*, the same expression found in the Creation Hymn of Genesis, Chapter 1, such as "the evening and the morning were the first day," and so on until the sixth day. There is no way that *ereb boqer* means the opposite of evening-morning, that is morning and evening sacrifices, as some contend. The Septuagint reads: "Evening and morning two thousand and three hundred days" (Alex.).

17. *Newell's Commentary*, p. 137.

18. *The Christian Observer*, November, 1810 (Vol. 9, No. 107), pp. 668–670.

19. *Ibid.*, July, 1828 (Vol. 28, No. 319), p. 415.

20. *The Morning Watch*, June, 1832 (Vol. 5, No. 2), p. 276.

21. *The Christian Observer*, November, 1810 (Vol. 9, No. 107), p. 669.

22. William Hales, *A New Analysis of Chronology* (London: Printed for the Author, 1809–1812), II, 564; *The Christian Herald*, September, 1832 (Vol. 3, No. 31), pp. 190, 191.

23. *The Christian Observer*, November, 1810 (Vol. 9, No. 107), p. 669.

24. *The Christian Herald*, September, 1832 (Vol. 3, No. 31), pp. 190, 191.

25. *The Morning Watch*, June, 1831 (Vol. 3, No. 2), p. 472.

26. *Ibid.*, June, 1832 (Vol. 5, No. 2), p. 276.

27. Archibald Mason, *Two Essays of Daniel's Prophetic Number of Two Thousand Three Hundred Days* (Glasgow: Maurice Ogle, 1821), pp. 21, 54.

28. William Cuninghame, *The Scheme of Prophetic Arrangement of the Revelation*, p. 80.

29. *Ibid.*, p. 79.

30. Edward Irving, *Babylon and Infidelity Foredoomed of God: A Discourse on the Prophecies of Daniel and the Apocalypse* (Glasgow: Chalmers & Collins, 1826), II, 222–225, I, 259.

31. John A. Brown, *The Even-Tide* (London: J. Offor, 1823), p. xlii.

32. William Cuninghame, *The Scheme of Prophetic Arrangement of the Revelation*, p. 81.

33. William Cuninghame, *A Dissertation on the Seals and Trumpets of the Apocalypse*, pp. 308, 309.

34. Edward Irving, Trans. of Manuel Lacunza, *The Coming of Messiah in Glory and Majesty* (London: L.B. Seeley & Son, 1827), I clxxxix, cxc.

35. Edward Miller, *The History and Doctrines of Irvingism*, I, 42.

36. Daniel Wilson, *On The Numbers in Daniel* (Madras: The Church Mission Press, 1836), p. 12.

37. Joseph Wolff, *Researches and Missionary Labours*, pp. 131, 262, 263; *Travels and Adventures of the Rev. Joseph Wolff* (London: Saunders, Otley, & Co., 1861), p. 466.

38. Edward Irving, Trans., *The Coming of Messiah*, I, iv, v.

39. Edward Irving, Trans., *The Coming of Messiah*, I, i.

40. Elliott, IV, 552.

41. For the narrative on Gaussen and Bengel I have consulted LeRoy E. Froom, *The Prophetic Faith of our Fathers* (Washington, D.C.: Review & Herald Publishing Assn., 1946–1954), III, 687–700, 297–299.

42. *Ibid.*, III, 673.

43. *Ibid.*, III, 674; Emma E. Howell, *The Great Advent Movement* (Washington, D.C.: Review & Herald Publishing Assn., 1947), p. 23.

44. Quoted in Froom, III, 674.

45. Quoted in Froom, III, 677.

46, Froom, III, 681–685.

47. Quoted in Froom, III, 683–686.

48. Quoted in Froom, III, 674.

49. Quoted in Froom, III, 679, 680.

50. Edward Irving, Trans., *The Coming of Messiah*, I, xxiii, xxiv, 3, 8; Froom, III, 307–309.

51. Edward Irving, Trans., *The Coming of Messiah*, I, xvi, xxiv; Froom, III, 309–314; Elliott, IV, 536–538, 543.

52. Edward Irving, Trans., *The Coming of Messiah*, I, xxvi, xxvii, 187, 199, 207, 219, 220, 223–225, 262; Elliot, IV, 538–543.

53. Froom, III, 313.

54. Elliott, IV, 551.

55. Miller, I, 130, 131.

56. *The Christian Herald*, July, 1835 (Vol. 5, No. 40), pp. 217–221.

57. William Cuninghame, *The Pre-Millennial Advent of Messiah Demonstrated from the Scriptures* (3rd ed., London: James Nisbet & Co., 1836), p. xv.

58. Alexander Reese, *The Approaching Advent of Christ* (Grand Rapids: Grand Rapids International Publications, Kregel, 1975), pp. 17, 18.

CHAPTER 4

1. Edward Miller, I, 38, 39.
2. *The Christian Herald*, September, 1833 (Vol. 4, No. 35), pp. 196, 197.
3. Elliott, IV, 552–554.
4. H. Grattan Guinness, D.D. *History Unveiling Prophecy or Time as an Interpreter* (London and Edinburgh: Flemming H. Revell Company, 1905), p. 288.
5. *Ibid.*, p. 287.
6. *Ibid.*, pp. 285–291.
7. Elliott, IV, 555.
8. *Ibid.*,
9. Guinness, p. 289.
10. Elliott, IV, 552.
11. Edward Miller, I, 28, 29;
    Elliott, IV, 538.
12. Edward Irving, Trans., *The Coming of Messiah*, I, xxvi.
13. *Ibid.*, I, xli, xlii.
14. *Ibid.*, I, xxxvii, xli.
15. *Ibid.*, I, xxxii, II, 251, 103.
16. *Ibid.*, I, xxxii, xxxvi.
17. *Ibid.*, I, xxix.
18. *Ibid.*, I. xxx.
19. Wolff, *Letter Addressed to the Citizens of Rome* (London: J. Hatchard & Son, 1849), p. 9.
20. *Ibid.*, *Travels and Adventures*, p. 237.
21. Froom, III, 407.
22. Edward Irving, Trans., *The Coming of Messiah*, I, 99.
23. *Ibid.*, II, 267, I, 114.
24. Miller, I, 47.
25. Edward Irving, Trans., *The Coming of Messiah*, I, v.
26. Quoted in Miller, I, 45, 46.
27. Miller, I, 53, 54.
28. *Ibid.*, I, 55, 56.
29. Robert Norton, *Memoirs of James and George MacDonald, of Port Glasgow* (London: John F. Shaw, 1840), pp. 171–176.
30. *Ibid.*, *The Restoration of Apostles and Prophets In the Catholic Apostolic Church* (London: Bosworth & Harrison, 1861), p. 15.
31. Samuel P. Tregelles, *The Hope of Christ's Second Coming* (London: Samuel Bagster & Sons, 1864), p. 35.
32. Miller, I, 61, 65; *The Morning Watch*, December, 1830 (Vol. 2, No. 4), pp. 869–873
33. *The Morning Watch*, September, 1830, pp. 587–593.

34. Harold H. Rowdon, *The Origins of the Brethren* (London: Pickering & Inglis, 1967), pp. 30, 31.
35. John N. Darby, *Letters of J.N.D.*, (Reprint Oak Park, Illinois: Bible Truth Publishers, 1971), III, 297–299, II,499.
36. Miller, II, 202, 203.
37. Dave MacPherson, *The Incredible Cover-Up* (2nd Printing, Medford, Oregon: Omega Publications, 1980), pp. 82–85, 31.
38. *Ibid.*, *The Great Rapture Hoax* (Fletcher, N.C.: New Puritan Library, 1983), p. 178.
39. Darby, *Letters of J.N.D.*, II, 230.
40. Rowdon, p. 82.
41. Darby, *Letters of J.N.D.*, III, 424.
42. Ernest R. Sandeen, *The Roots of Fundamentalism* (Chicago: The University of Chicago Press, 1970), p. 38.
43. *Ibid.*
44. Darby, *Letters of J.N.D.*, I, 131.
45. Harry A. Ironside, *The Great Parenthesis* (Grand Rapids: Zondervan, 1943), p. 33.
46. Richard W. de Haan, *The Middle East in Prophecy* (Wheaton, Illinois: Victor Books, A Division of S.P. Publications, Inc., 1974), p. 20.
47. Ironside, p. 33.
48. Philip Mauro, *The Seventy Weeks and the Great Tribulation* (Boston: Mass.: Hamilton Bros., 1923), p. 96.
49. *Ibid.*, p. 95.
50. Darby, *Letters of J.N.D.*, III, 424.
51. Mauro, p. 92.
52. Quoted in Margaret O.W. Oliphant, *The Life of Edward Irving* (London: Hurst & Blackett, Publishers, 1865), pp. 292, 293.
53. Quoted in Miller, I, 51, 56, 57.
54. Miller, I, 52, 64.
55. MacPherson, *The Incredible Cover-Up*, pp. 72, 73, 76, 77; Miller, I, 58, 60.
56. Quoted in Miller, I, 52.
57. *Ibid.*, I, 52.
58. Miller, I, 52, 53.
59. *Ibid.*, I, 58.
60. Quoted in Miller, I, 58, 59.
61. Miller, I, 143, 77.
62. *Ibid.*, I, 51, 59, 60, 73.
63. *Ibid.*, I, 59, 102, 103.
64. Quoted in MacPherson, *The Incredible Cover-Up*, p. 89.
65. Quoted in Miller, I, 74, 75.
66. *The Morning Watch*, December, 1830 (Vol. 2, No.4), p. 872.
67. Quoted in Miller, I, 72.
68. Miller, I, 72, 68, II, 243.
69. *Ibid.*, I, 99.
70. Quoted in Miller, I, 79.

71. Miller, I, 81, 82, 98.
72. Quoted in Miller, II, 237, 238.
73. Miller, II, 79, 238, 239.
74. Froom, III, 516, 517.
    Miller, I, 68–71, 98.
75. Miller, I, 135, 125, 147.
76. Robert Baxter, *Irvingism in its Rise, Progress, and Present State* (2nd ed. London: James Nisbet & Co., 1836), p. 10.
77. Miller, I, x, 5, 178, 179.
78. Baxter, p. 14;
    Miller, I, 135.
79. Miller, I, 57, 109, II, 120, 121;
    Baxter, pp. 11, 14, 15.
80. Miller, I, 109, 110, 135, 136;
    Baxter, pp. 14, 16.
81. Miller, I, 179, 180, 185, 292;
    Baxter, pp. 24, 25.
82. Miller, II, 36, 46; I, 81.
83. *Ibid.*, I, 262, 292, 293, 346, II, 79, 121.
84. *Ibid.*, I, 346.
85. Roland R. Hegstad, *Rattling the Gates* (Washington, D.C.: Review & Herald Publishing Assn., 1974), p. 9.
86. John F. MacArthur, Jr., *Charismatic Chaos* (Grand Rapids: Zondervan Publishing House, 1992), p. 20.
87. Hegstad, pp. 9, 10; MacArthur, p. 21.

CHAPTER 5

1. LeRoy E. Froom, *The Prophetic Faith of Our Fathers*, IV, 134, 144.
2. *The Christian Observer*, November and December, 1807, pp. 701–705, 774–777; April, 1808, pp. 209–211; January, 1810, pp. 16, 17.
3. Froom, III, 723, IV, 325.
4. *Ibid.*
5. *Ibid.*, IV, 143, 210–220.
6. *Ibid.*
7. *Ibid.*, IV, 402, 403, 407.
8. Sir Charles Lyell, *Principles of Geology* (New York, 1858), p. 495; Thomas Hunter, *Historical Account of Earthquakes* (Liverpool, 1756), pp. 72–74. *The New Encyclopedia Britannica* (Helen Hemingway Benton, 1976) X, 1031.
9. Robert Sears, *Wonders of the World*, p. 50.
10. *Ibid.*, pp. 50, 58; A.R. Spofford & Charles Gibbon, *The Library of Choice Literature*, VII, pp. 162, 163.
11. *The London Magazine*, December, 1755, p. 586.
12. Froom, III, 187, 188.
13. *The Gentleman's Magazine* (London), February, 1756, pp. 68, 69.
14. Froom, II, 675–677.

15. *Ibid.*, III, 187.
16. *Ibid.*, III, 188–190.
17. *History of Weare, New Hampshire,* 1735–1888 (Boston Public Library).
18. Samuel Williams, in *Memoirs of the American Academy of Arts & Sciences* (Boston, 1785), I, 234, 235.
19. "Vocabulary of the Names of Noted... Persons & Places," *An American Dictionary of the English Language,* 1882 ed.
20. Quoted in John W. Barber, *Connecticut Historical Collections,* p. 403.
21. Quoted in R.M. Devens, *Our First Century,* p. 90.
22. Quoted in *The Independent Chronicle,* (Boston), June 22, 1780.
23. Quoted in John W. Barber, *Connecticut Historical Collections,* p. 403.
24. John G. Whittier, "Abraham Davenport," *Complete Poetical Works,* p. 260.
25. Froom, III, 202, IV, 291.
26. *Ibid.*, III, 211, 212.
27. *Ibid.*, III, 230–233, IV, 290.
28. Quoted in Froom, III, 231.
29. *Ibid.*, IV, 183.
30. Quoted in Froom, IV, 183, 145, 146.
31. Elijah H. Burritt, *The Geography of the Heavens,* p. 163.
32. Denison Olmstead, *The Mechanism of the Heavens,* p. 328.
33. *The American Journal of Science,* XXV (1834), pp. 382, 372.
34. C.A. Young, *Manual of Astronomy,* p. 469.
35. *The American Journal of Science,* XXV (1834), p. 382.
36. Froom, IV, 295–297.
37. *Ibid.*, IV, 301–311.
38. *The New York Journal of Commerce,* November 14, 1833.
39. W.A. Spicer, *Our Day In the Light of Prophecy* (Washington, D.C.: Review & Herald Publishing Assn., 1918), p. 99.
40. Willard J. Fisher, "The Ancient Leonids," *The Telescope,* pp. 80–83.
41. G. Johnstone Stoney and A.M.W. Downing, "Perturbations of the Leonids," abstract of a paper read before the Royal Astronomical Society, March 2, 1899, cited in *Nature,* March 23, 1899, pp. 497, 498.
42. *Chambers' Astronomy,* 1889, I, 635.
43. Agnes M. Clerke, *A Popular History of Astronomy During the Nineteenth Century,* (1902 ed.), p. 338.
44. Sir Harold Spencer Jones, "Meteors," *Chambers' Encyclopedia* (1950 ed.), IX, pp. 332, 333.
45. Peter M. Millman, "The Falling of the Stars," *The Telescope,* May-June, 1940, p. 60.
46. Thomas Milner, *The Gallery of Nature* (London, 1852), p. 140.
47. Josiah Litch, *Signs of the Times, and Expositor of Prophecy,* August 1, 1840.

48. Josiah Litch, *The Probability of the Second Coming of Christ About A.D. 1843* (Published 1838), p. 157.

49. Josiah Litch, *Signs of the Times*, August 1, 1840.

50. Quoted in Roy A. Anderson, *Unfolding the Revelation* (Mountain View, California: Pacific Press Publishing Assn., 1961), p. 94.

51. Tallentyre, *Life of Voltaire*, p. 319.

CHAPTER 6

1. William Miller, *William Miller's Apology and Defense* (Boston: J.V. Himes, 1845), pp. 11, 12.

2. This biographical sketch and outcome of the movement he led is based on *William Miller's Apology and Defense*, and his letters; *The Advent Shield and Review* (Boston: Published by J.V. Himes, 1844), I, Number 1; Joshua V. Himes, *Views of The Prophecies and Prophetic Chronology* (Boston: Dow & Jackson's Power Press, 1842); Sylvester Bliss, *Memoirs of William Miller* (Boston: Published by Joshua V. Himes, 1853); Francis D. Nichol, *The Midnight Cry* (Washington, D.C.: Review & Herald Publishing Association, 1944); LeRoy E. Froom, *The Prophetic Faith of Our Fathers* (Washington, D.C.: Review & Herald Publishing Association, 1954), IV, 429–851.

3. Sylvester Bliss, *Memoirs of William Miller*, p. 65.

4. *Ibid.*, pp. 66, 67.

5. *Ibid.*, pp. 70, 71.

6. *Ibid.*, p. 70.

7. *William Miller's Apology and Defense*, p. 12.

8. Bliss, p. 72.

9. *Ibid.*, pp. 74, 75.

10. Joshua V. Himes, *Views of The Prophecies and Prophetic Chronology* (Boston: Dow & Jackson's Power Press, 1842), p. 12.

11. Bliss, pp. 72–77. Miller dated the commencement of the 2,300 years from "the seventh year of Artaxerxes the king" of Persia (Ezra 7:7) being 457 B.C., according to the "best chronologers" of his day. Modern Bible Dictionaries attest to the accuracy of this date: *The Zondervan Pictorial Bible Dictionary*; *The New International Dictionary of the Bible*; *The New Unger's Bible Dictionary*.

12. *William Miller's Apology and Defense*, p. 13.

13. *Ibid.*, pp. 24, 25.

14. Bliss, pp. 77–79.

15. *Ibid.*, p. 79.

16. *William Miller's Apology and Defense*, p. 22.

17. *Ibid.*, p. 19.

18. *Ibid.*, pp. 24, 25;
    Froom, IV, 761–783.

19. *William Miller's Apology and Defense*, pp. 28, 29;
    Froom, IV, 804–807.

20. *Midnight Cry*, October 11, 1844, p. 116.
21. Froom, IV, 822–826. Francis D. Nichol, *The Midnight Cry*, clearly documents and shows that the climactic hour for the expected coming of the Lord was not celebrated with extremism, or fanaticism, either in fields, or on housetops, or mountaintops, neither did the followers wear "ascension robes."
22. *William Miller's Apology*, p. 23.
23. *Signs of the Times*, January 31, 1844, p. 196.
24. *William Miller's Apology*, pp. 22, 23.
25. Letter, Dec. 3, 1844, in *The Advent Herald*, Dec. 18, 1844, p. 147.
26. William Miller, *Letter to Joshua V. Himes On the Cleansing of the Sanctuary* (Boston: Published by Joshua V. Himes), 1842, pp. 9, 13.
27. Bliss, p. 71.
28. Letter, May 3, 1843, in *Signs of the Times*, May 17, 1843, p. 85.
29. *Ibid.*
30. *William Miller's Apology*, p. 25.

CHAPTER 7

1. Hiram Edson, Fragment of a Manuscript on his "Life and Experience," pp. 8, 9. This segment of the Manuscript is located in George Knight, ed. *1844 and the Rise of Sabbatarian Adventism* (Hagerstown, MD.: Review & Herald Publishing Assn., 1994), pp. 123–126.
2. *Ibid.*, pp. 9, 10.
3. Ms., "Hiram Edson's Experience," as Related to P.Z. Kinne, quoted in William A. Spicer, *Pioneer Days of the Advent Movement* (Takoma Park: Review & Herald Publishing Association, 1941), p. 83.
4. E.G. White, *Testimonies for the Church* (Mountain View, California: Pacific Press Publishing Assn., 1948), I, 75–77.
5. "Declaration of Principles," *Signs of the Times*, June 7, 1843, p. 107.
6. E.G. White, *Life Sketches*, pp. 64–68.
7. James White, *A Word to the "Little Flock"* (Gorham, Maine: James White, 1847), p. 22; E.G. White, *Early Writings* (Washington, D.C.: Review & Herald Publishing Assn., 1945), p. 20.
8. James White, *A Word to the "Little Flock,"* p. 21.
9. Quoted in William A. Spicer, *The Spirit of Prophecy in the Advent Movement* (Washington, D.C.: Review & Herald Publishing Assn., 1937), p. 127.
10. E.G. White, Manuscript 140, 1905.
11. Editorial, "An American Prophetess," *The Independent*, August 23, 1915.
12. Edith Dean, *Great Women of the Christian Faith*, p. 230.
13. Unpublished Manuscript, "Ellen G. White in Vision, The Testimony of Eye Witnesses," Washington, D.C.: Ellen G. White Publications, July 3, 1952, p. 1.

14. James White, *Life Incidents, in Connection with the Great Advent Movement* (Battle Creek, Michigan: Seventh-day Adventist Publishing Association, 1868), pp. 272, 273.

15. James White, *A Word to the "Little Flock,"* p. 13.

16. E.G. White, *A Sketch of the Christian Experience and Views of Ellen G. White* (Saratoga Springs, N.Y.: James White, 1851), p. 64.

17. James White, editorial, "The Gifts of the Gospel Church," *Review and Herald*, April 21, 1851, p. 70.

18. *Review and Herald*, May 6, 1852, p. 5.

19. Letter: James White to Brother Bowles, Volney, N.Y., Nov. 8, 1849. Letter located in George Knight, pp. 183–186.

20. E.G. White, *Spiritual Gifts* (Battle Creek, Michigan: James White, 1860), II, 97–99.

21. E.G. White, *Special Testimony, Series B.*, No. 2, pp. 56, 57.

22. E.G. White, *Spiritual Gifts*, II, 97–99.

23. E.G. White, Manuscript 13, 1889.

24. E.G. White, *Selected Messages* (Washington, D.C.: Review & Herald Publishing Assn., 1958), Book I, 65; Testimonies for The Church, I, 39–41.

25. E.G. White, Letter in *Present Truth*, August, 1849, p. 21; also quoted in *Early Writings*, p. 43.

26. E.G. White, *Life Sketches*, p. 125.

27. *Adventist Review*, July 4, 1995, p. 21.

28. William C. White, "A Comprehensive Vision—II," *Review and Herald*, February 10, 17, 1938.

29. *Ibid.*

30. *Ibid.*

31. Arthur G. Daniells, *The Abiding Gift of Prophecy* (Mountain View, California: Pacific Press Publishing Association, 1936), pp. 308–321; D.A. Delafield, *Ellen G. White and the Seventh-day Adventist Church* (Mountain View, California: Pacific Press Publishing Association, 1963), pp. 58–62.

32. Virgil Robinson, *The Solusi Story* (Washington, D.C.: Review & Herald Publishing Association, 1979), pp. 14–29.

33. *Adult Sabbath School Lessons* (Nampa, Idaho: Pacific Press Publishing Association, January-March, 1997) Back Cover.

34. E.G. White, "The Need of Home Religion," *Review & Herald*, June 29, 1905, p. 8.

35. Fact Sheet, *Partners—American Bible Society and Church Missions*.

CHAPTER 8

1. Authors: Department of Education, *The Story of Our Church* (Mountain View, California: Pacific Press Publishing Association, 1956), p. 419.

2. E.G. White, *Spiritual Gifts* (Facsimile Reproduction, Washington, D.C.: Review & Herald Publishing Association, 1945), IV, 124.

3. *Ibid.*, IV, 125–131, 148.

4. *Ibid.*, IV, 127, 133–140, 142–146.

5. *Ibid.*, IV, 145.

6. *Ibid.*, IV, 128.

7. E.G. White, *Ministry of Healing* (Mountain View, California: Pacific Press Publishing Association, 1909), p. 327.

8. *Ibid.*, p. 298.

9. E.G. White, *Testimonies for The Church*, II, 347.

10. *Ibid.*, III, 157.

11. *Spiritual Gifts*, IV, 153, 154.

12. Warren L. Johns, Richard H. Utt, eds., *The Vision Bold* (Washington, D.C.: Review & Herald Publishing Association, 1977), p. 73. This book has been consulted for the subject of the health message and Battle Creek Sanitarium, including *The Story of Our Church*, and Richard H. Utt, *A Century of Miracles* (Mountain View, California: Pacific Press Publishing Association, 1963).

13. *The Vision Bold*, pp. 126–137.

14. E.J. Stevenson Jr., "A History of the Claremont Sanitarium South Africa (1897–1905)," Typescript Term Paper, November 23, 1972, pp. 1–24.

15. *The Story of Our Church*, pp. 368, 369, 376, 419.

16. D.E. Robinson, *The Story of Our Health Message* (Nashville, Tennessee: Southern Publishing Association, 1965), p. 302; "A History of the Claremont Sanitarium," p. 2.

17. *Seventh-day Adventist Yearbook* (Hagerstown, Maryland: Review & Herald Publishing Association, 1986), pp. 4, 491–538.

18. *University Scope*, VI, No. 2, February 5, 1969, p. 1.

19. *Adventist Review*, June 29, 1989, p. 16.

20. *University Scope*, VI, No. 2, February 5, 1969, p. 1.

21. *Adventist Review*, June 29, 1989, p. 17.

22. *Ibid.*, p. 18.

23. E.G. White, Letter 291, 1905.

24. E.G. White Ms. 152, 1901.

25. *The Story of Our Church*, p. 429.

26. *Ibid.*, p. 429; D.E. Robinson, pp. 343–363.

27. *A Century of Miracles*, pp. 32, 33; *The Story of Our Church*, pp. 430, 431.

28. *Review and Herald*, December 4, 1855, p. 78.

29. *The Story of Our Church*, p. 224; Robert W. Olson, "One Hundred and One Questions," Typescript booklet, Ellen G. White Estate, Washington, D.C. March, 1981, pp. 55, 56.

30. George W. James, *California—Romantic and Beautiful*, pp. 319, 320.

31. E.G. White, *The Great Controversy* (Mountain View, California: Pacific Press Publishing Association, 1949), p. vii.

APPENDICES

APPENDIX A

GREEK TERMS FOR SOUL AND SPIRIT

The Greek *psuche* is frequently used for *nephesh* (translated soul 428 times, and **life** 119 times—O.T.; A.V.) in the Greek Septuagint Version. *Psuche* is translated soul 58 times, and **life** 40 times, in the New Testament, Authorized Version. Many times *psuche* is translated soul, but is used as a periphrasis for person or self, examples:

1 Corinthians 15:45; Revelation 16:3, 6:9; 1 Peter 3:20; Acts 2:41; Romans 13:1; Matthew 11:29.

The Greek *pneuma* is frequently used for *ruach* (translated spirit 232 times, wind 117 times, and **breath** 33 times—O.T.; A.V.) in the Greek Septuagint Version. But in the Authorized Version of the N.T. *pneuma* is translated spirit, and not wind or breath, as in the case of *ruach*. For example, compare Luke 8:55 with Ezekiel 37:10.

APPENDIX B

HEBREW PARALLELISM

Unlike English poetry that has words that rhyme, Hebrew poetry has thoughts that rhyme, that is parallelism—parallel repetition of thoughts. The most common is Synonymous Parallels such as Psalm 19, verse 1:

First Line: "The heavens declare the glory of God"
Synonymously Paralleled with

Second Line: "And the firmament showeth His handiwork."

Other parallels of lines of thought include: (1) Antithetical or contrasting parallel lines; (2) Synthetic or completing parallel lines; (3) Alternating parallel lines.

Daniel 9, verses 25 to 27 do not present parallel lines in the usual Hebrew poetic form. But the literary structure presents contrasting and alternating parallels by actually splitting the verses into two clauses.

The *first* half of each verse
is contrasted and alternated
with the *second* half of each verse.

The passage of Daniel 9, verses 25 to 27 is laid out below, under the headings that summarize the content of each half of the verses. The lines under the A headings cover the *first* half of each verse. The lines under the B headings cover the *second* half of each verse.

v. 25. A. Messiah Prince to Come.
   B. City of Jerusalem to be Rebuilt
v. 26. A. Messiah to be Cut Off or Destroyed.
   B. Desolater Prince to Destroy the City.
v. 27. A. Messiah Crucified to bring an End to Sacrifices.
   B. Desolater Prince to be Destroyed.

The A column is focused on the Messianic Prince, and expressly related to, and intimately interwoven with the *timing* of the seventy weeks.

The B column events regarding the history of Jerusalem and the antagonistic desolater prince are related, but not *timed* to the seventy weeks.

It is evident from the literary structure above, that when the A column at Daniel 9, verse 27, uses the personal pronoun, "He," it has to be the Messianic Prince, and not the antagonistic prince that belongs to the B column only. Read verses 25 to 27 carefully, bearing in mind the structural division by means of columns A and B.

We'd love to send you a free catalog of titles we publish
or even hear your thoughts, reactions, criticism,
about things you did or didn't like about this
or any other book we publish.

Just write or call us at:

TEACH Services, Inc.
254 Donovan Road
Brushton, New York 12916-9738

1-800-367-1998

http://www.teachservicesinc.com

- IN The Fire
  1 JN 3:1
  JN 10 10
  JN 14:27
  Bold
  Faith
  Apostles